D1713368

Divided Minds and Successive Selves

Philosophical Psychopathology: Disorders in Mind
Owen Flanagan and George Graham, editors

Divided Minds and Successive Selves: Ethical Issues in Disorders of Identity and Personality Jennifer Radden

Divided Minds and Successive Selves

Ethical Issues in Disorders of Identity and Personality

Jennifer Radden

A Bradford Book
The MIT Press
Cambridge, Massachusetts
London, England

This book was set in Bembo by Asco Trade Typesetting Ltd., Hong Kong, and was printed and bound in the United States of America.

First printing, 1996.

Library of Congress Cataloging-in-Publication Data

Radden, Jennifer.
  Divided minds and successive selves : ethical issues in disorders of identity and personality / Jennifer Radden.
       p.   cm.
  "A Bradford book."
  Includes bibliographical references and index.
  ISBN 0-262-18175-4 (hc : alk. paper)
  1. Self. 2. Personality change—Moral and ethical aspects. 3. Dissociative disorders—Moral and ethical aspects. 4. Responsibility. 5. Identity (Psychology) 6. Self (Philosophy) I. Title.
RC455.4.S42R33   1996
616.85'23—dc20   95-46262
                                                                                    CIP

To the man I married

Contents

Series Foreword   xi
Acknowledgments   xiii

I   **Divided Minds and Successive Selves**   1

Introduction   3
Why It Matters   4
Modernist Misgivings over a Unified Self   6
The Framework and Sequence of Argument   7
A Reader's Guide   10
Preliminary Terminological Clarification   11

1   Heterogeneities of Self in Everyday Life   13
Perspectives   13
Disunity: Heterogeneities of Self at a Given Time   15
Discontinuity: Heterogeneities of Self over Time   18
More Puzzling Divisions: Self-Deception and Akrasia   20
The Heterogeneous Self: A Touchstone   23

2   A Language of Successive Selves   25
Identity and Uniqueness   25
The Language of Sameness and Difference   26
A Language of Successive Selves   28
A Metaphysics of Successive Selves   31
John Locke's Language and Metaphysics of Successive Persons   34

3   Multiplicity through Dissociation   37
Fragmentation: Unarguable Cases   37
Multiplicity   38
Ambiguities of Multiplicity   43
Dissociative-Identity Disorder and Multiplicity   46
Dissociative-Identity Disorder as Entrenched Self-Deception   54

4   Succession and Recurrence outside Dissociative Disorder   59
The Continuity Requirement   59
Personality Change Due to Disease and Damage to the Brain   60

Personality Change Due to Mood and Schizophrenic Disorders   61
Multiplicity Conditions and Ideological Conversion   66
Akrasia and Disorders of Impulse Control   68
The Separate "Selves" of Self-Deception   71

II   Successive Selves and Personal Responsibility   75

**5   From Abnormal Psychology to Metaphysics:
A Methodological Preamble   77**
Imagined Examples   78
Real Examples   82
Metaphysical Conclusions from Moral Convictions   83
The Presumption of Organicity   86
Multiplicity and Generalization   87

6   Memory, Responsibility, and Contrition   91
The Forensic Sense of Self   92
Memory and Responsibility   93
Moral Attitudes Attending Responsibility Ascriptions   95
Responsibility, Memory, and the Cognitive Components of
Contrition   96
Foreseeability and Prevention   99
Responsibility and the Successive Selves of Abnormal Psychology   99
"Real Selves" and Responsibility   105

**7   Purposes and Discourses of Responsibility
Ascription   109**
Discourses of Culpability and Discourses of Care   110
Therapeutic Contexts   111
Legal Contexts and Purposes   117
The Therapist's Role   120
Everyday Relationships   121

8   Multiplicity and Legal Culpability   125
Mental Disturbance and Criminal Law: Retributivist Presuppositions   126
Legal Guilt and the Successive Selves of Nondissociative Disorders   127
Dissociative-Identity Disorder and Legal Culpability   129
The Insanity Defense   131
The Defense of Unconsciousness   133
Suspended Personhood   135
Diminished Capacity   137
Guilty   139
Punishing the Innocent?   140

9   Paternalistic Intervention   143
Paternalism and Treatment Refusals   144
Who Decides and How?   145
Responsibility and Incompetence   146

Restoring the Authentic Self   150
The Proxy and Substituted Judgments of Guardians   154
"Best Interests" Reasoning   155
"Would Have Wanted" Reasoning   155
"Will Want" Reasoning and "Thank You" Theory   157

10   Responsibilities over Oneself in the Future or One's Future Selves   161
Advance Directives or Ulysses Contracts in Psychiatry   163
Not Enslavement but Unfairness   164
Attempts to Rebut the Moral Challenge   165
Weakness of Will, Changes of Mind, Promises, and Resolves   167
Self-Destructive Wishes   172
Responsibilities over Oneself or One's Selves   177

III   Successive Selves and Individualism   181

11   A Metaphysics of Successive Selves   183
Empiricist Theories of Personal Identity   184
The Role of the Imagination   186
Psychological Forms of Continuity   187
Psychological Continuity and Connectedness   188
Interpreting the Criteria of Survival or Singularity   191
Refining the Language of Successive Selves   192
Objections to Psychological-Continuity Theories   194

12   The Normative Tug of Individualism   195
Does Continuity Matter?   197
Moral Categories   198
Time-Spanning Emotions of Self-Assessment   200
The Concept and Acknowledgment of Agency   201
Judicious Trust   202
Self-Understanding   203
Vices and Virtues, and Their Moral Framework   204
Dependency Theses: Clinical Confirmation   205
Dependent "Goods": Are They Good?   205

13   Therapeutic Goals for a Liberal Culture   209
Seeking Integration in the Dissociative Disorders   212
Self-Knowledge in Insight Therapies   215
Helping the Client Help Herself: The Value of Self-Determination   220

14   Continuity Sufficient for Individualism   227
Continuity Sufficient for Agency   229
Continuity Sufficient for Our Moral Categories   230
Continuity Sufficient for Moral Concepts and Emotions   232
Continuity Sufficient for Trust   233
Continuity Sufficient for Self-Understanding   234

Continuity Sufficient for Virtues   234
Continuity Sufficient for Self-Determination and Autonomy   236
Life Changes in More Normal Lives   236

IV   Divided Minds   239

15   The Divided Minds of Mental Disorder   241
Divided Minds and Questions of Evidence   242
Behavioral Evidence for Coconsciousness   243
Separate awareness in dissociative-identity disorder   243
Alleged separate awareness in hypnotic states and commissurotomy   245
Subjective Evidence for Divided Minds   248
Thought insertion   248
*Depersonalization, derealization, possession states, and out-of-body
experience*   250

16   The Grammar of Disownership   255
Philosophical Accounts of Ownership   256
Hume, James, and the Self's Unity   259
The Meaning of Disowned Experience   263

Conclusion   267

Notes   273
References   291
Index   307

Series Foreword

The aim of the series is both interdisciplinary and uncharted: to offer philosophical examination of mental disorder, an area of intense and fascinating activity in recent years. The perspective of philosophy provides a richly synoptic vision of the forms, limits, and lessons of mental disorder, as well as its study and treatment. Potential topics include, but are not limited to, the following:

- How to explain mental disorder
- Dissociative personality and volitional disorders and what they tell us about rational and moral agency
- Disorders of consciousness and what they tell us about selfhood and self-representation
- The lessons of cognitive neuropsychology for the nature and function of mind
- Whether disorders are "rational strategies" for coping with trauma or stress
- Relationships between dream states and psychosis
- Neural-network models of pathology and their implications for the debate over the functional integration of mind/brain
- Culture-specific and gender-linked forms of psychopathology and their lessons for both the taxonomy of mental disorder and the scientific status of the study of mental illness
- Logical and epistemological relations between theories of mental disorder and forms of therapy
- Conceptual and methodological foundations of psychopharmacology
- Ethical and political issues in definition and treatment of mental disorder

The editors welcome proposals and submissions from philosophers, cognitive scientists, psychiatric researchers, physicians, social scientists, and others committed to a philosophical approach to psychopathology.

Owen Flanagan
George Graham

Acknowledgments

Much of this research was undertaken when I was an Ethics Fellow at Harvard University during 1991–1992, and I am grateful for the support of the Program for Ethics in the Professions, and, particularly, its Director, Dennis Thompson.

My thanks also go to friends and professional colleagues who offered comments on the several drafts out of which this manuscript evolved, particularly Dennis Thompson, Martha Minnow, Arthur Applbaum; my fellow Ethics Fellows Alan Wertheimer, Terry Moore, Bob Pearlman, Dan Brock, Andrew Stark, Sandy Levinson, Moshe Halbertal; members of PHAEDRA Jane Roland Martin, Susan Franzosa, Ann Diller, Barbara Houston, Janet Farrell Smith, Beatrice Kipp Nelson, Suzie Laird; my fellow moral psychologists Margaret Rhodes, David Wong, Larry Blum, Amélie Rorty, Ruth Anna Putnam, Steve Nathanson; my friends and acquaintances who offered clinical tales and confirmation from the trenches, Felicia Len, Joan Fordyce, Arnold Modell, Bennett Simon, Jim Sabin; and finally Rabbi Julia Neuberger, Phyllis Menken, Ed Hundert, Patricia Herzog, Stephen Braude, Etzel Cardeña, Owen Flanagan, George Graham, and Derek Parfit.

As the manuscript neared completion, I relied on the energy, effort, and sure judgment of my editors Teri Mendelsohn and Amy Pierce, my copyeditor Alan Thwaits, my research assistant Rachel Friesecke, and my computer wizard Derek Brandt. To each of these I wish to express my warmest appreciation.

For contributions ranging from editorial and philosophical assistance to moral support, sympathy, wit, and housekeeping, I gratefully acknowledge Frank Keefe and our children, Patrick, Beatrice, and Tristram.

I

Divided Minds and Successive Selves

Introduction

A cluster of questions about personal changes through time and the moral attitudes we adopt in the face of these changes were the initial impetus for this book. These questions have particular force in relation to the vivid forms of self fracture evident in mental abnormality. Tied to the context of abnormal psychology, where they most urgently require answers, these questions may be distilled into one: if people change radically as the result of mental disturbance or brain damage or disease, how should we acknowledge that change in the way in which we respond to them?

Some variants of this question have public-policy implications. If I make some contractual agreement with a person—say, get her consent to a mutual engagement—and that person then changes, is the contract binding? When someone commits a crime and subsequently undergoes extreme personality change, is he still rightly punished for that crime?

There are more immediate and intimate forms of the question. Should one maintain one's emotional attitudes toward the other person through such changes, or must these emotional attitudes themselves be adjusted? For example, should one later blame or reproach people for harm wrought when they were very different? Are emotional distance and alienation appropriate feelings to harbor toward a friend or loved one when he seems so transformed? Are agreements, promises, and more tacit engagements, earlier entered into, binding through such change? Should one feel betrayed if they are not? May we violate such engagements and agreements without accusing ourselves of betrayal?

These puzzles frequently play themselves out in the clinical context as well, arising as issues of psychotherapeutic ethics. How should a clinician respond to her transformed patient's later attempts to violate preestablished treatment plans? Does loyalty to the "earlier" patient who strove to secure appropriate therapy for himself require the therapist to thwart or resist these later efforts?

What links these questions together are deeply abstract and contested philosophical ideas about the self, about personal responsibility, about the unity of the self at a given time, and about what philosophers call personal identity, the notion that the self or person remains one and the same, singular and unvarying, through time.

So, to discover answers to our question about attitudes toward people who radically change, we must explore questions of philosophical theory. What sort of thing is a self? Is it rightly described as unified at a given time and as continuous as it passes through time? When, if ever, should we speak of one self having changed so much as to have been succeeded, at least temporarily, by another? Should we adopt a special way of speaking, or "language," a language of successive selves, to describe the extremes of duality and even multiplicity found in abnormal psychology? Only when we have explored more far-flung questions such as these can we return close to where we began and ask, How do our usual notions of personal responsibility adjust to the idea of a single body housing more than one self?

Why It Matters

Why is it important to find answers to the questions about extreme personal change, and our attitudes toward those who undergo it, that stimulated this inquiry? There are a number of reasons, some immediate, pressing, and practical, others more theoretical; some perennial, others new.

Many of these questions have been with us as long as have the mental disturbances and brain conditions that result in radical personal change. Do I betray my brother as I plot to hospitalize him for manic excesses that render him, temporarily, like a different person? If I plan for an anticipated phase of mental disturbance of my own, should my plans be respected over the resistance I may show to them later when, much changed, I undergo that mental disturbance? Families, friends, and clinicians have always struggled with these issues about how to act and feel toward others transformed by mental disturbance and disease, as have patients and prospective patients anticipating radical change in themselves.

There is added urgency over the topic of the self's unity today because of developments in psychiatry, abnormal psychology, and psychopharmacology. Advances in psychotropic medication have resulted in the possibility of effecting therapeutic personality change: now as never before, psychiatry can alter people in radical ways, creating new dispositions, moods, attitudes, and responses. With this potential for controlling personality change at hand, it is imperative that we clarify the inclination to construe personal identity in terms of personality, and that we attempt to understand how this construction affects, and is affected by, our central moral categories concerning personal responsibility.

Moreover, because of diminishing skepticism over severe dissociative states and increases in the estimated prevalence of such conditions—or at least an increase in their accurate diagnosis[1]—there is added pressure to understand the meaning of sameness and change when these terms apply to personality or character. If one body can house multiple personalities, our rules for counting personality must be resolved. These developments have already given rise to new legal issues and ethical dilemmas. Should one self of a multiple be held culpable for the misdeeds of another? The first legal cases in the twentieth century resting on this question have been heard in the last two decades.[2]

Theoretical developments have also prepared the way for a study of the kind undertaken here. A remark in Robert Louis Stevenson's tale *Dr. Jekyll and Mr. Hyde*, has a prescience that today is striking. "I hazard the guess," Dr. Jekyll ventures, in his long letter of explanation toward the end of the story, that man "will ultimately be known for a mere polity of multifarious, incongruous and independent denizens" (Stevenson 1886, 49). If we do not yet view the person as Jekyll predicts, nevertheless that vision is more familiar now than ever before. Allusions to divided, fractured, fragmented minds and to multiple, successive selves are nowadays commonplace in both theoretical and empirical studies. We no longer accept unquestioningly the various Western traditions these concepts challenge, including the Cartesian-Kantian one associated with individualism, which posits a single, unified, unvarying subject of experiences in every human breast.

Social scientists, for example, have come to acknowledge the experimental evidence and phenomenological support for, and folk understanding of, a less unified picture of the person. Phenomena like self-deception and weakness of will, split-brain experiments (where neural connections between the two hemispheres of the brain are severed), even the motivational inconsistencies between "economic" and "social" man (Elster 1987), have led to a range of analyses of the multiple, divided, or fragmented self. In some of these analyses, separate but coexisting selves are understood figuratively, in others more literally; they are construed as separate agents in some, merely as separate aspects in others; as rare cases in some, as inevitable features of human nature in others.

In addition, the last decade has seen increasing awareness within philosophy and the social sciences of the normative basis of "methodological individualism," the view that only the properties of individual humans can explain social phenomena. With recognition of alternative, more holistic methodologies, theorists have made renewed efforts to articulate and explain the normative tug of individualism: the social and theoretical interests individualism serves and its links with our moral categories of agency, autonomy, and personal responsibility. Once explained and articulated, these considerations cast will light on our notion of the self and on the custom of attributing a single self to an individual for his or her lifetime.

Other aspects of the tradition of individualism too have been a focus of potentially subversive and radical reassessment. For example, the theory of personal identity underlying the tradition has been directly questioned. To philosophers like Derek Parfit (1971, 1973, 1984), the seeming unity of the self reflects no more than a succession of qualitatively similar, overlapping, and causally related psychological traits.

Modernist Misgivings over a Unified Self

This analysis is situated within the discourse sometimes identified as "modern" or "modernist," at least in that there remains adherence to many of the basic epistemological categories derived from the Enlightenment and from traditional scientific and philosophical method. Postmodern deconstructions of the self, it is true, are also associated with claims as to the self's disunity, discontinuity, and fragmentation, and with doubts over its identity. Indeed, postmodernism has ushered in the purported "death" of the modern subject. In place of the traditional Enlightenment conception of a unified and autonomous self, it has embraced, in the words of one observer, "the flux which moves beyond the scope of control or integration" (Taylor 1989, 462).

The unity of the modern self has also been the subject of profound reevaluation and reassessment within modernist discourse, though. And the concern of this book will be such "modernist" misgivings. Do the relative unity and continuity of a merely empirical self warrant retaining, limiting ourselves to, or relinquishing, the identity language associated with the singular and unvarying self of Cartesian and Kantian theory? Are some selves significantly less unified than others at a time and across stretches of time, as the result of mental disturbance, brain damage, disease, or pharmacological intervention? If we are conceptually free to relinquish the assumptions by which a single, unchanging self inhabits the same body for its spatiotemporal lifetime, at least in the normal case, what normative considerations might nevertheless disincline us from doing so? What can we learn about and from the moral notion of responsibility when we acknowledge that a body may, in unusual cases, house more than one self?

Some of the clinical descriptions examined here, particularly those of the conceptually and clinically problematic "multiples," are the ultimate postmodern phenomena: dizzyingly ambiguous, fragmentary, and elusive. Nonetheless, questions such as these about the moral and philosophical significance of the way the self comes apart in psychopathology cannot be formulated or addressed as readily in postmodernist language: they seem to require and presuppose the concepts and fabric of modernism.

The Framework and Sequence of Argument

This essay elucidates two ways in which the oneness of the self is ruptured in everyday experience and in psychopathology. "Divided minds," disunities and fractures of self at a given time, are conceptually distinguishable from "successive selves," breaks and discontinuities between earlier and later self stages viewed across stretches of time.[3] Rarely evident in normal experience, these fractures and ruptures of the self are usefully highlighted through an examination of case material from abnormal psychology. Here each is vividly reflected, sometimes in unrelated disorders. The patient who suffers from "thought insertion" complains that her mind is invaded by the ideas and feelings of another person. This is a divided mind, at least from her subjective perspective. Yet it may be a relatively unvarying trait through time: the troubling "possession" of which she complains may be a constant. In contrast, we see a succession of selves in the person whose unaccountable swings from manic elation to depressive despair seem to change who she is from one phase to another. At any given time she may possess a mind undivided; more, the quality of unrelieved elation or despair she experiences might seem to exceed the mix and fluctuation of mood we associate with normal experience.

Divided minds force us to clarify our thinking about human subjectivity. They provoke interesting ethical and legal issues when they result in a succession of "selves" sustained through stretches of time and alternating, or potentially alternating, control of the shared body. As its postulates are in certain respects more ambitious, the metaphysics of successive selves invites answers to the important questions about attitudes we should adopt toward those who change radically as the result of mental disturbance. And since my emphasis here is on the practical implications of these phenomena on ethical, therapeutic, and legal theory and practice, successive selves are my initial concern.

Part I begins with a reminder of the divisions and heterogeneities associated with the normal self. I introduce conceptual distinctions and identify a "language of successive selves"—locutions that, by disregarding the traditional identity presumptions underlying the ratio of one person or self to a body per lifetime, permit us to speak of a body as housing more than one self, sequentially or simultaneously. Instances of apparent multiplicity in abnormal psychology, such as dissociative-identity disorder and the cyclical personality changes associated with manic-depressive disorder, seem to invite us to speak of more than one self concurrently or sequentially housed within the same body. The application of the language of successive selves to these disorders allows definition and refinement of terms like 'self' and 'multiplicity'. A language of successive selves may be a mere *façon de parler*. But it may reflect a deeper metaphysics of successive selves. With what metaphysical commitments we adopt a language of successive selves remains to be resolved. This question motivates, in part II, the extended analysis of personal responsibility and culpability as they arise in relation to extreme multiplicity. I explore the implications of allowing these clinical descriptions to challenge our traditional concepts of personal identity, but they reveal methodological issues of great complexity. How we decide to proceed in the practical settings where policy is required will be influenced by our decision over whether to adopt a nontraditional metaphysics of successive selves. But our intuitive responses to these practical and particular matters will influence that decision. Our guide must be an elaborate and methodologically hazardous process of "reflective equilibrium," in which responses to cases temper and influence theory making.

My inquiry in part III furthers the notion of a metaphysics of successive selves by introducing contemporary neo-Humean philosophers, such as H. P. Grice and Derek Parfit, in whose ideas such a nontraditional metaphysics can find theoretical grounding. But other strands of thought are also interposed here: contemporary formulations about the blandishments of individualism. There are purportedly weighty reasons to maintain the notion of an individualistic, singular self and to favor the methodology of individualism.

Finally, in part IV, we return to divided minds. My analysis here addresses theoretical concerns associated with clinical material and uses clinical material to further our understanding of the concepts of self, consciousness, and subjectivity. When divided minds are understood to entail simultaneous, separated centers of awareness and when the behavioral evidence and the introspective evidence are distinguished from one another, the support for ascribing divided minds to cases from psychopathology is weak. The behavioral evidence is equivocal, and the introspective evidence proves insufficient to shake the inviolable subjective unity presupposed in these clinical descriptions.

The conclusions I draw in this essay are of several different kinds. First, we will discover answers to three questions about the informal language of successive selves: Are there practical reasons to use it? Are there theoretical reasons compelling us to see it as merely figurative?

Are there normative reasons to eschew its use? When clarified, we will find that the language of successive selves has particular work to do in the context of understanding, and undertaking therapy with, some forms of mental disorder. Moreover, if we adopt a metaphysics of the self like that of the neoempiricist Parfit, we may use such a language nonfiguratively when we speak of the successive selves found in abnormal psychology. Finally, if we adopt a singularity-conserving "survival" threshold for our metaphysics, we need not fear losing valued concepts and categories—like culpability and responsibility—associated with individualism.

This exploration was stimulated by a set of questions—some personal, some clinical, and others policy-related—about what attitudes we should adopt in the face of the radical personality change and even multiplicity of selves exhibited through mental disturbance. We will find a modest number of answers to these questions too through our analysis of the language and metaphysics of successive selves.

Yet what are in some ways the most important and far-reaching conclusions of this inquiry will not be helpful in any practical or even personal setting. In this sense, the questions that proved the impetus for the beginning of this investigation do not adequately define its middle and end. Viewed as a whole, the essay that follows emerges as an extended effort to show the complexities and methodological dangers that stand in the way of achieving a resolution, rather than a set of matching answers, when we engage with this particular set of questions. As such, many of its conclusions are negative, others are nuanced and qualified.

A Reader's Guide

This discussion is multistranded and located at the borders between several fields of inquiry, each with its distinctive discourses and concerns. Thus, although it contains overarching themes and theses of interest to each discipline, the essay that follows has been constructed to be read selectively. The following observations provide a guide to the selective or theory-wary reader. Chapter 2 offers a simplified outline of the set of theoretical distinctions required for the analysis; these are explored more fully in the notes and in chapter 11. Chapters

1, 3, and 4 present empirical descriptions from everyday life and abnormal psychology that provide the data for claims about the unity and continuity of the self. Personal responsibility is a theme throughout part III, but the practical and policy-related questions about multiplicity are raised in chapters 7 to 10. The central argument concerning the normative tug of individualism is to be found in the first pages of chapter 12 and in chapter 14. And finally, the conclusions and discussion about divided minds in part IV, although they represent a contribution to philosophical theory, add only indirectly to the framing questions concerning multiplicity and personal responsibility.

Preliminary Terminological Clarification

In the vast and varied literature on the self, there are diverse conceptions and many different understandings of the self's divisions, heterogeneities, and discontinuities, and these will be distinguished and ordered in the pages to come. But three brief explanations are required at the outset. First, we need some definition for the theoretical and theory-saturated construct of the self. Let us work with the following: a self = an embodied repository of integrated psychological states. The nature of the repository and the degree and kind of integration are intentionally left vague in this formulation to accommodate the diverse understandings of the self to be explored; each term will be clarified and sharpened through that exploration.[4]

Next, unity. We speak of the unity of the self in two slightly different ways. Normally, a oneness and harmony to the heterogeneity of the experiences of a person *at a given time* allows us to say that they are all the person's experiences. Distinguishable from this is the normal connectedness between a person's experiences *as they are scattered over time*—the linked and enduring nature of sets of traits and experiences through time that allows us to say they are all attributable to the same person. These may be distinguished as unity and continuity, respectively. A want of the first kind of unity, which we find in the divided minds of mental disorder, I will call *disunity*. A want of the second kind, the unity of the person over time, which invites an analysis of successive selves, I will call *discontinuity*. Some theorists have employed the adjectives 'synchronic' (referring to a given time) and 'diachronic' (referring to stretches of time) in noting the distinction between the self's relative unity or oneness at a given time and its apparent loose identity or continuity through stretches of time (Daniels 1979, de Sousa 1976, Shoemaker 1986, Wilkes 1988, Korsgaard 1989). While I will emphasize the contrast between diachronic and synchronic disunities of the self, I will avoid these terms. I will use the term 'disunity' for those heterogeneities or disunities of self that occur at a particular time (i.e., for synchronic disunity); 'discontinuity' will portray the heterogeneity and lack of oneness exhibited by selves through stretches of time (i.e., their diachronic disunities).

The exploration that follows, then, will pursue two sorts of questions: those concerning disunity—'Are these (present) experiences all mine (hers)?'—and those concerning discontinuity—'Am I (is she) the same person now as I (she) was at some earlier time?'

Finally, a comment on the place of perspective. The self's disunity and discontinuity may be understood introspectively and from the more detached perspective of the public stance. Our understanding of the self's disunity and discontinuity vary according to the introspective and public perspectives, and these different perspectives yield different senses or understandings of the notions of disunity and discontinuity, and of the self. What subjectively feels like a divided mind may publicly be a united one; what publicly looks disunited or discontinuous may subjectively feel like one or a series of normal changes. Which perspective should be honored when they indicate divergent and even contradictory judgements and prescriptions, as we will see later, is a philosophical question with far-reaching implications, and so calls for a careful and considered decision.

1

Heterogeneities of Self in Everyday Life

If we inquire first not into where the self's apparent heterogeneities are problematic but where they are not, we confront normal psychology, its common or garden variety. Elements of discontinuity and disharmony are present here, but they are not found strange, awkward, or requiring special explanation, either by ordinary or specialized understanding. Everyday life experience reveals selves as less than perfect, homogenous unities. At a given time they may be both experienced and publicly observed as made up of distinguishable parts and divisions; through time they undergo changes.

The findings of this chapter, then, will be limited and free of theorizing. By beginning where the self's assorted heterogeneities, disunities, and discontinuities are unproblematic, or relatively so, and revealing the sources on which we rely for our precritical sense of the wholeness or oneness of the normal self, I hope to have clarified some ordinary notions of unity and continuity by the time we reach the rare and extreme cases of disunity and discontinuity we seek to understand.

In particular, this chapter will lay the groundwork for what follows by delimiting what will be deemed unity and disunity, continuity and discontinuity, sameness and difference. Our everyday, precritical notion of the self's unity, which will yield our touchstone, allows us to see a unified self as comprising parts and as changing through time.

Perspectives

Even the commonest and least remarkable heterogeneities of self, such as the psychological changes we undergo as we mature or the states of conflict and ambivalence to which we are subject, may be understood in several ways and from several perspectives. One may recognize a want of oneness or harmony within the self both when one regards the self at some given time and when one regards it as it persists through time. It may be recognized in ourselves by ourselves, or in us by others, or recognized by no one.

First, disunity and discontinuity. Heterogeneities, or disunities at given moment in time, are distinguishable from failures of oneness or continuity through time, we know. The interruptions resulting from sleep affect the self's psychic continuity through time, to take the simplest example. Conflicting wishes, on the other hand, challenge our experience of the self's inner unity at a given time; they may be said to reflect disunity. The collection of heterogeneities enumerated below includes some that illustrate disunity within the self and some that illustrate the self's discontinuity through stretches of time.

Next, subjective and public perspectives. Another important contrast is between the self's heterogeneity as it is understood from within, or introspectively, and as it is understood from the more detached perspective of the public stance. Felt or introspectively apprehended disunity, such as the struggle we experience as the victims of conflicting and incompatible desires, may not be seen to threaten the integrity of the self from the outside, or publicly. Disunity not recognized from inside may reveal itself as a fractured or heterogeneous self to the public observer—as in self-deception or the apparently incompatible desires expressed in alternating inconsistent preferences through time.

What we can discover about discontinuity and change of the self through time is not so critically a function of perspective as is our understanding of the self's disunity at a given time. Viewing ourselves across stretches of time, we come to know changes in ourselves in ways that are closer to the ways in which others know the changes in us. We often adopt a public perspective, or something very like it, when we take the long view and contemplate our past and future selves. The statement "I am a different person now from the person I was them" may well be based on something detached, publicly observable, and objective. Rather than an intimate comparison of the remembered feeling of past states (my sadness or despair then, for example) with those I now experience (my present equanimity) my sources may be a comparison between earlier and later behavior and behavioral dispositions (I used to be so moody, always crying into my brandy, and now nothing seems to trouble me)—precisely the sources used by others to make such a judgement.

To distinguish public from more subjective perspectives, then, is not to embrace an unyielding dichotomy, either between self and other or between subject and object. First, the individual may adopt a public perspective toward her own states and experiences, we just saw. This perspectival shifting and distancing commonly takes place as immediate experiences recede in time to become memories. It is particularly common and significant after mental disturbance works radical personality change and fractures an individual life into parts.

Second, the practice of empathic understanding and response allows others, including therapists, to leave the public standpoint and approach the subjective perspective associated with introspection (Margulies 1989, Meyers 1994).

While not consistently correlated with self and other, or subject and object, and also not sharply delineated at its borders, this distinction between subjective and more public perspectives is nevertheless recognizable, and it will prove morally significant when we come to consider questions of responsibility ascription later in this book.[1]

Disunity: Heterogeneities of Self at a Given Time

The mind or self is far from coextensive with consciousness. It is commonly acknowledged that parts of our mental lives take place beyond conscious awareness. Although the infusion of Freudian theory into our everyday thinking on this matter has served to emphasize this point, an appreciation that there exist mental workings of which we are not aware far antedates Freudianism and is widespread. (Some theorists object that this source of every day heterogeneity is insufficiently stressed, nonetheless [Kristeva 1991, 192].)

Such an appreciation also exceeds Freudianism. Experimental psychology has established that behavior is affected by stimuli whose reception went unnoticed by the subject. Thus awareness, at least as measured in these studies, by verbal report, is not an accurate indication of the effect stimuli have on behavior. Moreover, the machinations of mental capacities like memory, or memory-based recognition, remain substantially unavailable to awareness. I know the outcome of such machinations, the knowledge itself, but I do not experience the process by which memory retrieval is effected—this process remains unconscious. So one division of the self widely acknowledged and accepted as holding universally (if at all) marks its conscious and unconscious aspects. This is only one, fairly prosaic way in which we often seem to presuppose the self to be made up of parts. But it is one that, by definition, does not present itself to immediate introspection. Only by adopting the detached, public view of the observer may we see that the mind comprises unconscious as well as conscious elements.

Next, consider how it is when we cannot decide how to act or believe because of a set of conflicting assumptions, desires or beliefs. We experience ambivalence, or are of two minds, as it is colloquially put. Here disunity is felt and suffered. Consider too the several disharmonies between our mental states. A certain degree of consonance is usual between a person's assumptions, beliefs, values, and desires, for example, yet this degree is compatible with that person's encompassing and even struggling with conflicting states. Rather than an unusual or problematic state, being of two minds is a most commonplace and natural experience. Some assumptions, beliefs, values, and desires are in conflict, and to recognize this is normal. Perhaps it is human too: a degree of harmony so great as to preclude all ambivalence, if such a state is imaginable, suggests a different style of intelligence—perhaps of divine or artificial origin. A related point has been emphasized by the philosopher Harry Frankfurt. It is distinctly human, Frankfurt (1971) has pointed out, to experience "second-order" desires—desires about what we want to desire. (Others have captured this distinction more colloquially, speaking of the conflict between desires and values [Watson 1975, 1977; Segal 1991].) To entertain two orders of desire is to be creatures of conflicting desire and inner duality: to want one thing and to want to want another.

Some degree of integration is brought about by agency itself: a single source of direction or control that aligns thought and action. Yet these are not always aligned. We give in to wayward impulses—acting contrary to our second-order desires or despite them—and these misalignments too are unsurprising.

There are other divisions and breaks in awareness. We talk to ourselves, inwardly and sometimes aloud, and this behavior seems least paradoxical if we postulate an inner "audience," an aspect distinct from the speaker to whom such words are directed. We also divide our attention, doing two things at once, like singing while we drive or monitoring a side exchange, or a TV screen, while we engage in conversation. Habitual action and response seem to be at odds, in a certain way, with what receives full attention.

Altered states of consciousness like daydreaming and meditation suggest another disunity. They result in a sharper division between the "background" and "foreground" experiences than that to which we are accustomed in more ordinary exercises of selective attention. There is also the complication introduced by unbidden thoughts, welcome and unwelcome. A tune runs persistently through one's head; an image or memory floats up uninvited. Here the coherence imposed through a willfully directed train of thought or through controlled acts of attention is interrupted.

The contents of consciousness comprise a kind of heterogeneous unity when considered at a particular time. At any moment we are the subject of a plurality of experiences and states. Yet these experiences and states *are* simultaneous, or are at least experienced to be so, and are thus united temporally.[2] They are all mine, moreover, and mine alone. They seem centered in my spot of spatiality, the particular, unique place from which I derive my point of view. James captures the sense of this kind of unity in the following passage:

In this room—in this lecture room, say—there are a multitude of thoughts —yours and mine—some of which cohere mutually, and some not.... My thought belongs with MY other thoughts, and your thought with YOUR other thoughts. Whether anywhere in the room there is a MERE thought, which is nobody's thought, we have no means of ascertaining, for we have no experience of its like. (1890, 220–221)

Now it seems obvious that these ways in which our lives and selves are marked by a want of oneness, wholeness, and homogeneity are the very stuff of normal human experience. They are eminently unpuzzling. Indeed, the puzzle lies with the person not subject to these inner complexities and, we might say, this inner richness.

So much seems true at least when we regard these heterogeneities in temporal isolation, or from the perspective of a given moment in time. Yet a person's peace of mind, even the ability to undertake coherent action, may be threatened by a pattern of disharmonies and heterogeneities, even if the disharmonies and heterogeneities are of this seemingly innocent kind. We may come to regard as troubled, neurotic, and opaque the person so torn or divided. James describes a "heterogenous personality," for instance, where, as he puts it, a strong degree of heterogeneity may make havoc of a person's life. James's portrayal of such people is immediately recognizable. There are those, he says, "whose existence is little more than a series of zigzags, as now one tendency and now another gets the upper hand. Their spirit wars with their flesh, they wish for incompatibles, wayward impulses interrupt their most deliberate plans, and their lives are one long drama of repentance and of effort to repair misdemeanors and mistakes" (James 1890, 145).

James pictures an extreme, though this passage is free of psychiatric language. But his description serves to remind us that, in lesser and unsurprising degrees, we are all subject to these vagaries and zig zags, these wayward impulses, wars between spirit and flesh, and wishes for incompatibles. And it reminds us that the view at a slice of time may conceal heterogeneities more perspicuous when viewed over time.

Discontinuity: Heterogeneities of Self over Time

From the longitudinal perspective over time too, experiences exhibit a degree of sameness or continuity while being recognizably discontinuous. There is also the inexorable change we all observe and experience through childhood and youth. The developments of capacity, disposition, moral and emotional response, can transform an infant between one month and five years (already strikingly altered in physical appearance and physical abilities), a child between six and ten, a youth between thirteen and sixteen.

Consciousness usually presents itself as a relatively coherent and continuous "stream," to use James's metaphor. My experience now is united with my experience yesterday through a succession of intermediate, overlapping states. Breaks within my conscious awareness result from lacunae or lapses in my experiential memory and the losses of consciousness undergone during sleep. Further and different interruptions to the sequence and coherence of my mental life are brought about by dreaming. But such interruptions little disturb my sense of lived continuity, since they are predictable and often shared. Moreover, my bundles of experience vary against a backdrop of cognitive, emotional, and attitudinal dispositions, habits, and capabilities that remain relatively invariant. Like the earth's crust, these dispositions usually shift and alter only gradually and imperceptibly.

Both as we observe it in others and from within ourselves, however, the normal, adult self's constancy and unchanging continuity through time is less than absolute. Changes in these dispositions occur. Accommodations are made for new ideas, changes in circumstances, and capacities. And our ability to adapt and develop as the result of new experience is commonplace. Nor are all these "natural" changes gradual, as some cases of conversion illustrate.

Although strongly linked with religious life, the notion of a change in personality brought about by adopting an intensely felt belief or passion, or by an influential experience, exceeds the strictly religious or spiritual context. "Life-changing" or "life-altering" experiences come in many different guises, particularly in a secular age (Flanagan 1991, 1994). In *The Varieties of Religious Experience* (1902) James portrays not only cases of "counterconversion" (the transition from orthodoxy to infidelity) but also cases of, for example, a sudden conversion to avarice and cases of falling in and out of love. On this broad understanding that encompasses more than religious experience, conversions point to one way in which personality change may be both radical and rapidly occurring in those who are psychologically normal. It is part of our concept of radical change of this kind to suppose it thoroughgoing enough to affect all of the person, not only her beliefs and desires but also her long-term dispositions, behavior, and moods. James quotes the New England Puritan Joseph Alleine on this point, and although Alleine refers to religiously effected change, we can readily recognize that his description extends beyond that case. Conversion, Alleine says, "is not the putting in a patch of holiness; but with the true convert holiness is woven into all his powers, principles, and practice. The sincere Christian is quite a new fabric, from the foundation to the top-stone. He is a new man, a new creature" (James 1902, 188).

Such thoroughgoing change may be very rapid, even dated to a single experience, a single moment. Yet it may also be more gradual. Indeed, James objects to the notion that true religious conversion need be dramatic or sudden. Rather than something divine, he argues that what makes the difference between a sudden and a gradual convert is that those suddenly affected have undergone a period of "subconscious incubation" (1902, 153).[3]

Conversions, then, constitute an important example for us. They may be religiously motivated or not; they may be rapidly effected or not. But once effected, in the cases that are illustrative here, they will be radical and thoroughgoing, transforming of foundation, and topstone, to produce a "new creature." And despite the sometimes sudden and always extreme personality changes with which they are associated, religious and other "conversions" are usually regarded as intelligible: we suppose that they are explained in loosely rational terms. A woman previously submissive and downtrodden sometimes will undergo such radical "conversion" upon exposure to feminist ideas and ideals. She will reassess her life—her relationships, her goals, how she presents herself and feels, her beliefs and desires—and so her behavior and dispositions. Given that she has come to adopt a new set of beliefs, we see nothing puzzling or incoherent about the radical changes in her behavior and dispositions that ensue. Thus, if the change is rapid and radical but seemingly rationally embraced, we treat it as we would the slow personality changes described earlier, and we think of it, like them, if not as prudent, then at least as normal.

None of the heterogeneities discussed thus far is controversial. There is widespread agreement, among philosophers and nonphilosophers alike, over the normal disunities of self here illustrated and the normally explained changes and discontinuities of self through time.

More Puzzling Divisions: Self-Deception and Akrasia

In many cases the apparent heterogeneity of the self expressed through holding contradictory beliefs and desires is also unproblematic. But instances of each of these forms of disharmony has been adduced in support of some theory or thesis concerning the self's fragmentation, disunity, discontinuity, or multiplicity, so these categories deserve special attention here. Moreover, the holding of incompatible beliefs and desires that respectively emerge in self-deception and weakness of will (or what philosophers call "akrasia") are rightly seen as more problematic and puzzling for philosophical accounts of the self.

We may hold contradictory beliefs quite unwittingly. We often fail to recognize the inherent contradiction in a set of beliefs because of the complexity of the relationships between them, for example. No heterogeneity of a serious or puzzling kind seems to be reflected by these cases, though, because we feel sure that were the individual aware of the contradiction, the pull of consistency would result in the unifying step required: one belief would be relinquished. Apparently wittingly holding contradictory beliefs also often reflects an innocent and unproblematic heterogeneity of self. We engage in it when we adopt aesthetic, symbolic, empathetic, and wishful stances or attitudes (Radden 1984). Reading a work of fiction, we knowingly enter into a state of believing both *p* (the heroine exists) and not *p* (she does not exist). It is a constituent part of an emotional response to the heroine's plight that we entertain the false belief that she exists while knowing she does not and never has. When we identify with another person (*X*) empathetically, putting ourselves in her shoes and feeling as she does, our emotional response seems to presuppose constituent beliefs, such as 'I feel *X*'s pain', knowingly held simultaneously with contrary beliefs, such as 'I do not feel *X*'s pain'. Finally, our pleasure when we engage in wishful thinking and imagine ourselves rich depends on the (false) belief that we are rich, which we entertain simultaneously with our knowledge that we are not.

Wishful thinking is closely related to, and often seems to occasion, self-deception. But self-deception, which also appears to involve knowingly holding conflicting or contradictory beliefs, presents a more serious challenge to the notion of the self's oneness and will require a separate and fuller treatment later. While commonplace, self-deception and weakness of will, or akrasia, are puzzling.

A consideration of inconsistent desires reveals some of the same features that we have seen in inconsistent beliefs. Economists and social scientists have uncovered assorted inconsistencies in the preferences exhibited in human behavior. For example there are "preference reversals," where people make intransitive choices (preferring *a* over *c*, even though *a* and *c* are substantively equivalent [$a = b$, $b = c$]) or they alternate between one preference and another, incompatible preference. (Thaler 1980, Tversky and Kahneman 1981). The first of these is easily explained, and any suggestion of disunity attached to it dispelled, if we remember that although *a* and *c* are substantively equivalent, the way the choice is described, or as social scientists put it, "framed," may influence how *a* and *c* are evaluated. Cast as a percentage of a number, an outcome may elicit different responses from when it is put forward as a raw score, for example. Inconsistent preferences of this kind may be irrational, but they are hardly inexplicable or, as has been suggested, an indication of significantly fractured selves.

Knowingly holding incompatible preferences is more difficult to understand. Sometimes alternating preferences are the result of an inner struggle; at other times they are not—a difference that is critical. When there is no struggle, the simplest explanation, akin to the caveats above about framing, applies. It seems more plausible to conclude either that the individual is unaware of the inconsistency (it is an unwitting confusion, which we would expect eliminated upon its disclosure) or that the individual's preference system cannot be characterized as baldly as it has been and must contain hedges and qualifications that would account for the apparent inconsistency. Conflicting preferences accompanied by, or resulting from, a felt struggle within the person, however, are more difficult to understand and more suggestive of deep disunity. They are instances of the philosophical category of akrasia, to be discussed later. Like self-deception and unlike the other phenomena enumerated here, akratic behavior is puzzling.

In conclusion, unremarkable heterogeneities of self found in everyday life have two features of significance for us. First, they are universal, or next to universal. To greater and lesser degrees, they are ascribable to everyone and anyone. This means that they must be taken into account in a rather different way from the rare phenomena found in, for example, abnormal psychology. Yet their ubiquity is not sufficient to mark off and distinguish these habits of mind and behavior. Other phenomena that seem to challenge the usual notion of the self's unity—self-deception and weakness of will, or akrasia, for example—are also as widespread. But unlike self-deception and akrasia, which have been a source of paradox, the heterogeneities described here are neither puzzling nor strange. Indeed, some of them seem so central to our notion of a human self that we would question whether a more unified self than they allow were truly human.

When we turn from divisions and disunities in the self viewed at a single time to discontinuities and changes that emerge when the self is understood as an entity persisting through time, we find that these latter cases presuppose, in addition, a certain explanatory framework. This is what philosophers distinguish as the "rational" or "intentional" framework, associated with human action and the notion of behavior as not merely goal-directed but as motivated and explained by reasons (Dennett 1969). Even when they are abrupt and radical, normal causes, such as changing one's mind through rational persuasion or adapting one's behavior to newly acquired beliefs and desires, are sufficient to account for these discontinuities. Unremarkable heterogeneities, then, aside from those associated with conflicting beliefs, preferences, and desires, are readily explained by reasons.

The Heterogeneous Self: A Touchstone

Whatever approach we adopt in our exploration of divided minds and successive selves, we must acknowledge these unremarkable heterogeneities. Ordinary selves are at best only relatively continuous through time, and at any particular time their unity or oneness is not simple. In the discussions that follow, these observations about the unremarkable heterogeneities of the singular self we encounter in everyday life will be treated as a given and a touchstone. Other evidence and observations will be measured against this standard of oneness, and no further effort will be made to defend the merely relative unity of the self revealed in the examples enumerated here. Any thesis concerning the self's disunity, fragmentation, multiplicity, or discontinuity through time must find support elsewhere: these empirical observations are spoken for. They reveal heterogeneities of the self compatible with our usual notion that the self is one.

A Language of Successive Selves

The philosophical ideas associated with identity offer a framework for understanding how we are able to speak of a single body housing more than one self throughout its lifetime. Yet the concept of identity, like the concept of self, is complex, many-faceted, and open to misinterpretation. Some initial clarification is required of the different ways in which 'identity' may be understood; of the distinction between perfect or numerical identity and qualitative sameness or similarity; of the personal identity presumptions underlying our commonsense supposition that selves come just "one to a customer," in the phrase of a contemporary theorist (Dennett 1991); and finally, of the status to be ascribed to, and the scope for, the seemingly figurative and secondary "language" of successive selves, which belies these personal identity presumptions.

Identity and Uniqueness

In its concern with questions about the self's sameness through time or identity in the sense of singularity (oneness at a given time) and invariance (the trait of remaining unchanged through time), philosophical inquiry into personal identity considers what enduring physical or psychological traits provide grounds for the judgment 'It's the same person.' Yet it is not the individuating particularity of these attributes that I emphasize here—my body's distinguishing features, your distinctive personality and memories. Rather, it is what you and I share in common: having *some* enduring psychological and bodily characteristics, rather than none.

Nietzsche has remarked that at bottom, every human being knows quite well that he is only in the world one time, uniquely. For no accident, however strange, Nietzsche insists, will shake together for a second time "such an oddly bright sundriness" into "the sameness" that a person is (1966, 1:287–288). Identity in this sense of uniqueness illustrated by Nietzsche focuses not on sameness through time but on difference and differentiation from other persons. Like the self concept, of which it will be a part, a person's identity in this sense of her "oddly bright sundriness" is detailed, rich, and embroidered: in serving to individuate us one from another, it captures all our uniqueness, our selves as social and cultural particulars. This richer, social and cultural notion of identity is inexpressibly important to human lives, as some theorists have recognized (Flanagan and Rorty 1990). But it will not enter our discussion initially. In this chapter, my concern is with the person's sameness or identity in the thinner sense of sameness through time.

The Language of Sameness and Difference

The fact that we customarily speak as if selves were unities though they are heterogeneous—containing parts and changing through stretches of time—should deter us from two errors of thinking about sameness and difference. It would be a mistake to suppose that something must be simple, i.e., without parts, for us to see it as one at a given time, and it would be wrong to suppose that a thing must remain entirely unchanging for us to speak about it as remaining the same through time. Forewarned so that we may avoid these two errors, we still must navigate difficult waters when we use language making reference to the self's singularity and invariance through time. Ambiguities and complexities are involved in these judgments. Some of these may be illustrated by reference to the way we speak of the identity of nonhumans, ordinary material objects like curtains and refrigerators. We might say both (a) and (b):

(a)   It's the same curtains (though I dyed them a different shade)!

(b)   The curtains are not the same as before (because I dyed them).

Context and an explanation of the kind provided parenthetically in each of (a) and (b) prevent us from becoming confused by this ambiguity in most cases. Native speakers of English are adroit at distinguishing when 'the same *x*' bespeaks singularity as in the spatio-temporal continuity of "particulars" (as entities like curtains are called [Strawson 1959]) from the qualitative sameness that rests on invariance of attributes such as color.[1]

Minds, persons, and selves differ from more mundane spatio-temporal particulars like curtains and refrigerators. Nonetheless, it is possible to recognize significant parallels between the ambiguities of the language of sameness and difference in which we speak about such material objects as curtains and refrigerators and how we judge continuity and discontinuity in human beings. Speaking of selves or persons, we employ a matching pair of meanings to those noted in the judgments above about curtains.

(a') Jane is the (same) person I went to school with!

(b') Jane is not the same person since becoming a feminist.

There is no incompatibility between these two claims ((a') and (b')). In the first instance, (a'), sameness probably implies spatiotemporal continuity, while in the second, (b'), the customarily slow progression and continuation of psychological attributes like beliefs and desires is recognized to have been radically interrupted through an experience or a cluster of significant events: Jane's becoming a feminist. Jane has undergone personality and perhaps character change.

In people, as in curtains, sameness understood in these qualitative and (in this case) psychological terms frequently does diverge in the way suggested by the example of (a') and (b'). Like a set of curtains, a person is wont to remain at once the same and yet not the same through a stretch of time.[2] Our customary language affirms traditional and commonsensical presumptions such as the notion that just one person or self will be housed in each body for that body's lifetime. But because of the ambiguities attached to 'sameness' noted above, we may acknowledge that alongside our customary language, there coexists another way of speaking, another "language." Such a language enables us to say 'She's not the same person' without precluding that the person or self remains the same in other empirical respects, is, for example, spatiotemporally continuous. This additional language of sameness and change emerges naturally and surprisingly commonly in discussions about the case material of abnormal psychology.

Despite the parallels between (a) plus (b) and (a') plus (b'), we now must recognize a difference between the two attributions of sameness and difference found in them. (There are other differences as well [Mackie 1976, chap. 6], although they are not important to us here.) Without concern, we can say that our use of 'the same curtains' in (a) is a literal one, whereas in (b) it is not. 'It's not the same curtains' is a figurative and secondary use of 'the same curtains'.[3] In contrast, when we turn to (a') and (b') and speak of the sameness of persons or selves, we will see that it is not so clear how or whether this distinction between literal and figurative usages applies.

Because the discourse of exact similarity or qualitative sameness in which we say 'She's not the same person since she became a feminist' also makes reference to sameness and difference through time, it too involves identity, loosely understood. To refer to this last way of talking about identity, I will make use of an expression introduced by the philosopher Derek Parfit (1984) and speak of the language of successive selves. Let me define the phrase. A *language of successive selves* refers to that set of locutions about the sameness of selves or persons that emphasizes judgments based on qualitative sameness, or similarity.

A Language of Successive Selves

In one important way, even the person who undergoes radical psychological changes though time remains the same, whether or not these changes are accompanied by alterations of physical appearance. Bodily continuity unites earlier and later temporal stages of our bodily selves, through which, as particulars with a unique spatiotemporal pathway in the empirical world, unique identifying reference can be made and reidentification through time is possible. This bodily continuity is not to be confused with bodily appearances.

Unlike appearances, bodily continuity is invariant. My spatiotemporal continuity can be no greater or less than yours. My outward bodily appearance, in contrast, may change more or less than yours. You may bald, fatten, and lose an eye; I may remain apparently unchanged. The language of successive selves admits of degree. It allows that some people may be less united through time than others. So the continuities and discontinuities of selves implied in the language of successive selves will rely on features likely to vary: outward bodily appearance and nonbodily, psychological criteria. And indeed it does. We may say 'He's a new man since losing that 40 pounds.' And, more important for my discussion, we appeal to features of personality and character, and changes in nonbodily dispositions and traits, when we employ the language of successive selves and judge, for example, 'She is not the person she was.' Put another way, the language of successive selves allows us to acknowledge changes that leave people different, in qualitative respects, from how they were.

This notion of qualitative sameness or similarity will be especially important for us to examine, as we will see in later chapters. The informal criteria by which we distinguish multiplicity (separate selves) and unity in discussions of everyday and psychiatric phenomena clearly appeal to some kind of nonbodily attributes. Bodily and in physical appearance, the person divided or fractured by dissociative disorder, extensive self-deception, or brain disease may remain unchanged.

Two important questions must be asked here about the language of successive selves, one concerning its scope and the second its nature. First, should this language have exclusive application to the extreme discontinuities found in abnormal psychology? Or may we continue to apply it—as many now do—to the ruptures and breaks in otherwise ordinary selves and lives wrought by religious experience and ideological conversion?

That a language of successive selves seems fitting for descriptions of religiously or ideologically induced personality change seems undeniable. Cases of personality change encountered in abnormal psychology share strong similarities with these conversions, we will see. But they also differ. For example, the changes resulting from religious and ideological conversion (although not the conversion experience itself: the salient experience or the voice from God) are usually explained by means of a "rational" or "intentional" framework. Not only within a community of believers—the other folk in the revivalists' tent, let us say—but also among those skeptical of the convictions in question, there is a generosity of interpretation toward religious and ideological transformation. A link posited between thought and action, it is allowed, is comprehensible to observer and convert alike. This will be true, for the most part, just when the fine line between religious or ideological change and pathology is preserved.

When the terms of the language of successive selves have been clarified and analyzed, it will become apparent that this feature of religious and ideological change is significant. Thus, while conversions resemble forms of mental disturbance, they will prove more problematic examples of successive selves than the personality changes encountered within the clinical field.

A second question concerns the nature of this language of successive selves. Must the language be seen as *figurative*? Is it, as the *OED* reminds us, nonliteral in being exaggerated and allegorical or failing to take words in their primary sense? Certainly this is how it is treated in the informal settings in which it is usually introduced. It is a loose, vague, and limited form of reference with few, or at least few resolved, implications. It is employed, after all, within the linguistic context of the customary and more common language honoring the presumptions of the "one self to a customer" rule. Moreover, it is employed within a world in which few changes are at once so abrupt and so radical as to invite the use of a looser language of successive selves. As it is presently used, then, the language of successive selves seems less literal than the personal-identity language with which it is contrasted.

But to determine whether this language of successive selves *must* be judged as figurative and secondary, we have to resolve issues not merely of language but of metaphysics. The concepts of person and self are theory-laden and contested constructs: they do not make unproblematic reference to the material or bodily entities or attributes with which they are associated.[4] In this respect, as we saw, persons and selves are unlike curtains. If we seek a parallel, angels might be more fitting. Consider the following:

(c)   She was an angel to me, coming in and cooking while I was sick in bed.

(d)   There are angels in heaven.

If the distinction between literal and figurative usages applies at all, (c) is figurative. But whether the distinction applies, and whether (d) is a literal use, will depend on the speaker's and/or hearer's metaphysical beliefs. 'Angel' too, we might say, is a theory-laden and contested construct.

A Metaphysics of Successive Selves

For some theorists of personal identity, it is unimaginable that we should treat a language of successive selves as anything more than figurative and metaphorical, because this language cannot provide us with the means of uniquely identifying and reidentifying persons through time—a requirement that is central to many of our human purposes. This view is expressed in philosophical debates about what are called the criteria of personal identity, the traits people possess in virtue of whose continuity through time we make judgments of singularity and invariance.[5] Some philosophers have insisted that the spatiotemporal continuity of the body (or the brain) is the source of personal identity judgments (Wiggins 1967, Williams 1973). On such an account, the continuity of persons or selves is just as strict—no more and no less, and for the same reasons—as the relative and imperfect identity of other material objects we judge to remain the same through time (curtains, refrigerators, etc.). This may not be identity strictly so called, which does not admit of degree. But it is the workaday spatiotemporal continuity we need to identify and reidentify particulars. On this theory, the continuation of the body is at least necessary for personal identity.[6]

Not all philosophers judge bodily continuity to be the, or even a, criterion of personal identity. The normal person in everyday contexts has a high degree of continuity of several kinds. As well as the continuation of the body through its spatiotemporal path, there is also continuity of enduring psychological states and dispositions, memory, the stream of consciousness, and persisting capabilities and skills. (Notice that some of these are directly observed only by adopting a subjective approach and appealing to introspection, some are publicly observable from the more detached perspective of the other, and some may be observed from either stance.) Theorists arguing for one or another of these enduring, empirically observable sources of continuity as criteria for personal identity urge that not each of them is equally vital for our judgment that the same person or self is perpetuated through time.

Several contemporary thinkers have pointed to the continuity of psychological attributes in answer to questions about the singularity and invariance of the person or self through time (Grice 1941; Quinton 1962; Parfit 1971, 1973, 1984; Shoemaker 1963, 1968, 1970, 1979, 1984). These attributes, which in normal cases, at least, provide a quite high degree of continuity between earlier and later stages of a person's psychological life, are portrayed in several different ways. Some have been seen to be occurrences—recurring, dateable, experienced states that link earlier and later stages of one's psychological history. Others have been regarded as overlapping or continuing dispositions to do, feel, remember, believe, or will. As long as these attributes are taken to be psychological *occurrences* (particular, dateable, introspectable events in consciousness), there will be interruptions in this continuity, of course, such as those that result from sleep. The sequence will be less like a stream (to use James's metaphor for consciousness) and more like a serialized newspaper story. Only by treating these traits as dispositions or capabilities with causal powers (we remain disposed to do, feel, remember, believe, and will even while asleep) can we countenance their uninterrupted continuity.[7]

One influential theory emphasizing the importance of the continuity provided by psychological traits is that of Derek Parfit, and for the sake of simplicity I will make use of his theory, although other theorists, such as Sydney Shoemaker, have elaborated accounts of comparable depth and detail. On Parfit's analysis, the continuity of psychological states explains the traditional ways we speak of the self as invariant. Memories, dispositions, personality traits, and behavioral tendencies form a causally related and overlapping series in most people's lives sufficient for us to speak of the same person as surviving— though not as maintaining "identity," strictly understood—through stretches of time.

Theories such as this rely on some form of psychological continuity to ground and explain normal judgments of singularity and invariance, and together with the quarrel dividing theorists over psychological and bodily continuity criteria for personal identity, they will be explored more fully in chapter 11. These metaphysical questions about the sort of thing a self is and the criteria for its continuing identity or survival through time are complex and must await an analysis of the normative context.

And answers to these deep questions will affect whether, and in what way, a language of successive selves may be said to be figurative or nonliteral. If bodily continuity is required for personal identity, then, indeed, the language of successive selves will be seen as strongly metaphorical or figurative, at best. Literally, selves or persons are, or are to be identified with, bodies: the "one to a customer" rule, on this view, is based on metaphysical necessity, not arbitrary decision. If, on the other hand, we accept some version of psychological-continuity theory, then selves, and perhaps persons too, are rather different sorts of things, and it ceases to be clear that the language of successive selves need be, or even can be, construed as figurative. Rather, it has to be taken more literally. For those embracing a successive-selves metaphysics, the *figurative* language would be our customary, singularity-conserving language reflecting the "one to a customer" rule, and the literal language, that of successive selves.

Moral- and policy-related questions over the personal responsibility attributable to the successive selves associated with mental disturbance force us to focus on what is at stake when there is divergence from traditional identity theories and presuppositions. Indeed, so interdependent are moral and metaphysical reasoning, that our moral responses to these questions about responsibility contribute to our decision whether to adopt a metaphysics of successive selves.

Is the language of successive selves merely figurative? Since moral responses in part determine the plausibility of metaphysical theories, one way to begin to find out is to explore these moral responses, as we will, in part II. In the last chapters of this book (part IV), we will return to theories of personal identity, like Parfit's, that permit us to embrace a metaphysics of successive selves. Until the moral and normative issues are explored and these theories laid out, we may remain agnostic about whether we are employing a figurative language or adopting a new metaphysics of the self.

If this language of successive selves proves merely figurative, committing us to no exotic metaphysics of the self, it is nevertheless a convenience—and once clarified, an exceedingly useful one, we will see—in application to particular kinds of mental disturbance. So it will remain if, aided by Parfit's theory, we eventually recognize the language of successive selves to reveal a deeper metaphysical truth about the nature of the self.

John Locke's Language and Metaphysics of Successive Persons

John Locke, who was an important seventeenth-century contributor to the discussion of personal identity, noted the language identified here as the language of successive selves. He draws attention to our ways of saying a person is "not himself" or is "beside himself," in which, he concludes, "it is insinuated, as if those who now, or at least first used them, thought that self was changed; the self-same person was no longer that man" (Locke 1690, 75). This passage is interesting in illustrating the entrenched and persistent voice of the language of successive selves, or, as Locke would have it, successive persons. But Locke wished to make metaphysically ambitious use of the distinction between man and person, not merely to report usage. More than one man cannot inhabit a body over its lifetime, on Locke's view, but more than one person conceivably can. 'Person', he insists, is a different kind of term, at once more important morally, and more flexible, than 'man'. While 'man' adheres to the requirements for spatiotemporal particulars—conforming to the "one to a customer" rule—'person' need not. And 'person', not 'man', is the forensic term, to which ascriptions of praise and blame, connoting responsibility, attach.

Suppose that I wholly lose the memory of some parts of my life beyond the possibility of retrieving them, he speculates, "yet am I not the same person that did those actions, had those thoughts, that I once was conscious of, though I have now forgot them?" His answer: "We must here take notice what the word 'I' is applied to; which in this case is the man only. And the same man being presumed to be the same person, 'I' is easily here supposed to stand also for the same person. But if it be possible for the same man to have distinct incommunicable consciousness at different times, it is past doubt the same man would at different times make different persons" (Locke 1690, 195–196).

For Locke, the same body would in this case house one *man* but different *persons*. Like the twentieth-century theorist Derek Parfit, Locke accords singularity to the person on the basis of a continuity of psychological, rather than bodily, traits. Were such continuity to fail, successive persons, or, we may say, successive selves, would result.

To refine the terms of our language of successive selves, we must examine the intriguing case descriptions from abnormal psychology. Here we find real people apparently exemplifying Locke's speculations about the possibility of the same man with "distinct incommunicable consciousnesses at different times."

Multiplicity through Dissociation

Certain clinical case material strikingly belies the identity presumption by which bodies house one person, or self, throughout their bodily lifetime, and this material will be the subject of the next two chapters. Particularly germane here is the sustained separation of ordinarily integrated mental processes, which we find in severe cases of dissociative disorder.[1] It is illuminating just where the relative oneness and apparent seamlessness of most normal experience is not. Here is where empirical descriptions provide an important complement to theoretical and conceptual claims about self identity. Here also lies the opportunity to refine and clarify the notions, like 'multiplicity' and 'separate self', necessary to a language of successive selves.

In this chapter I formulate multiplicity criteria—a set of conditions concerning personality and agent patterns, fractured awareness, and continuity, which are all met in strong cases of several selves sharing a single body. Such strong cases are few, and none provides incontrovertible evidence for the phenomenon of multiplicity, however. Not surprisingly, since it is the exemplar and standard from which, among others, these criteria have been derived, the description of Dr. Jekyll and Mr. Hyde constitutes one such strong case. Others come from descriptions of severe dissociative disorder, although the interself epistemology revealed in such descriptions will require adjustments to, and a weakening of, the multiplicity criteria.

Fragmentation: Unarguable Cases

The evidence suggesting the presence of separate selves housed in the same body, or *multiplicity*, must be distinguished, first, from that suggesting the total disintegration of the self, or *fragmentation*. Oliver

Sacks (1970) has illustrated some of the devastating amnesias that result from disease and damage to the brain. These are so encompassing that with only fragmentary memory, even from moment to moment, their sufferers are condemned to lead a life of unimaginable transience and superficiality, what Sacks calls, "a sort of Humean froth, a meaningless fluttering on the surface" (1970, 37). Amnesia, or memory incapacity, here destroys the unity or wholeness of the self. At least temporarily, its victims appear, as Sacks says of his patient Jimmie G., "de-pithed, de-souled and scooped out," or, we might say, *without self.*

Sacks' analysis of these cases of amnesia serves as vivid confirmation and illustration of the centrality of unity in relation to the notion of the self. If there were no memory to link experience through time, Sacks shows, there could be no self. Some degree of unity is required for us to ascribe selves to the bodily shells with which they are associated.[2] Persons, in some moral sense, these patients may remain, but selves they have not.[3] (Not all organic memory loss is as widespread or as permanent as this. Amnesias of shorter duration, those resulting from epileptic and other brain disorders, for example, sometimes allow the patient to feel and behave apparently normally during the lapse, although reciprocal amnesia prevents subsequent memory of it.)

Other disorders appear to cause dissolution of the self comparably severe to the cases Sacks describes. At its most extreme, for example, the loosened associations; poverty of context; and repetitive, incomprehensible, and apparently meaningless speech patterns of schizophrenia suggest a devastating want of integration and continuity.[4] Although maybe only temporarily, its victims appear as depithed, desouled, and scooped out as Jimmie G.

I will reserve the word 'fragmentation' to describe extremes such as these, and I will speak of divided selves or minds to refer to the less extreme forms of disintegration, fracture, disunity, and heterogeneity to be explored in the rest of this chapter.

Multiplicity

Considered from a public perspective and at a single slice of time, the multiple suffering extreme dissociative disorder is portrayed as both aware and not aware of the same experience at a given moment and in this way exemplifies a disunited self. Introspectively, she may not experience herself thus, though. Multiples bring many complaints when they seek therapy. They speak of blackouts, time lapses, headaches, and inexplicable happenings. But they must sometimes be told that they are *many*, not *one*. The experience of patients suffering from schizophrenic disorder who entertain thoughts that they feel are not their own may be more fractured, introspectively, than that of the multiple, with her headaches and blackouts; patients whose "thought insertion" seems to render them prey to others' thoughts, constitute more consistent evidence of subjectively experienced disunity of self. (States of "copresence" in multiples sometimes offer descriptions of subjectively experienced duality rather like that of the subject of thought insertion, we will see.)

Longer study of multiples reveals to the observer several apparently separate patterns of agency and separate personalities. This suggests more: multiplicity. But again, such a view is not given to the multiple, at least until dissociative barriers are reduced.

When we leave the simpler hypothesis of the self's disunity for more complex claims about its discontinuity through time and its possible multiplicity, we need to clarify the conditions for attributing separate selves to the same spatiotemporal person. Many discussions about separate selves seem to presuppose that one, several, or all of four conditions are involved here. First, if we are tempted to postulate separate, persisting subselves, rather than fleeting self fragments, there will be evidence of separate sets of propositional attitudes: beliefs, values, goals, desires, and responses. These will be expressed in distinguishable patterns of motivation and behavior—separate agendas, we could say. Call this the *separate-agency condition.*

Second, if we are inclined to speak of separate selves, they will probably reveal other distinguishing personality traits than those reflected in their separate agendas. Physical and emotional style, temperament, gender and cultural identity, moral disposition, idiosyncratic history, and self concept—all are part of what we mean by 'personality', broadly interpreted to go beyond mere agent patterns. And multiplicity implies the presence of more than one such distinct personality. This may be called the *separate-personality condition.*

A question now arises about the individuating function these criteria serve. Once we acknowledge the possibility that one body might house separate selves, a distinction must be recognized between intrapersonal and interpersonal individuation. Let us designate our terms. Let X be the composite person, publicly identifiable as a spatiotemporal particular. X comprises separate selves (self 1, self 2, self n). If one of X's separate selves (self 1) is characterized by personality traits of sufficient number, variety, uniqueness, or uniqueness of combination to identify and reidentify self 1 between one time and another (t_1-t_2), these will be sufficient to distinguish self 1 from another separate self (self 2).

Will such interself differentiation also suffice to distinguish X from whole person Y (or some separate self of whole person Y)? This seems likely. It requires only that Y (or Y's separate self) has a different set of traits. The separate selves (self 1 and self 2) thus serve to individuate both interpersonally and intrapersonally.

Agent and personality individuation of this kind presuppose a certain continuity of the purported self, or selves, through a stretch of time. We cannot establish the presence of a second self distinguished in terms of either agency or personality unless we see patterns of its presence.[5] This is for two reasons. First, 'self' is a dispositional or trait term, as are 'person' and 'character'. To attribute a self to its attendant body is to refer not to a datable occurrence but to a tendency to respond in certain ways over stretches of time. This is true also of particular personality or character traits. 'Emotional warmth', for example, may refer to a momentary and datable display of warmth. But to attribute it as a personality trait presupposes the possibility of more than one, temporally separated occasion at which it will be displayed. Agent patterns similarly require time to reveal themselves.

How do we formulate this point about continuity? We might say that a plausibly ascribed separate self must have continuity, offering an additional *continuity condition*, or we might treat continuity as a presupposition of the other two criteria. Which way we choose to say it is probably not important. These are not precise formulas, as the considerable overlap between the first and second two conditions attests. (Reference to agent patterns is certainly one way to indicate personality, even if personality is not captured fully in agent patterns.)

Finally, on the part of at least one self there will be some form of incomplete or disordered awareness, or disordered memory, in excess of that found in normally integrated people. This disordered awareness too is central to the inclination in the theorist to postulate a multiplicity of selves. An integrated mind can always introspect its simultaneous conscious contents, as philosophers have pointed out (Grice 1941).[6] In a divided mind, epistemic barriers prevent this state of transparency. At least one separate self cannot introspect the simultaneous conscious contents of the composite whole (the person) with which it is identified. Thus we get a *disordered-awareness condition*: introspective awareness of simultaneous conscious contents is not possible for at least one separate self, due to disordered or incomplete awareness or memory.

Although 'amnesia' is widely used to describe the forms of dissociatively wrought memory disturbance accompanying many claims about multiplicity, I will not use the term here, for it brings its own problems. In particular, two misleading connotations are avoided by using the term 'disordered awareness'. The suggestion that what is now unavailable to recall was once an object of awareness for the subject and the implication that total unawareness always prevails are two features that, we will see, the empirical descriptions require us to reject.

Retrospectively understood, disordered awareness results in, or becomes, disordered memory. This is not merely *forgetting*, or *not remembering*, however; these latter two expressions also convey that memory fails to reproduce what once had entered awareness. Disordered memory will also include the consequences of initial failures of awareness—blackouts, for example. Moreover, 'disordered memory' covers distortions and omissions in the quality of experiential memory, as well as the lacunae resulting from lapses into complete unawareness.[7]

The conditions identified here may be formulated as loose multiplicity criteria thus:

1. *Separate-agency condition*   Separate selves will have separate agendas.
2. *Separate-personality condition*   Separate selves will exhibit distinct, non-agential personality traits singly or jointly. These two conditions (separate agency and separate personality) will suffice for interself and intraself identification and reidentification.
3. *Continuity condition*   Separate selves will persist through time.
4. *Disordered-awareness condition*   Disordered awareness on the part of at least one self will result in disordered memory in the subject in excess of that found in normal people.

Conditions 1 to 4 represent a somewhat agreed on, and perhaps even intuitively obvious, account of multiplicity.[8] Where do they come from? The answer is not difficult: our imagination, our customary ways of identifying and reidentifying others, the influence of Freudianism with its emphasis on parts of the self influencing thought and action and yet prevented from entering conscious awareness, our deeply human fondness for positing homunculi—and tales such as Stevenson's. Dr. Jekyll and Mr. Hyde fulfill each condition to the fullest; indeed, they form a standard and exemplar of multiplicity. Each self in the story pursues radically distinct agendas. Each exhibits well-rounded and roundly contrary personalities. There is disordered awareness, since Dr. Jekyll had to discover Hyde's evil deeds after the fact and had no memory of Hyde's rampages.

The homunculus has been a common motif in much post-Enlightenment thinking, and homuncular models remain importance today for theorizing in the cognitive sciences.[9] As widely understood, the homuncular model merely stresses a division of the person into two or more interacting subsystems, each with its own agent features and even personality. Freud's version of this homuncular thinking goes further, and better captures what is usually understood by multiple 'selves' inhabiting the same body, in its stress on barriers to awareness and memory created by these divisions.

When the spatiotemporal continuity and distinctness of persons is not sufficient for their identification and reidentification, we appeal to just such criteria as conditions 1 to 4. Very often, of course, appeal to spatiotemporal continuity is sufficient for such identification and reidentification. If we seek to distinguish and define others, and must do so without reference to bodily characteristics, we turn to features of personality, agency, and awareness. We make deductions based on evidence from personality when in answer to 'Who did that?' we say, 'It must be Sara's doing; only she would think of that.' Attempting to establish the identity of a shadowy figure in a photograph, we depend on agent patterns in concluding, 'The woman whose face is concealed must be Mary; she said she planned to come.' We also appeal to the continuity of awareness attributable to a person in establishing an otherwise uncertain identity. Responding to 'Who was the fourth member of the committee?' we say 'Paula said she went that night; it must have been she.'

The multiplicity conditions enumerated above thus constitute loose criteria for one of the terms of the language of successive selves: multiplicity. And the tale of Dr. Jekyll and Mr. Hyde provides an exemplar and shaping case of separate selves. With one exception, these conditions are to be understood as criteria, not as necessary and sufficient conditions, for multiplicity. The exception is the continuity condition, condition 3, which may stand as something akin to a logically necessary requirement, or a precondition, of the separate-agency and separate-personality conditions, because to attribute a self, whether multiple or unitary, does seem to imply temporal duration. But conditions 1, 2, and 4 should not be read as more than a guide by which we can hope to range different cases around the central or prototypical one or ones. Moreover, no discoverable boundary, sharp or fuzzy, will permit us to say that separate aspects of a person have become, or have ceased to be, separate selves. This is not so much a process of discovery as one of decision. And degrees of plausibility attach to our use of this language, so we will be identifying cases to which it attaches with more, rather than less, plausibility, not judging instances of a natural class. (In his recent discussion of the prototypes for multiple personality, Ian Hacking [1995, 23, 34] has reached conclusions very similar to these.)

Ambiguities of Multiplicity

We may better understand the strengths of these intuitive multiplicity criteria if we consider two possible ambiguities surrounding their application to unproblematic cases such as Dr. Jekyll and Mr. Hyde.

First, there are ambiguities in how agency may be understood in the separate-agency condition. Presumably, the behavior of whole person X, who houses more than one self, when it is observed over a stretch of time, will be erratic and inexplicable in comparison with that of a normally integrated person. She will at least *invite* explanation in terms of separate agent systems alternating control of her body. It is likely, on the other hand, that much, perhaps most, of X's behavior will still appear purposive, even integrated. She will rise from her bed, dress, eat, catch the bus, finish sentences, engage in and complete activities, and exercise many skills and capabilities. How do we choose which set of observations to emphasize, we might ask: her integrated behavior or her lapses from it? Or should we compare the erratic behavior of composite person X with her less erratic behavior, attributing unitary agency as long as *most*, or even *some*, of her behavior seems to derive from a single agenda?[10]

The same divisions and questions arise at a more general level when we consider whether to speak of the composite person (X) as one or many, and a resolution to these questions about multiple agency will emerge from an examination of them.

Part of the puzzle in the Jekyll and Hyde story involves Dr. Jekyll's indecision over how to feel about Hyde's presence. Should he judge himself a unity or a duality? Stevenson teases his readers with this question without answering it, however, and we find more certainty in clinical and popular tales of dissociative disorder. I will shortly subject dissociative-identity disorder to a rigorous analysis in terms of the multiplicity criteria. For my purposes of illustration here, it is sufficient that dissociative disorder is an instance of multiplicity in the intuitive and preanalytic terms widely embraced today. From a subjective point of view, the multiple who, through therapy, has come to acknowledge her multiplicity often feels herself to be several selves. Prior to therapy, moreover, these patients show a bizarre tendency to avoid the first-person singular in natural conversation. Describing the adjustments of multiples who have sought therapy, one clinician reports that multiples experience feelings of "loneliness" after their successful psychic reintegration (Putnam 1989).

Yet from a public point of view, the unity of the person is indubitable and palpable in several respects. Not only are these patients spatiotemporal unities, but as agents, they apparently proceed through much of their lives in the orderly, purposive way indicative of a single, integrated source of agency. Compared with the disintegrated, incoherent, erratic public selves of the discontinuous and disunited victims of neurological disease and damage, described by Sacks (1970), multiples are moderately unified characters.

Must we choose? Does attributing multiplicity (i.e., several selves) to one person preclude our speaking of that person as an identity or unity?

There are two ways of describing the behavior of the composite person X, it was just illustrated, and they reveal that there are several different purposes at work when we make judgments of unity and multiplicity in relation to agency and more generally. Will not the context permit us to distinguish what is going on when we assert that a multiple comprises *one and many* agents or selves? It is entirely possible to speak thus and be understood. While clumsy, even '*X* has several selves inside herself' is roughly intelligible; its explication requires only that 'self' allows of more than one meaning here.

Such fracture of the concept of self will not be without costs in some contexts, certainly. And some purposes will militate against it. If, for example, importance attaches to Locke's recognition that the self is what he calls a forensic concept, with moral work to do, then admitting of difference senses of 'self' will require us to establish which is the morally significant one. (This task is undertaken in chapter 6.) Or if integration is seen as a therapeutic goal for multiples, as generally it is, then to reduce obstacles to that unification, there may be reason to deemphasize a separation of selves and to speak instead about parts or aspects of a single self, as has been recommended (Putnam 1989), rather than of separate selves.

Nonetheless, it seems possible to countenance multiplicity within unity. And similarly, of the apparently ambiguous evidence about the composite person's source of agency, at once diversified and unified, we may say that the composite person reveals one and many agendas.

A second kind of ambiguity concerns whether selves are sequential or simultaneous. Is the sequence of appearances and reappearances associated with multiplicity as it is understood here a succession of selves, we may ask, or is it the manifestation of members of a set of coexisting selves?

At this general level, the answer seems to require a decision, and not one of philosophical moment. The notion of having a self may be analyzed dispositionally. To have a self is to be inclined to respond in certain ways. Thus a person may not presently manifest any of the traits we think comprise her self, yet we continne to attribute that self to her. (She is so good at languages, we say of the girl who sleeps.) A loose rule exists here, presumably. There is more tendency to speak of selves as co-existing or simultaneous where, and to the extent that, rapid and frequent alteration, and even apparent recurrence or rotation, take place. If Hyde had reappeared for months at a time at ten year intervals, we might be more inclined to regard him as having replaced Jekyll, sharing a body with him only serially.

With regard to both the succession and rotation of selves associated with dissociative identity disorder and, for instance, the cyclical mood disorders, it may be appropriate to speak of separate selves simultaneously, and/or sequentially, inhabiting one body. However, as we will see later, such a description does not license us to attribute simultaneous *awareness* to more than one self inhabiting one body. It is because the concept of a separate self is dispositional that the possibility of separate selves coexisting is unproblematic here.

Further ambiguities in the multiplicity criteria may be resolved by examining the descriptions from abnormal psychology that most apparently fit them: those of multiple-personality disorder, or, as it is now known, dissociative-identity disorder, the most extreme among a range of dissociative disorders. (Some changes of emphasis and definition have accompanied this name change, although they need not concern us here.)

Dissociative-Identity Disorder and Multiplicity

Defined in terms of a disturbance or alteration in the normally integrative functions of identity, memory, and consciousness, dissociative-identity disorder is portrayed as involving two or more distinct and often widely differing identities (personalities) or personality states, each an integrated and complex unit with its own relatively enduring pattern of perceiving, relating to, and thinking about, the environment and itself (American Psychiatric Association 1994).[11]

The terminology associated with this condition at present has no orthodoxy or even consistent usage. I will maintain the following conventions here. 'Dissociative-identity disorder' refers to the syndrome. 'Person' applies to the unitary whole, whether a spatio-temporal, bodily entity or a public identity or both. 'Multiple' refers to the person who has or suffers the dissociative disorder. The term 'self' is used to indicate each of the alternative personalities comprising the multiple. (Thus self 1, self 2, self *n*.) The term 'reigning' ('regnant') indicates the state of a self when presently embodied and in what some have referred to as "executive control" of the shared body (Braude 1991, 44).

Descriptions of dissociative-identity disorder amply fulfill the agency, personality, and continuity conditions of multiplicity. This is incontestible and fairly obvious; in these respects such descriptions could be said to form an exemplar of multiplicity—almost, like Jekyll and Hyde, a shaping case. But descriptions of dissociative-identity disorder reveal an "interself epistemology," i.e., an awareness of other selves' experiences and existence, of great complexity. To determine whether and in what way these descriptions fulfill the disordered-awareness condition, we must examine this distinctive epistemology and clarify ambiguities in our present formulation of this condition.

More generally, in fixing the terms of the claim that descriptions of dissociative-identity disorder reflect multiplicity, we have several additional tasks. The goal of most therapy with multiples is an integration or fusion of the separate selves, resulting in a single, normally unified whole. At what point in the dynamic progression toward this state of unified awareness are we to say that the description of multiplicity ceases to apply? When do several separate selves reduce, by elimination or integration, to one self, with at most separate aspects or dimensions? This determination will rest at least in part on how the disordered-awareness condition is understood.

How aware are the multiple's selves of each others' experiences and existence? What is the nature of her interself epistemology? A variety of possibilities have been described, from total amnesic ignorance, such Dr. Jekyll's, to what is sometimes known as coconsciousness, where one self enjoys seemingly direct access to the experiences of another. The analysis that follows suggests that three forms of disordered awareness distinguish these cases: total unawareness of states one could be expected to have experienced, of the kind usually associated with the term amnesia, "disowned" experiences of states one could be expected to have experienced, and "nonagential" experience of states one could be expected to have experienced.

Consider first the state of total unawareness. The presence of amnesic barriers between separate selves is a regular feature of dissociative-identity disorder. But it presents problems to the diagnostician. Evidence of amnesia is not always a presenting symptom. Patients subject to amnesic gaps of experience since childhood may not recognize them; those who recognize that they are different may resort to confabulatory, false "memories" to conceal their lapses. At best, amnesia must present itself indirectly. The clinician must draw inferences from evidence of lost periods of time, "blackouts," and inexplicable happenings, such as the patient's experience of finding herself in possession of articles she does not remember acquiring or of discovering herself in a strange place with no knowledge of how she came there. These experiences are indeed what most commonly impel the multiple to seek psychiatric help.

Apart from the immediate concerns of the diagnostician, however, it seems apparent that some degree of disordered awareness, or what is often called "dissociative amnesia," on the part of at least one self will always be present. A total unawareness of states that the self could be expected to experience forms a central and defining feature of dissociative-identity disorder.[12] Yet this total unawareness is by no means the only, and perhaps not the commonest, feature of multiples' interself epistemology. We must look also at the notion or notions of "coconsciousness."

The term 'coconsciousness' has been the bearer of several different meanings since its introduction by Morton Prince in his early case descriptions of multiple personalities (Prince 1906, Beahrs 1983). Because of the ambiguity the term carries, we might begin by rehearsing Stephen Braude's (1991) understanding and definition of 'coconsciousness' and associated terminology.

On Braude's taxonomy, self A is said to be *coconscious* with self B when one of two states obtains between the two selves. A may be "cosensory" with B or "intraconscious" with B. A is *cosensory* with B when both A and B seem to be simultaneously aware of external events, such as sights and sounds. A is *intraconscious* with B when A claims knowledge of B's mental states, such as feelings, beliefs, and memories.

Attitudes felt by selves toward one another and one anothers' experiences are also distinctive, some have thought defining (Braude 1991), characteristics of relations among selves. When aware of the experiences of other selves, each self may regard the other's roughly as we regard another, spatiotemporally distinct person's experience. The other self's experiences lack a felt quality of "mineness," or ownership, and are described in the public language of the third person, not the first-person singular. For example, Joan (self 1) recounts that Mary (self 2) believes p, by saying 'Mary believes p'. This contrasts with the language of the first-person singular ('I believe *p*'). But it also contrasts with the language that normally unified people adopt when confessing to ambivalence. 'Part of me believes *p*', 'I would like to believe *p*', 'I half believe *p*', or 'I am in two minds about the fact that *p*', we would say. The multiples' locutions spring from a felt inner division much greater than these imply.

Braude (1991) has also introduced terminology to help us speak of the puzzles of self-ascription found in dissociation. Two or more states are *coreferential* when they may be ascribed to the same person. A state is *indexical* when a person believes it to be her own (i.e., to be assignable to herself). A state is *autobiographical* when a person experiences it *as* her own. These are not sharply separated categories, but they admit of clear cases. A clearly indexical, autobiographical claim would be 'I feel sad.' A clearly nonindexical, nonautobiographical one, 'Jane Austen experienced great grief over the death of her sister.'

Among related dissociative phenomena such as depersonalization and hypnoid states, Braude (1991) has argued, multiples alone comprise distinct "apperceptive centers," i.e., the autobiographical and indexical states of each self are (respectively) largely nonautobiographical and nonindexical for the others.

These epistemic relationships and attitudes among the selves making up multiples are far from permanent, or even static, however. (Herein lies some of the dizzying and elusive quality of such case material and the incoherence associated with the actual experience of relating to multiples.) Initial ignorance on the part of one self of the experience and memories of another—the acquisition of additional indexical states—may quickly be dispelled. Both in diagnosis and subsequent therapeutic endeavor, hypnosis has been successfully employed, for example, in breaking or reducing these barriers. But it often leaves disordered awareness or memory, nonetheless. Although self 1 has acquired access to self 2's experiences and actions, this awareness is limited and alienated, lacking a sense of ownership. (Thus self 1 acquires additional indexical states without acquiring autobiographical states.)

Multiples report not only degrees of coconsciousness but other forms of interaction among selves. One self may report hearing, or having heard, the voice(s) of another (one or more) selves, or may report talking with another. These interactions invite comparison with delusory and hallucinatory phenomena, and confound diagnosis because of this. However, nosological considerations, and even some phenomenological report, are widely believed to require that we maintain a sharp distinction. A multiple's inner conversations are not to be confused with the hallucinated voices of schizophrenia and, we are told, are recognizably distinct.

Also, varied relationships over agency and control pertain among the separate selves of dissociative-identity disorder. Although one regnant self exerts executive control, other selves may at the same time influence the regnant self and indirectly interfere with her autonomy—by voicing critical or cautionary comments to the regnant self, for example. They may also challenge her autonomy more directly. Experiences as of "possession," or what some theorists have called "dissociated will," have also been reported (Spiegel and Cardeña 1991). Here the embodied or experiencing self feels directed by the will of another, in whose presence she is no more than a passive and obedient instrument. We may question the distinctiveness of this experience, many parallels to which are found in the delusory "made" experiences of schizophrenic disorder, but this discussion I will defer until chapter 15.

The multiple's awareness is incomplete in a third respect, then. It is sometimes what I will here call "nonagential" experience. An action took place. It was brought about by the multiple's bodily movements, but not through her own agency.

Nonagential experience is a notion without parallel in normal experience. The closest, but still distant, analogy is involuntary movement caused by another source of agency outside one's body (I am pushed by something), or one's initiating an action with an unintended effect (I mean to close the door and succeed in jamming the cat's tail).

We may best acquire the flavor of this epistemic complexity by reviewing the well-known case of Miss Beauchamp, analyzed and meticulously described by Morton Prince (1906). Christine Beauchamp, as Prince portrays her, comprised a total of four selves. First was B-I, who consulted with Prince because of depression, fatigue, headaches, and nervousness. She was reserved, refined, and religious. Under hypnosis other selves multiplied, including Sally. Sally was aware of all the mental life of B-I, despised B-I, and described her impersonally, i.e., she knew of B-I's experiences but did not claim them as her own. Being light-hearted, irreverent, and sociable, Sally had a character that differed markedly from B-I's. B-I was ignorant of Sally's existence and "lost" the stretches of time when Sally was reigning. She also suffered the results of Sally's hostile plots against her. Next came B-IV, a personality whose actions but not mental life, were known to Sally. B-I was again ignorant of B-IV.

Deeper under hypnosis a fourth self emerged, an apparent amalgam of B-I and B-IV, whom Prince names B-II. This underlying self identified herself with, and shared character traits with, both B-I and B-IV and was aware of their experience, though she knew nothing of Sally.

However, the relationship with B-I and B-IV was also asymmetrical: neither B-I nor B-IV was aware of B-II. Although initially hypnotic trance was required, Prince became able to elicit these different subselves by other means. Moreover, it emerged that Sally and B-II had alternated control for many years and were joined since a more recent trauma six years previously by the loosely rotating ascendancy of each of the newer selves B-I and B-IV.

Prince's therapeutic endeavors rested on a series of presuppositions. There was, he believed, an initial self, the real or authentic Christine Beauchamp. Fractured as the result of psychic trauma, this original or basic self must be restored to ascendancy, even at the cost of extinguishing pretenders to that position. Prince determined that B-II was the real Miss Beauchamp. This was in part because she identified herself with, and embraced, two selves (B-I and B-IV); she was in this sense more basic, or general, than any other self. In part it was because her memories anteceded those of others (for example, B-IV, whose memory span covered only the previous six years), which gave her some claim to being the original self. And it was in part because Prince deemed her personality better balanced and more in conformity with moral and mental health norms.

Although several philosophers have been drawn toward the descriptions of the purported phenomena of multiple personality, or dissociative-identity disorder, few have agreed on what such phenomena show. A number of distinguishable philosophical inquiries and findings have been stimulated by these odd cases. One is a question that concerns us here: the question of how these phenomena should be described. Do we want to acknowledge the presence in one body of distinct selves or, as others have suggested, "persons" or "minds"? Or do we want to insist that these separate psychological entities are merely separate aspects or components of a single self, person, or mind?[13]

The often contradictory and puzzling behavior associated with dissociative-identity disorder is explicable—and, it seems, is only explicable—by postulating two or more sources or "selves" alternating control or agency, each equipped with distinct agendas. We know, moreover, that these selves are often strikingly dissimilar—indeed, contraries—in respect to their nonmotivational traits and patterns. Although they may share more traits than is customarily acknowledged,[14] nevertheless their distinguishing "personality" characteristics are often sufficient for intraself identification and reidentification. And while some selves may be cognizant of the states of mind and activities of other selves through internal and introspectable means—"listening in," recollection, or other forms of shared awareness—total unawareness on the part of at least one self is invariably present, at least initially.

On the basis of our criteria it seems fairly clear that we should we treat dissociative-identity disorder as an instance of multiplicity. But we must return to the notion of disordered awareness to resolve another question: how many of the multiple's separate "selves" comprise this multiplicity? If disordered awareness were limited to the case of total unawareness, then at least one of the selves in descriptions of any given multiple will fulfill our final condition for a time and count, with Jekyll and Hyde, as a separate self. This approach has the drawback that epistemic changes in the relationships between selves would result in rapid and fluctuating changes of separate-self status.

Such changes of status are the inevitable outcome of successful therapeutic intervention with multiples. From being a multiple, the patient is rendered a unitary whole; from being full-blown separate selves, the various separate parts are eliminated or are reduced to aspects of a single self. But the complex and dynamic interself epistemology that prevails before this final, and more permanent, alteration of status argues against such an analysis until this stage is reached. A fluid shifting back and forth, where aspects become separate selves, only to return to aspects again, spells confusion. Moreover, it prevents the application of our formal framework. Selves must persist through reasonable stretches of time for the dispositional language in which we characterize their distinguishing traits to get purchase. (This is the continuity condition.) If the multiple houses a rapidly fluctuating number of selves, varying from day to day or week to week, it violates this requirement. Unless we are prepared to withhold the ascription of multiplicity from all these cases and apply it exclusively to the fictional case of Jekyll and Hyde, we must seek an alternative, less stringent interpretation of the notion of disordered awareness. It must be one by which it is possible to claim and maintain the status of separate selves for all or most "selves" in these descriptions of dissociative-identity disorder until or close to the point of permanent integration.

This end may be achieved by allowing the notion of disordered awareness to include three separate forms of incapacity:

1. Total unawareness of states the multiple could be expected to have experienced
2. "Disowned" experiences of states the multiple could be expected to have experienced
3. "Nonagential" experience of states the multiple could be expected to have experienced

The first of these is the epistemic relationship between Jekyll and Hyde and is also the initial, pretherapeutic status of at least one of each multiple's selves. The second and third forms capture features associated with the several relationships between these selves possible through coconsciousness.

By interpreting the disordered-awareness condition to include (1) through (3), we are able to place dissociative-identity disorder beside Jekyll and Hyde as an instance of multiplicity. At least until completion of successful therapeutic fusion or integration, most, if not all, of the subsystems making up the multiple will rank as separate selves.[15]

The tale of Dr. Jekyll and Mr. Hyde was fiction, not fact. But the parallels between Stevenson's story and the phenomenon portrayed in descriptions of dissociative-identity disorder may be closer than is often supposed. Certainly, such descriptions have a fictional ring. There are reasons to question the evidence supporting an ascription of this diagnosis in any given case, as some of those attempting to draw

philosophical conclusions from such seeming multiplicity have recognized (Hacking 1986, 1995, Dennett 1988, Glover 1988, Braude
1991). The set of symptoms making up dissociative-identity disorder
appear peculiarly susceptible to misdiagnosis; they have been successfully falsified; they seem unusually vulnerable to distortion and
fabrication.

Early skepticism about the possibility of this disorder has been
somewhat overcome within clinical psychiatry, however. This is sufficient reason to acknowledge that something like the phenomenon as
described may be empirically possible, while allowing that the terms
in which it is described could prove misleading, exaggerated, or even
conceptually incoherent in certain respects. On the other hand, it
would be naive to dismiss or diminish the extent to which the purported phenomenon of dissociative-identity disorder appears to be a
cultural product, rather than a natural kind.[16]

Dissociative-Identity Disorder as Entrenched Self-Deception

Within medical psychiatry, dissociative-identity disorder is understood to be a symptom cluster, or syndrome, and a mental disorder,
with the distinctive ontological status that this entails. It is known to
us from this context, and even without our embracing all the medical
psychiatric assumptions it often conveys, we are unlikely to equate
dissociative-identity disorder with the more common and less severe
forms of dissociation we encounter in everyday life. This, however,
is what I propose we must now do. If we restrict our attention to
descriptions of these clinical forms of multiplicity, temporarily setting
aside the medical psychiatric assumptions within which such descriptions are usually embedded, we can see that dissociative-identity disorder may be redescribed as extreme self-deception.

Confusion surrounds and obscures this equation. It is not immediately obvious, because of the different discourses within which
self-deception and mental disturbance are customarily introduced. In
the next chapter I will provide a closer analysis of the puzzling yet
ubiquitous condition referred to as self-deception and, in extreme
cases, its successful fulfillment of each of the multiplicity criteria. But
here I will emphasize the different discourses obscuring our recognition that dissociative-identity disorder is also severe self-deception.

A cluster of features distinguish the discourse of self-deception: its status as a functional term, its literary and philosophical parentage, and finally, the scope and ubiquity of the human trait it captures.

First, self-deception is a "functional" term: it does not participate in the syndrome discourse of psychiatric nosology. The nearest equivalents to 'self-deception' in clinical terminology are perhaps 'denial', 'repression', and, depending on the context in which it is introduced, 'delusory thinking'. As this suggests, self-deception presupposes a notion of psychology and the mind associated with only one branch of abnormal psychology: the dynamic, homuncular models of psychoanalytic thinking and theory. There is neither a condition nor a syndrome that corresponds to 'repression', 'denial', or 'delusory'; rather, these terms describe a symptom that may form part of several different psychiatric diagnoses. The same is true for 'self-deception'.

Second, despite these apparent affinities with psychoanalytic reasoning and assumptions, 'self-deception' is not a term favored in psychoanalytic writing. (There are exceptions.[17]) Rather, we associate it with literary portrayal, where its subtlety, its elusive there-you-see-it, there-you-don't quality, can most successfully be conveyed, and we associate it with philosophical analyses. To appreciate why the term 'self-deception' is found in literary and philosophical discourse rather than psychiatric or even psychoanalytic discourse, we must remind ourselves of the third feature noted above: its ubiquity. In its simplest forms, self-deception seems to be a commonplace of everyday life. In its more subtle and complex elaborations, self-deception becomes a long-term disposition and motivational pattern, shaping self-concepts, habits of mind, choice, action, and awareness. Philosophical discussion, particularly, has served to obscure or diminish this difference between mild and entrenched self-deception. But where there is an entrenched and distinctive personality (self 1) that has a distinguishable agenda and is able to manipulate the self of conscious awareness (self 2) only by enjoying some separate awareness of its own from which self 2 is excluded, then we should have no reason to withhold the ascription of multiplicity. Indeed, with self-deception as extreme as this, we have reached a condition indistinguishable from that usually entitled multiple-personality disorder, or dissociative-identity disorder.[18]

Some of the everydayness of self-deception, and the apprehension that enables us to see it as more, and as something close
to multiplicity, is conveyed by the philosopher John King-Farlow
(1963). Self-deception is often analyzed in the simplest, homuncular
terms as a duality of deceiving and deceived, or conscious and unconscious sources of agency. But not by King-Farlow. We have so
many reasons, he remarks, for

> wanting to have our cake, for wanting to eat it, alone, to share it, to trade it
> for the latest issue of *Analysis* (though we know we just haven't time to keep
> up with all that onerous reading), to make it a burnt offering for Godot, etc.,
> etc.; since we are often quite aware of these competing reasons or goals, and
> since we are conscious of believing that each should have *the* deliberative
> priority, a person is quite often usefully looked at, with reference to his
> consciousness, as a large, loose sort of committee. There is a most irregularly
> rotating chairmanship. The members question, warn, praise, and *deceive* each
> other . . . : the one who at present holds the chair (and the chair is not to be
> identified with consciousness or fullness of assent) is in the best position to
> cow or gull the others. They debate, share jokes, cross-check the facts about
> yesterday's sensations, and carry on group activities very much as would a
> group of flesh and blood individuals. Some fall half asleep from time to time,
> and many more are caught off guard by various factions within the com-
> mittee and driven out into the corridor to stamp their feet or moan dis-
> tractingly through the keyholes. (1963, 135)

This account reaches multiplicity from the evidence of self-deception.
Yet my earlier analysis would suggest that King-Farlow's claim requires qualification. For the separate selves of multiplicity can plausibly be ascribed to extreme cases only.

To acknowledge these parallels between clinical descriptions of
dissociative-identity disorder and the results of extreme self-deception,
I must stress, is not to propose a terminological reduction. Placed in
and anchored by the distinctive purposes and presuppositions of their
separate discourses, these terms each have a separate part to play in our
understanding of the human mind.

The case of Dr. Jekyll and Mr. Hyde forms the standard and exemplar, representing the fulfillment of all multiplicity conditions. And
aspects of dissociative-identity disorder, or extreme and entrenched
self-deception, also strongly support a judgment of multiplicity. For
this very reason, however, these two examples cannot guide us over
another set of questions that might be asked about the concept of

multiplicity: What sort of traits, and how many, form a separate agenda and a separate personality? What is the relationship between the four conditions (separate agency, separate personality, continuity, and disordered awareness)? In the absence of one or another, are there ever, and is there equal warrant or reason to speak of, separate selves? To explore these questions, we need to look at more problematic cases, and we will do so in the following chapter.

Succession and Recurrence outside Dissociative Disorder

Equipped with loose criteria for multiplicity, we can now examine the more problematic candidates for the status of successive selves, including some conditions familiar from everyday life, such as ideological conversion, akrasia, and self-deception less extreme than those types introduced in the last chapter. In addition, we will explore personality changes resulting from a number of clinical conditions.

The evidence from clinical psychology offers a plethora of seeming candidates for multiplicity, candidates proposed by theorists and elected by some clinicians. But my refinements on the notions of self, separate self, and multiplicity require me to accept a more modest yield from the clinical data. My language of successive selves applies best to two kinds of multiplicity. The first is that attributable to the separate selves of dissociative disorder, which, we saw, may be described as the result of extreme and entrenched patterns of self-deception. The second, explored in this chapter, is found in the succession and recurrence of distinct selves sometimes resulting from other, non-dissociative conditions, in particular, affective or mood disorders and schizophrenia.

The Continuity Requirement

Each of the phenomena discussed in this chapter exhibits at least some degree of continuity. This is necessary for us plausibly to speak of these phenomena as separate selves, and it serves to preclude some states and conditions resulting in fleeting disunities or discontinuities of the self, such as hypnoid states, out-of-body hallucinations, depersonalization and derealization experiences, and the brief changes and personality facets found in descriptions of borderline personality disorder. Such fleeting facets bespeak only momentary or extremely short-term discontinuities of self. These may be regarded as separate-self fragments, but they are less than separate selves.

Personality Change Due to Disease and Damage to the Brain

The primary focus of this chapter will be personality changes that result from mental disorder. But we will begin elsewhere: with personality changes due to diseases and damage to the brain (some of which, we will see, fulfill all the multiplicity conditions). These will allow us to recognize conceptual distinctions important for the rest of the discussion.

Many personality changes are associated with identifiable damage to and disease of the brain. When, in a violent accident, an iron rod passed through Phineas Gage's head, his dispositions and behavior were altered, while leaving unaffected his motor and sensory functions (Damasio et al. 1994). His physician J. M. Harlow, reporting the case in 1896, offered this description of how the head injury left Gage.

His physical health is good, and I am inclined to say that he has recovered. Has no pain in the head, but says it has a queer feeling which he is not able to describe. Applied for his situation as foremen, but is undecided whether to work or travel. His contractors, who regarded him as the most efficient and capable foreman in their employ previous to his injury, considered the change in his head so marked that they could not give him his place again. The equilibrium or balance, so to speak, between his intellectual faculties and animal propensities, seems to have been destroyed. He is fitful, irreverent, indulging at times in the grossest profanity (which was not previously his custom), manifesting but little deference for his fellows, impatient of restraint or advice when it conflicts with his desires, at times pertinaciously obstinate, yet capricious and vacillating, devising many plans for future operations, which are no sooner arranged than they are abandoned in turn for others, his mind is radically changed, so decidedly that his friends and acquaintances said he was "no longer Gage." (Harlow 1868, 327)

Personality change transformed Gage's identity from the moment of his accident on. Harlow's account fails to note if there were retrospective amnesia blotting out his patient's life before the accident, as is often true with such cases. But if there were, we would be required to concede that the new Gage was a separate self.

Several conditions of presenile and senile dementia where the patient suffers deterioration of parts of the brain bring changes no less radical than those resulting from head injury, albeit the alteration is usually less dramatic than Gage's. In the often heart-breaking changes from irreversible degenerative diseases of the brain, we are sometimes inclined to judge that while the original self has been extinguished, no alternative self has succeeded it, however. Not all personality change allows us to speak of succession or multiplicity.

Even where a second personality replaces the earlier one, more-over, some "successions" are considerably less dynamic than the changes associated with multiplicity as identified in the last chapter. Injury to and disease of the brain are often irreversible, and inasmuch as they are, the succession of a resulting "self" will be inexorable. There may be *succession* but not *rotation* of selves. (This difference seems to influence certain normative judgments we would make about how such patients ought to be treated, we will see later.) Not all per-sonality changes resulting from nondissociative conditions are inex-orable in this way, however. Temporary disease of and reversible damage to the brain, much substance-induced personality change, as well as conditions such as schizophrenia and mood disorders, each seem to allow us to recognize very different personalities not only replacing one another through time but also exhibiting rotation. If not as complex, fast-paced, and mercurial as the rotation of selves portrayed in descriptions of dissociative disorder, nonetheless this ro-tation of personalities is analogous to it.

We must now determine when and how successfully these separate, successive, and rotating selves constitute multiplicity, as I have defined it. Clinical descriptions of schizophrenic, and particu-larly of mood or affective, disorders yield some of our strongest cases here, and since they remain the focus of the later themes explored in this book, they will provide the central cases for discussion in this chapter.

Personality Change Due to Mood and Schizophrenic Disorders

Taxonomically and clinically, the personality changes associated with the occurrence and course of mood and schizophrenic disorders differ importantly from the multiplicity associated with dissociative disorder. These disorders are not classified in terms of the resulting personality changes that their clinical descriptions reveal. They are defined and understood in other ways. The personality changes are more of a product—and often not a central one, clinically—of other symptoms and states at the heart of the condition. A patient's beliefs and desires, mental capabilities, or mood might gradually transform the complex of dispositions making up her personality. But with nondissociative conditions such as schizophrenia and mood disorders, her primary symptoms are the cognitive, volitional, or affective states or mental capabilities themselves, rather than the resulting changes. In addition, personality change unfailingly characterizes none of these conditions as it does dissociative disorder. In nondissociative conditions sometimes there will be great variation between the earlier and later parts of the self, variation so extreme as to strongly invite the language of successive selves. But in other cases, such differences are slight. Personality change admits of degree, and while schizophrenia and mood disorders may result in radical and transformative change, neither consistently does so. Methodologically, this is a significant difference, of course. We must choose our cases and remember that if we posit successive selves, we speak not of all but of some cases of each kind of disorder.

A brief illustration will serve to remind us of the alterations wrought by severe mental disorders such as these: the case of Mr. M.'s manic phase.

Mr. M., a thirty-three-year-old postal worker, had been married for eight years. He and his wife lived comfortably and happily in a middle-class neighborhood with their two children. In retrospect, there appeared to be no warning for what was to happen. On 12 February Mr. M. let his wife know that he was bursting with energy and ideas, that his job as a mail carrier was unfulfilling, and that he was just wasting his talent. That night he slept little, spending most of the time at a desk, writing furiously. The next morning he left for work at the usual time but returned home at 11 a.m., his car filled to overflowing with aquaria and other equipment for tropical fish. He had quit his job and then withdrawn all the money from the family's saving account. The money had been spent on tropical-fish equipment. Mr. M. reported that the previous night he had worked out a way to modify existing equipment so that fish "won't die anymore. We'll be millionaires." After unloading the paraphernalia, he set off to canvass the neighborhood for possible buyers, going door to door and talking to anyone who would listen (Davidson and Neale 1986, 196).

At least temporarily, Mr. M. had become incorrigibly optimistic and "provocative," (Davidson and Neale 1986, 196), traits hitherto uncharacteristic of him. His personality had radically altered. Loosely speaking, at least, he had become a new person. And the loose figurative language of successive selves is commonly applied to these kinds of clinical cases too. We speak of hospitalization and pharmacological treatment as restoring the victim of a schizophrenic episode to her former self, just as we say the victim of a degenerative brain disease is not the person she once was and just as, after his brain damage, Phineas Gage's friends and acquaintances declared him "no longer Gage."

May we speak of the earlier and later self stages occurring in these nondissociative disorders as separate selves? It does seem plausible to do so. These conditions sometimes result in successive and even recurrent selves. First, they strongly exemplify the separate-personality and separate-agency conditions. The separate selves of schizophrenic and mood disorders may reveal comprehensive personality change, each separate self pursuing distinct agendas and each exhibiting significantly different emotional and behavioral dispositions and propositional attitudes. These separate selves may be relatively permanent structures, lasting weeks, months, or years in some cases, and in others, alternating in cyclical swings. Second, they reveal forms of incomplete awareness and deficient memory at least comparable to, although distinguishable from, the disowned and nonagential awareness found in descriptions of multiples' coconsciousness.

Mr. M. exemplifies the separate-personality and separate-agency conditions. The person he became during his manic episode—provocative, optimistic, reckless, ambitious, and energetic—contrasted sharply with the man he had been, and the one he would again become. This manic self would serve to distinguish him not only from his previous and subsequent selves but also from other, spatiotemporarily distinct persons. In addition, his mission gave him a new set of desires and goals, which would be sufficient agency for intraself and interself individuation.[1]

And the disordered-awareness condition? There is a difference between conditions such as Mr. M.'s and dissociative-identity disorder, and this requires emphasis and explanation.

Because in cases such as Mr. M.'s we speak of selves succeeding one another in the same body through time, rather than simultaneously inhabiting that body, the disordered-awareness condition always requires retrospective interpretation here. Mr. M.'s multiplicity will be recognizable only as a defect or peculiarity of memory, not one of immediate awareness. Moreover, while there is, in dissociative-identity disorder, a total amnesic unawareness of at least one of the multiple's selves for the mood and schizophrenic disorders of psychiatry, these alterations of personality seem able to occur without significant *loss* of memory between the earlier and later "selves." On the other hand, changes resulting from schizophrenic and mood disorders commonly exhibit through time memory *distortion* and *selectivity* in excess of that associated with more continuous personal lives. Though remembered, experiences may not feel like experiential memories as we usually know them, particularly when viewed from some distance in time. In this respect, the disorders discussed here find their closest parallel not to the case of Dr. Jekyll and Mr. Hyde but to the coconsciousness found among the selves in dissociative disorder, where one self knows of, but disowns, the experience and actions of another, and knows of them with nonagential memory only.

A brief aside is required here. Within the theoretical tenets of dynamic psychology, patients such as Mr. M. are seen to suffer a manic defense serving to conceal underlying depression. Thus, it may be said, their memory is deficient in ways entirely analogous to the memory deficiencies associated with the multiples' dissociative amnesia: the manic reaction prevents its sufferer from acquiring knowledge of feelings of depression. Although this theoretical interpretation is appealing, particularly in light of the empirical data, it presupposes allegiances not shared by all in psychiatry and beyond the scope of the empirical approach adopted in this essay. Thus the focus here will be on the more limited claim that memory distortion and selectivity often mark retrospective awareness in such cases; this deficiency will prove sufficient for the purposes guiding our inquiry.

To Mr. M., restored now to his earlier personality and agent patterns (or something close to them) and as the retrospective rememberer of the manic episode, the changes that occurred in him were far from normal. They are remembered as an unsought, unwelcome, unnatural, and foreign visitation. Mr. M. will likely recall this episode later in nonagential terms (not 'I did *x*', but '*x* happened to me'); similarly, he might look back on his manic excesses without the characteristic sense of mineness or ownership that we normally associate with personal memories.

It is important to notice that this application of the disordered-awareness condition requires not only retrospective interpretation but also an interpretation from the perspective of the subsequent, restored Mr. M. And such restoration may be a long time coming or may not come at all. This suggests that the disordered-awareness condition will be fulfilled, on this interpretation, only in conditions that exhibit a rotation of personality changes, of the kind we typically find in the cyclical mood or affective conditions such as Mr. M.'s and in the shifting course seen in schizophrenia.

The issues of perspective that have arisen here require further attention. To those observing him from without—his therapist, his perplexed family, and "himself" at a later date—these strange changes in Mr. M.'s personality, behavior, and motivation resulted from his mental disorder. Yet from Mr. M.'s point of view at the time, it is clear that he took this personal alteration to be normal. His new knowledge and ideas naturally led to his changes. Indeed, given that knowledge and those ideas, it would have been puzzling, from his perspective, if they had not. From the subjective and immediate perspective, those changed by such mental disorders often feel and understand such changes within the framework earlier identified as rational or intentional. Freely and knowingly, it seems to them, they have allowed newly acquired beliefs and desires to affect their states of mind; from a changed state of mind have sprung altered behavioral dispositions.

This will not always be so. Sometimes the changes feel as strange and inexplicable to their subjects as they appear to others, even at the time they are experienced, and later in this book I will examine the various forms of disowned or "ego-alien" experience associated with some of these states. Moreover, sometimes a retrospective portrayal of such an episode will accommodate a divided analysis. The subject concedes that the original shift in beliefs and desires may not have been freely and knowingly acquired. Yet she remembers subsequent action taken in the light of these beliefs and desires as stemming from her own agency. (We will see an interestingly parallel analysis to this in retrospective explanations of religious conversion.)

True, it will not always happen, but the same person (speaking spatiotemporally) sometimes will at different times recognize past personal change from both of these two differing perspectives. And the cases of importance to our analysis here are just those where this occurs: where the immediate and subjective understanding of behavioral and motivational changes takes place within a rational or intentional framework—as was obviously so in Mr. M.'s case—until a perspectival shift occurred. For at the point of such a shift, at least, Mr. M.'s memory of past experience would reflect a disowned and/or nonagential awareness that would allow us to ascribe multiplicity.

Next I will examine three kinds of personality change found in everyday life, to each of which theorists have informally applied the language of successive selves or attributed some form of multiplicity: ideological conversion, akrasia, and less extreme and entrenched self-deceptions than were introduced in the last chapter.

Multiplicity Conditions and Ideological Conversion

Refining the notion of multiplicity allows us to resolve a question introduced earlier (page 29). The language of successive selves seemed at first so fitting for cases of religiously or ideologically wrought personality change in otherwise normal people. But should it be extended to such cases?

The separate-agency and separate-personality conditions are amply met in these changes, which by their nature are transformative and thoroughgoing. The "new creature" (see page 19) that results is by definition equipped with a different personality (or we may say 'character', since moral qualities are so deeply affected in these changes), and a changed set of agent dispositions. And certainly continuity is guaranteed: these are often changes that endure for the rest of the convert's life. But the subject of these changes gives no evidence of disordered awareness and memory.

To the convert, the conversion experience is often abnormally or supernaturally caused; it transforms his very being without his volition. But after the transformation, the person he has become acts on his new beliefs and desires in ways that he and the public world around him can explain within a rational or intentional framework. (The born-again Baptist's new found generosity to the needy flows naturally and intelligibly from the new beliefs and values he has acquired: his saviour preached a love of the dispossessed.) With the passing of time, the convert's actions are fully recalled, with full agent memory, and continue to be understood within an intentional and rational frame. And if we persist in speaking of conversion here, rather than mental disorder, it is in part because this is so and in part because the passage of time brings none of the perspectival shifts discussed in relation to mental disorder.

Thus it seems that while the separate-personality and separate-agency conditions invite us to speak of multiplicity in these cases of religious and ideological conversion, they are less appropriate subjects for the language of successive selves than are the several forms of mental disorder we have been considering.

Several phenomena that have been described in the language of successive selves fall short of multiplicity because they do not exhibit sufficient distinction of personality and agency between the purported separate selves involved. Akrasia or weakness of will, much self-deception, hypnoid states, and commissurotomy have each been interpreted as evidence for some form of multiplicity. Yet in each case the purported second, separate self ascribed has insufficient personality uniqueness to allow intrapersonal and interpersonal identification and reidentification. By the criteria for multiplicity established here, then, ascriptions of multiplicity to akrasia, much self-deception, hypnoid states, and commissurotomy must be problematic.

Two conditions will be explored somewhat more fully: akrasia and self-deception. (I should warn that what follows is not intended as a comprehensive analysis of either concept, nor of the relationship between them. Such analyses, which have been undertaken by others, are beyond the scope of this essay.) Akrasia requires special attention because there are "akratic" conditions that, because of the pervasiveness, persistence, or intensity of the overpowering impulses involved, exceed the simple akrasia common in everyday life, and that affect their victim's functioning to such a degree that they are ranked as pathology or psychological incapacity. Self-deception must be considered because extreme self-deception is indistinguishable from the cases of multiplicity already identified, though otherwise described.

Akrasia and Disorders of Impulse Control

Weakness of will, or what philosophers call akrasia, is familiar to all of us from personal experience and from our moral, literary, and philosophical traditions. We know well the feel of temptation, internal struggle, successful resistance, and succumbing to weakness. By standard philosophical definition, an akratic action *a* is one where a person acts voluntarily and intentionally under a description of *a* that on some level she takes to be contrary to her judgment about the preferred course for her to take in that situation.[2]

Cast in the language of a hierarchy of desires introduced by Frankfurt (1971), akrasia reflects a conflict between first- and second-order desires. The first-order desire prevails over the second order "volition": my desire to smoke, for example, overrides my second-order wish to refrain from smoking. Important moral distinctions are associated with the extremes of these disorders of impulse control.[3] Our concern is not with these moral differences, however, but with the alleged multiplicity such states exhibit.

If we appeal to our criteria, we find little reason to attribute multiplicity to the akratic. The disordered-awareness condition is not met, nor is the separate-personality condition. Moreover, I will show that the separate source of agency present in akrasia is insufficiently differentiated for interself identification. Yet akrasia deserves close attention, nonetheless. This is because it is a philosophical notion that ranges over commonplace weakness of will and deep mental disorders, rather as we saw self-deception does. Not only has akrasia been interpreted by theorists as a reflection of multiplicity. So too have the disorders of impulse control with which akrasia, in its more extreme forms, must be equated. And although the alleged separate selves sometimes attributed to the akratic are not strong instances of multiplicity, as the term is understood here, nevertheless it is true that in both therapeutic and self-help contexts, a language of successive selves has been utilized in countering these forms of akrasia.

At the heart of our understanding of akrasia are some descriptions Augustine (400) offers of struggle against weakness, not only because of the graphic and personal style of the *Confessions* but also because this account has formed our traditional view of these experiences. The "controversy" in Augustine's heart, which he understands as "naught but self against self," is over the need to give up his worldly habits. Of his delay in wholeheartedly turning from a worldly to a spiritual life, and the shame wrought by that delay, Augustine writes, "I tried again, and wanted but very little of reaching it, and somewhat less, and then all but touched and grasped it; and yet came not at it, nor touched nor grasped it, hesitating to die unto death, and to live unto life; and the worse, whereto I had been habituated, prevailed more with me than the better, which I had not tried" (400, 140–141). Augustine portrays this kind of incontinence as a struggle between wills, one of which fails to will entirely because it fails to command entirely. He concludes, "Were [the will] entire, it would not even command it to be, because it would already be. It is, therefore, no monstrous thing partly to will, partly to be unwilling, but an infirmity of the mind, that it doeth not wholly rise, sustained by truth, pressed down by custom." (400, 138). And so there are two wills, he proposes, "because one of them is not entire; and the one is supplied with what the other needs" (400, 138).

What conclusions about the unity of the self may be drawn from the fact that we sometimes struggle within ourselves as Augustine did, knowing what we should do yet failing to do it? Against the Manicheans, whose theory postulated two *selves* housed in the same body, Augustine insists that two *wills* inhabit a single soul, substance, or mind. And this insistence has prevailed, until recently, in much of the tradition that followed him.

But contemporary interpretations of akrasia show less restraint. A much quoted passage by the social scientist Thomas Schelling reveals a conclusion closer to the Manicheans' when he observes that people "behave sometimes as if they had two selves, one who wants clean lungs and a long life and another who adores tobacco, or one who wants a lean body and another who wants dessert, or one who wants to improve himself by reading Adam Smith's theory of self-command [in *The Theory of Moral Sentiments*] and another who would rather watch an old movie on television" (Schelling 1984, 58).[4]

Like 'self-deception', 'akrasia' is a philosophical and literary term. And the concept of akrasia applies to a range of weaknesses, from the most trivial, captured in Schelling's remarks, to the persistent and incapacitating impulse disorders known to psychiatry. Although it is not part of the syndromic, clinical language in which these disorders are usually described, such disorders too are captured by the philosophical dualistic picture of a "controversy" in the akratic's heart.

A separate-selves analysis of akrasia like Schelling's is not infrequent in therapeutic contexts where impulse control is sought. Separate-selves language has proven to be a vivid heuristic for conceptualizing and offering recommendations concerning self-control, for example, as the following passages from a discussion of overeating reveal: "On previous diets I had always said 'No' to my Fat Self. This time . . . I needed to say 'Yes' to my Thin Self" (Lay 1986, 68). "Practice the 'yes' tactic on behalf of your Thin Self, not your Fat Self, which has its own resistance tactic for saying 'Yes' to itself, and never for *your* benefit. This is why you must observe and learn to distinguish between your opposing food desires. Your Fat Self may attempt to confuse you as to which desire you are saying 'Yes' to." (Lay 1986, 75).

The separation of "selves" introduced into discussions of moral weakness, ambivalent motivation, and impulse disorders cannot claim to rank fully as separate selves, however. It is more accurate to refer to them as separate sources of agency or wills (Augustine), since their conative features alone serve to distinguish them. First, as we saw, both of the akratic's purported selves remain fully transparent to one another. Thus the disordered-awareness condition remains unfulfilled. Second, the personality differentiation is insufficient for inter-self identification. The unidimensional, undifferentiated lower self that beckons Augustine toward carnal temptation appears to be little more than a bundle of impulses toward sex. The wily Fat Self portrayed here is defined by, and reducible to, its desire for food. As such, neither alleged self is sufficiently complex and distinguishable to rank as a separate identity.

With his last pair (the self who would improve himself warring with the self who prefers the comfort of an old movie on television), Schelling takes us beyond the usual fleshly temptations and, in so doing, approaches personality traits that might serve to differentiate.

But these traits either challenge the continuity requirement or fail to differentiate sufficiently for the interself identification we require. Thus assumptions about human nature allow us to posit the simpler bodily appetites as enduring traits. It is not so evident that the pair described here—to read a particular book or indulge in a movie—are more than fleeting whims. And if they *are* more, then it seems to be because they are understood so broadly as to fail to differentiate this self-improver and that comfort seeker from other persons with these general, common traits.

The Separate "Selves" of Self-Deception

'Self-deception' names a mental function that, in its most extreme and entrenched manifestations, may be equated with multiplicity. But most self-deception is something less, as we will now see.

Unwittingly holding contradictory beliefs is a common and unremarkable feature of being human. Because we suppose that with awareness of her inconsistency a person embracing conflicting or contradictory beliefs would be strongly motivated to relinquish one, and would do so without particular difficulty or resistance (although perhaps with some reluctance and regret), contradictory beliefs invite no serious speculation about the self's disunity or multiplicity. Self-deception too is usually thought to involve entertaining conflicting or contrary beliefs. But when self-deception is involved, entertaining contradictory beliefs is more complicated and *is* puzzling, because of one additional, key paradoxical ingredient. On a standard, philosophical definition, self-deception involves holding conflicting or contrary beliefs knowingly.

Although this definition successfully distinguishes self-deception from unwittingly holding contradictory beliefs, it is not sufficient to demarcate self-deception from a number of other aspects of our experience (Radden 1984). So it will be important to give some examples to illustrate the sorts of self-deceiver we are talking about.

Well knowing it to be untrue, we persuade ourselves that our homework is complete, that there will be time enough to finish it later, or that it doesn't matter to us if it goes unfinished—and we retire early to bed.

Fictional portrayals richly illustrate elaborations wherein self-deception becomes entrenched habits of mind, choice, action, and awareness. And it is from such elaborations that most philosophical analyses of self-deception have been derived.[5] But clinical descriptions also illustrate self-deception. One of the most intriguing of Freud's cases was that of Daniel Schreber, a man whose *dementia paranoides*, as Freud (1911) diagnosed it, included florid delusions and resulted in extreme dysfunction. Even in as severe a psychiatric disorder as Schreber's, Freud's account of what he calls the mechanism of symptom formation may be seen as self-deception. Schreber deceives himself into persecutory delusions to prevent conscious awareness of his homosexual impulses. This is not the language that Freud employs; he speaks instead of repression. For self-deception is a philosophical and literary term, not usually, we saw, a psychoanalytic or psychiatric one. (Nor, it is true, would all clinicians analyze Daniel Schreber or paranoia in the way Freud did.)

Rather than a brief attempt to prolong pleasure or avoid pain, illustrated earlier (I deceive myself into retiring to bed early), self-deception may become the basis for entrenched and comprehensive patterns of behavior and thought. The habitual and systematic self-deceiver may be more familiar under other clinical descriptions, but the term self-deception well describes these cases.

Thus self-deception may be described as resulting in several selves, each of sufficient "lifespan" and differentiation of agency and personality for our multiplicity conditions. And when disordered memory or limited awareness results, this will be multiplicity, or by another name, dissociative-identity disorder. But so widespread is self-deception and so apparently rare are these extremes that these remain aberrant cases. The separate "self" that is deceived is not in general a personality, as we have understood this notion, nor has it a distinguishing agenda sufficient for intrapersonal identification. In an important discussion of these topics, Jonathan Glover reaches a similar conclusion. Only sometimes, he emphasizes (Glover 1988, 28–29), is the motivational story in self-deception more particular, detailed, and distinguishing than it is in commonplace akrasia.

Philosophy has something to learn from abnormal psychology and from real-life psychiatric, neurological, and psychological clinical details. Philosophy can also teach the disciplines of abnormal psychology and contribute insight into the ethical and moral dilemmas of psychotherapeutic theory and practice. However, the complex enterprise of drawing philosophical conclusions from empirical descriptions, on the one hand, and contributing philosophical distinctions and theories to an understanding of those facts, on the other, is fraught with methodological dangers. It is toward these dangers that I now wish to direct our attention.

II

Successive Selves and Personal Responsibility

From Abnormal Psychology to Metaphysics: A Methodological Preamble

Quite recent interest in the case material of abnormal psychology has led philosophers to offer interpretations of clinical phenomena and to seek conclusions that reach beyond the particularities involved— conclusions pertaining to all minds and selves, abnormal and normal, to the nature of consciousness, and to moral claims about responsibility. It is these conclusions and this warrant to go beyond particular cases that are the subject of the present chapter.

There are special limitations associated with proceeding in this area of philosophical inquiry without reference to the sort of case material that suggests multiplicity, disunity, and discontinuity of selves, it will be shown here. Philosophers attempting to draw theoretical and philosophical conclusions by exclusive appeal to *imaginary* and *unrealistic* examples are entitled to few definitive conclusions. But even when we turn to real clinical descriptions, the uncertainties and imponderable questions associated with the assumptions and theories we bring to an interpretation of the case material must give us pause. These uncertainties and imponderables not only make for conceptual confusion, they also invite a serious risk of circularity and vacuity. In particular, the philosophical method of appealing to moral intuitions to establish metaphysical conclusions, despite its widespread use, is difficult to apply. Moreover, the kind of all-encompassing generalizations and conclusions about ordinary minds and selves that we are tempted to derive from case material are vulnerable to overstatement. Only with unflagging attention to methodology may we avoid these hazards and find conclusions useful for either discipline, abnormal psychology or philosophy.

This chapter begins with a discussion of the role of real-life examples in aiding an understanding of metaphysical issues about the self. Next I introduce and explore a set of related methodological issues concerning the relationship between moral and metaphysical claims about persons, selves, and identity. Finally, we reach questions of generalization from abnormal cases.

Some philosophers whose interest has been drawn to this kind of odd and sometimes bizarre case material have judged it to direct us toward fairly extensive conclusions in the philosophy of mind— conclusions about all minds, and about the nature of consciousness in general. I have reservations about several of these generalizations. They are often overstated and unwarranted, and again, I will show that the fault lies with a want of attention to method.

Real cases from abnormal psychology require theory for their interpretation, and philosophical theory of the self, in turn, must accommodate these real cases. When we tackle normative, policy-related questions, this interdependence becomes a constant danger because of the likelihood that circularity and inconclusive inference will result. Generalization about all selves from the phenomena introduced earlier must be limited, moreover. Split brains will permit generalizations about the self but are not evidence of multiplicity, as we understand the term here. Dissociative disorders, like dissociative-identity disorder, whose causes are not understood, bespeak multiplicity but will not permit generalization to the normal case.

Imagined Examples

In deriving conclusions about the self and identity, philosophers have had two sources: clinical descriptions and imaginary, or "science fiction," examples. Use of the methodology of the thought experiment is familiar from other areas of philosophy. It is especially richly embroidered in discussions of personal identity and dates from at least as far back as Locke's famous request (1690, 216) that we imagine the mind of a prince magically transferred to the body of a cobbler. More recently, contemporary philosophers have derived support by appeal to hypothetical situations. Thus Bernard Williams (1973, 46) asks us to consider that there might be "some process" to which two persons *A* and *B* could be subjected and as the result of which they might be said to have changed bodies. And Parfit proposes imaginary operations whereby, upon the fatal injury of his body, his brain is divided and each half placed in the skull of his two brothers, thus producing in each resulting person the belief that "he is me" (Parfit 1984, 354).[1]

Especially in the context of theories of personal identity, the methodology of appealing to imaginary, science-fiction examples has been subjected to objections, as the damning remark of the well-known logician Willard Van Orman Quine illustrates: "To seek what is 'logically required' for sameness of person under unprecedented circumstances is to suggest that words have some logical force beyond what our past needs have invested them with" (1972, 489).

More recently, other philosophers have criticized the methodology of science-fiction examples. I will comment on the thorough-going attack marshalled by Kathleen Wilkes (1988). Wilkes's concerns are several. Basic scientific principles, she points out, require a statement of the background conditions against which the variable under consideration is examined. Without such a statement, the presence of intervening variables must taint any alleged inference drawn. Yet the "possible worlds" of philosophical thought experiments are typically unspecified and insufficiently described. When we have such thought experiments, as she puts it, the inference is necessarily problematic, because of the uncertainty concerning the relevant background conditions (Wilkes 1988, 8). In a world such as that proposed by some theorists of personal identity, where we split like amoebas, "everything else is going to be so unimaginably different that we do not know what concepts would remain 'fixed,' part of the background; we have not filled out the relevant details of this 'possible world,' except that we know it cannot be much like ours" (Wilkes 1988, 12).

A related problem is to be found in the nature of the imaginative exercise itself and the presumption that imaginability, conceivability, or describability serve indifferently as reliable indicators of logical and/or theoretical possibility. Being able to frame a mental picture of some imaginary phenomenon, Wilkes stresses, is not enough of a basis on which to build conclusions about what we would say if such things *did* happen, when we believe that they cannot happen in any possible world. What actually can and does happen, she concludes, "is usually more gripping than what the perfervid imagination dreams up from the philosopher's armchair." And with this, Wilkes abjures all imaginary examples and proposes, like Quine, that we limit our study to, as she puts it, "the sorts of things that can (really, actually) happen to the object we call a person, and the implications that wait to be drawn from those things" (1988, 1).

I am in some sympathy with the positive aspect of Wilkes's program, as the earlier chapters of this book attest. There is much to be learned about the self from empirical psychology. Both normal and abnormal cases can contribute to our understanding immeasurably. And to the extent that armchair philosophizing has stood in the way of making appeal to real cases, then Wilkes is surely right to question its role. But there are several very different questions that it is possible to ask about the self. And the different concerns they express are not comparable when it comes to this methodological debate over the use of real rather than imagined examples. Concerns about the self's disunity and even multiplicity at a given time require at most a limited contribution from the armchair. For these concerns, we would do better to consider the significance of real cases studies —the "disownership" experiences of schizophrenia and clinical descriptions of multiple personalities and commissurotomy patients —not to mention everyday weakness of will and stress-induced depersonalization.

But some questions about personal and self identity, while they cannot always or perhaps ever be answered if we imagine away the body, nevertheless cannot be answered *unless* we do just that. For the answers, the body must be magically, imaginarily removed. Although flights of what Wilkes disparages as science fantasy may ultimately prove barren, we are forced to engage in them. If we are debating the significance of memory continuity in attempting to determine criteria for personal identity, for example, the basic principles of scientific method to which Wilkes herself appeals would seem to require us to eliminate (through imagination) the maverick variable of spatio-temporal continuity. Such thought experiments may not usually, or perhaps ever, yield the conclusive and unequivocal answers we hope for. I share Wilkes's suspicion of the ability of thought experiments to generate findings, in part because they rely on a degree of agreement and intuitive obviousness rarely if ever found in fact. Nevertheless, such experiments seem still to rest on one—indeed, the only— methodologically defensible approach. If we want to prove that X at t_1 and Y at t_2 are one and the same person, we could never conclude that the mere fact of psychological continuity of some kind between

t_1 and t_2 (e.g., that provided by overlapping memory dispositions) is the source of our judgment of identity and the basis for identification and reidentification. To establish any nonphysical criterion for identity as not only sufficient but also necessary, in the way that Locke thought memory to be, we must exclude the influence of spatio-temporal continuity. And it is unclear how else to do so, as Locke recognized, except by imagining psychological traits apart from bodily traits.

We are left, then, with a dilemma. Stripping our example to the bone to eliminate extraneous variables recommends itself as methodologically appropriate. Yet a process of reclothing, or reembodying, is required before any claim applies to the real world. And such a process, as Wilkes's and Quine's comments emphasize, must be sloppy, biased, or ambiguous.

For some, though not all, of the reasons Wilkes gives, we would do well to eschew science fiction examples. I have two additional doubts about the usefulness of such examples. First, the different perspectives and purposes that we bring to our concern over the self's unity and continuity vary. The particular questions about identifiability and reidentifiability that suit the imaginative exercises of elimination involved in science-fiction thought experiments from only one of several kinds of inquiry into the unity and continuity of selves. At best, then, thought experiments will be of limited use. However, and this is my second point, these science-fiction cases typically rely on an intuitive response, often focused around moral issues like responsibility.

Appealing to intuitive responses elicited by particular science-fiction cases involves an exacting methodology that philosophers too rarely acknowledge. What seems intuitively obvious is an empirical question. Few convictions or even "moral certainties" have the universal agreement that can obviate an empirical investigation. And discussions about personal identity, it is my impression, reveal radical, intuitive disagreement. They are dogged not only by disagreement but also by uncertainty. We have cases over which it is not clear what to say. Our intuitions not only fail to concur but founder entirely. In responding to Quine's criticism, quoted above, of his use of imaginary examples, Parfit replied that there are agreements of this universal kind. I think he is almost certainly wrong, and at least the burden of proof lies with him.[2]

One imaginary case, that of Dr. Jekyll and his homunculus Mr. Hyde, is an exception to these observations about the dangers of imaginary cases. This tale is important to the discussion of the standards by which we determine multiplicity or separate selves. Stevenson captures and represents the temptation to posit a homunculus, which is a recurrent motif throughout post-Enlightenment philosophy and literature. As such, the duality of Jekyll and Hyde is an exemplar and shaping case of successive selves, to which we can helpfully appeal in trying to understand the notion of multiplicity and the way this notion informs case descriptions of mental disorder. Moreover, because the case of Jekyll and Hyde is described by a skillful writer of fiction, it comes with the detail, narrative context, and imaginative plausibility that are typically wanting in the underdescribed examples introduced within philosophy, of which Quine and Wilkes have rightly complained. Imaginary and fanciful, the product of armchair speculation—Mr. Hyde is all of these. But as our best known and most deeply internalized homunculus in the English literary and cultural tradition of the last hundred years, he has a special and valuable place in the philosophy of psychology.

Acknowledging these difficulties with imaginary cases, we now consider what can be learned from the real-life descriptions favored by Wilkes.

Real Examples

Pertinent, fascinating, and challenging as they are, real examples from case material and everyday life remain elusive and ambiguous. A definitive interpretation of these phenomena often seems difficult to establish. Should we say that those who suffer dissociative-identity disorder reveal disunity at a time as well as discontinuity through time, or should we merely describe their divisions, viewed across time, as discontinuity? Are they better seen as a divided mind or merely as successive, alternating selves or awarenesses? This question, we discovered, the facts cannot completely answer. Choices and decisions met us at every turn, no matter how apparently pertinent the case. Interpretation was called for. And where does our interpretation come from? We seem to turn back, ineluctably, to theory and metaphysics, to normative assumptions and posits, to nonobservable claims about the self and its unities.

At this juncture, however, a sense of familiarity besets us. Metaphysical theories of the self too call for choices and decisions. There are no apparent metaphysical facts of the matter, so intuitively clear and incontrovertibly true as to broach no denial, that will allow an immediate and definitive interpretation of the empirical data. Rather, metaphysical and theoretical accounts offer an embarrassment of riches. Moreover, we often seek to arbitrate between theoretical positions by appeal to examples and empirical case material and our intuitive response to such descriptions. Thus we have come full circle. We are back to cases, real or imagined.

This method conforms loosely to the back and forth motion by which we proceed when we seek principles of justice through what the political philosopher John Rawls (1971) entitled "reflective equilibrium." It is circling and iterative. Neither theory alone nor appeal to our basic, unanalyzable convictions over particularities (situations, actions, and case descriptions) alone will yield what we seek in philosophical analysis of this kind. Our intuitive reactions serve as curbs and stabilizers to theory; appeals to theoretical principles in turn feed and shape intuitive reactions.

Metaphysical Conclusions from Moral Convictions

The kind of back and forth play between cases and theory just outlined will be found in the chapter that follows (chapter 6), where the thesis is introduced that responsibility and its attendant emotions of contrition and remorse require continuity of memory. This thesis is a primary one, we will see, asserted without further principles or theory and supported through appeal to intuitive agreement about cases. We are not inclined to hold a man whose present amnesia prevents him from remembering his past responsible for his forgotten deeds, it has been asserted.[3]

Notice the structure of this argument. It aims to confirm a metaphysical principle that memory continuity is necessary for responsibility. (Memory alone would not be sufficient, presumably, since several conditions can prevent us from ascribing full responsibility, including compulsion, which is compatible with full memory.) It does so by appeal to a case, that of the amnesiac, that, even if it is imaginary, is nevertheless a real-life case, something that does in fact occur when damage and disease affect the brain and when mysterious "psychogenic" factors intervene to expunge part of a person's experience and knowledge of his or her identity. This argument presupposes that to punish a man for deeds that, through amnesia, he cannot remember would be wrong and an injustice. Our tacit intuitive agreement assumed, the argument returns from the case to the principle, which is that memory is a necessary condition for responsibility.

This particular version of the argument is strictly theoretical; philosophers proposing it have made no attempt to apply these findings outside of philosophy. Were their interest in these questions practical and policy-oriented, were they focused, let us say, on the legal culpability of those suffering psychogenic amnesia, then the bones of the argument could be seen to conform to the circling and iterative pattern of reflective equilibrium. From a first-order moral question about the culpability of a certain group of defendants, we are directed to a theoretical principle (responsibility requires memory). Then support for this principle is sought by appeal to intuitions about specific cases (the case of the amnesiac man). They are not the same cases as those that raised the first-order moral question, of course. That would be circular. (Moreover, if we had clear and concurring moral intuitions over the cases in question, then the whole inquiry would be unnecessary.) Rather, they are analogous cases.

This is not always a vicious or unhelpful circle, as its circling method may suggest. But we must focus our attention on the confusion and risk of unconscious circularity attendant on the methodology required for drawing conclusions of the kind we seek. In some discussions the vagaries to be found both when we appeal to theory and when we consider particular cases rightly discourage us from deriving substantive conclusions.[4] It is true, not all of the questions it is important to ask, even those with very specific policy consequences, are so inhospitable to the method of reflective equilibrium by which we turn from metaphysical theories and principles to cases and back again. Sometimes, when carefully applied, this method will yield substantive answers; at least it will enhance our understanding of the issues involved, narrow and clarify the conclusions open to us, and serve to guide those whose educated but ultimately personal decision it must be.

Among the questions raised in this book, some are primarily conceptual. For example, should we regard the very distinct personalities exhibited by the sufferer of manic depressive disorder as separate selves or as parts of the same self? Although this question is important in part because moral and ethical questions depend on it, on the face of things it is distinguishable from any normative conclusions its answer might be taken to invite or dictate. Others questions, while they immediately introduce values, are very general in form. An example, which we will explore in chapter 6 is, Are separate selves responsible for each others' deeds? The answers sought in questions of both kinds are germane to the more specific ethical questions that arise in the context of psychotherapeutic and psychiatric theory and practice: Should we use drugs to establish chemical sanity in a mentally ill defendant? Are we entitled to override the wishes of the mentally ill patient if at some earlier time that patient has made known that she does not wish for any treatment? Should the multiple who takes the stand as a defendant in the courtroom be asked to swear separately for each personality? As we saw above, the search for conceptual certainties often requires an examination of moral intuitions and convictions about particular cases, and questions of morality depend on and appeal to philosophical and metaphysical theories of self. Thus the seeming independence of conceptual, moral, and metaphysical issues is more apparent than real. Nonetheless, less explicitly normative the set of questions most straightforwardly benefit from philosophical analysis and the introduction of theory. Empirical facts of the matter cry out for theoretical interpretation. Until we understand the conceptual criteria involved, we cannot hope to assess the confusing reports from therapists working with multiples or the paradoxical findings of split-brain experiments. Only in the context of philosophical theory are we able to weigh a question like the one raised earlier: should we regard the very distinct personalities exhibited by the sufferer of manic depressive disorder as separate selves or as parts of the same self? While not absent, the dangers of circularity and vacuity sketched above seem less apparent here, particularly if the philosophical analysis restricts itself to the tasks outlined: enhancing our understanding of the issues involved, narrowing and clarifying the possible conclusions, and offering methodological guidance.

Some of the greatest risks accompany attempts to find answers to the boldly and explicitly moral questions raised above concerning responsibility. Here the hazardous reflexive play between our reactions to and intuitions concerning particular cases and examples, on the one hand, and tenets of philosophical and metaphysical theory, on the other, are at once most essential and most complex.

Are separate selves responsible for each other's deeds, it is asked. Several distinct arguments will emerge when we explore this matter. Two apparently emphasize concepts, theory, and metaphysical principles (the first focuses on the methodological and moral individualism embedded in traditional conceptions of responsibility; the second on the Lockean intuition that memory continuity is required for responsibility). Another argument appeals to intuitive responses to individual cases. Whether we approach our answers by way of theory or by appeal to moral responses to particular cases, however, we will discover that none of these arguments alone is sufficient for the task. Each contains separate and serious pitfalls of its own, only overcome by appeal to tenets of theory and to particular intuitions to cases, respectively.

The Presumption of Organicity

A further complexity in establishing answers to moral questions about the responsibility of the mentally disturbed is introduced by the presumption of organicity. This notion arises with the taxonomic distinction between functional and organic disorders, a distinction increasingly avoided in psychiatric classification because of its purported endorsement of mind-body dualism. However named, mental disorders whose origins are understood and established (hitherto classified as organic disorders) are distinguishable from those disorders (hitherto known of functional disorders) whose causal antecedents remain obscure and even controversial. The widely held presumption of organicity refers to the assumption or expectation that future research will disclose abnormalities of the brain to be the origins of functional conditions as schizophrenia and mood disorders, whose causation presently remains undetermined, and this knowledge will render these disorders analogous in every way to the organic disorders of psychiatry and neuropsychology, whose etiology is better understood.[5]

This presumption is strongly present in medical psychiatric understanding of many conditions such as schizophrenia and mood disorder. The difficulty is this: To the extent that organicity is presumed, it interferes with the conclusions we are entitled to draw from the reactive attitudes we adopt toward the deeds of those who suffer such conditions. When we are confronted with a moral conviction to exculpate or forgive, the theoretical challenge is to draw a single and unambiguous metaphysical implication or explanation from it, as we saw in the earlier discussion of the interpretation of moral intuitions. But the presumption of organicity provides a competing explanation for moral convictions and intuitions to excuse the sufferer of a mental disturbance. Any given impulse to excuse may derive from the presumption that the mental disturbance in question is organic in origin. This presumption, combined with the conviction that diseases excuse, is also sufficient to explain it. Thus the presumption of organicity lurks beneath any discussion of moral convictions about these cases and presents an impediment to this methodological goal of drawing a single unambiguous metaphysical explanation of our attitudes.

The presumption of organicity must be seen, then, as a maverick variable that will interfere with and act to disqualify or taint any metaphysical theory about selves we may have hoped to support by appeal to such moral intuitions. Because, and to the extent that, this presumption is absent from our understanding of dissociative disorders, we can usefully explore them in tracing the relation between ascriptions of responsibility, identity, and memory. For the theoretical purposes of this book, the last mentioned feature of dissociative-identity disorder is an advantage.

Heeding these warnings and recognizing the methodological dangers that stand in the way, I will attempt in the following chapters to find a solution to these important moral questions.

Multiplicity and Generalization

Before leaving these methodological issues, I must review a set of conclusions philosophers have sought that involve less overtly normative issues. Philosophical contributions to knowledge have included efforts to interpret the puzzling clinical descriptions of dissociative-identity disorder and even commissurotomy in order to draw general conclusions of a more strictly metaphysical or ontological kind as to the nature of minds and selves. At the very least, these rare phenomena prompt us to rethink our traditional categories and assumptions about the self's identity, unity, and continuity in application to these cases. But they may do more. Not only how these particular cases should be understood but also what this understanding shows about all minds or selves have been the subjects of philosophical analysis. Although I am not of the opinion that many, if any, useful general conclusions are to be extrapolated from these rare cases, several philosophers have been more sanguine on this point, and it will be useful to rehearse and consider their arguments. I will look at interpretations of two phenomena: multiple-personality disorder and the post-operative behavior of commissurotomy or split-brain patients.

Daniel Dennett (1988) is one philosopher sensitive to these issues of generalization. He has explored them in relation to the peculiar forms of divided consciousness resulting from commissurotomy—an operation that involves partial or complete severance of the cerebral commissures, the bundles of nerve fibers joining the two hemispheres of the brain.[6] I will not examine these split-brain cases fully in this book, but Dennett's claims about them are pertinent for us, because of the more general methodological assumptions they reveal. The fact that commissurotomy patients normally act as if they were a unity, he says, shows either (1) that the self is only split in particularly contrived circumstances or (2) that the unity of normal life is an illusion.[7]

Extreme and unlikely as it might seem, the position expressed in (2) has been adopted by some theorists (Gazzaniga 1970; Puccetti 1973a, 1981; Nagel 1971). And Dennett also accepts a version of (2), asserting that we all have a split consciousness in the sense that much of conscious thinking seems to be a variety of particularly efficient and private talking to oneself (Dennett 1988).

These conjectures reach far beyond the evidence provided by commissurotomy patients, however. Another philosopher, Marks, identifying the error in the argument that if there are two minds or persons in split-brain patients after their commissurotomy operation, there must have been two minds or persons in them before it, has put the point this way: "The explanation of how there can be two minds after the operation requires only that there be, before the operation, a single mind which is potentially, not actually, two" (1980, 29).[8]

A disjunction matching the one posed by Dennett over the significance of commissurotomy may be formulated in relation to dissociative-identity disorder. The possibility of dissociative-identity disorder shows either that (3) the self is split in particularly contrived, or as the result of unusual, circumstances or (4) that the unity of normal life is an illusion.

In the case of dissociative-identity disorder, however, to seek to establish (4) is to take a step without warrant. Indeed, in one respect it is to go beyond the license taken by Dennett and others in deriving (2) with regard to commissurotomy. With commissurotomy, an inference may be drawn from what is true of split-brain patients to what could be expected for any of the rest of us, were we subject to commissurotomy and placed in replicated experimental situations. No comparable inference is warranted from dissociative-identity disorder, however. Dissociative-identity disorder is a "functional" psychiatric disorder, whose natural history and causal origin or etiology remains unknown. The mind and brain of the multiple may be extremely unlike that of the normal, unified person. We do not know. This ignorance, together with the likelihood of differences so deep, must preclude any generalization, however modest, to the normal case.

Thus dissociative-identity disorder, offering us the strongest and one of the few plausible real cases of multiplicity, will yield no generalizations. We may reasonably speak of a multiple as comprising multiple, separate selves. But this ascription gives us no license to draw general conclusions as to the multiplicity of ordinary minds. It allows us to say multiple selves are logically possible, of course. But license to imagine separate selves was granted to us by Stevenson with the publication of *Dr. Jekyll and Mr. Hyde.*

Memory, Responsibility, and Contrition

This chapter and the four that follow form part of a broad exploration of the categories and concepts surrounding ascriptions of responsibility and how they pertain when we look at the successive selves we find in abnormal psychology. Apparently absent in these cases is our usual identity presumption that a single self inhabits one body throughout its lifetime. So we must wonder about the judgments we make about personal responsibility. One person is usually not held responsible for the deeds of another, unless that person was the indirect cause of those deeds. Might it be that one self should not be held responsible for the deeds of another self housed in the same body? Because disturbances of awareness and memory are a feature of multiplicity, my discussion here is centered around the way in which, as Locke believed, an absence of memory might prevent us from attributing responsibility. But we will also notice how a comparable conclusion may be derived from application of contemporary moral theories of hierarchical desire, which equate responsibility with the rule of the "real" self.

Important here is the relationship between memory continuity and some of the attitudes we adopt toward wrongdoing: particularly the contrition, remorse, and penitence we feel over our own misdeeds. Together with the notions of foreseeability and preventability, these moral attitudes help explain the purported link between responsibility and memory.

As Locke recognized, memory is connected with ascriptions of responsibility. This is a complex and difficult connection to understand, particularly if we introduce a traditional notion of personal identity to explain it, as Locke did, or if we fail to acknowledge the role of culpable forgetting. Nonetheless, by identifying responsibility ascription with the reactive attitudes generally accompanying it, we can find a plausible answer to the question of why and how disordered memory of the kind attributable to successive selves might serve to protect one self from responsibility for another's deeds. To the extent that memory of ownership and agency is absent or deficient—so long as this memory failure is not itself culpable—responsibility is diminished. Put more positively, the forensic sense of self requires subjectively experienced continuities and memory of ownership and agency. More particularly, we saw that both the disorders of memory found in multiples and those that often divide earlier and later selves resulting from other, nondissociative disorders serve to prevent our according full responsibility between separate selves.

In addition, these conclusions concerning the responsibility of successive selves are explicable by appeal to contemporary hierarchical theories of self and desire. The forensic sense of self is also one that requires government by a "real self" and by second-order desires.

The Forensic Sense of Self

'Person', for Locke, is a forensic term "appropriating actions and their merit" (1690, 198); 'man' is not. Ascriptions of praise and blame connoting responsibility attach to the person, not the man. Locke's discussion, quoted earlier, anticipates matters strikingly close to our concerns in applying these theories to cases of mental disturbance. Should I wholly lose the memory of some parts of my life beyond the possibility of retrieving them, he speculates, I would be the same man, but not the same person. His argument: if the same man had "distinct incommunicable consciousness" at different times, then the same man would at different times be different persons (Locke 1690, 195–196).

Which, then, we must ask, is the forensic sense of self in our inquiry, playing the critical role Locke assigns to 'person'? Or, since other contexts and purposes may call for a different analysis of responsibility from that encountered here, which are the forensic senses? More than one empirical continuity loosely links the earlier and later parts of most ordinary human lives. So how do we know which is the important forensic continuity to which responsibility—in the retrospective way in which Locke understands it—attaches?

Traditionally, philosophers have been able to bypass this question. 'Person' has been taken to be univocal. A unitary criterion determines personhood or personal identity, and only persons are responsible, i.e., fit objects of praise and blame, appropriate subjects of guilt and remorse. But our inquiry into selves has revealed several competing criteria by which selves may be identified: publicly, through bodily identity and personality, and subjectively, through the continuity of awareness and memory. We must determine which of these different understandings of self is the forensic one we seek. And although Locke's theory of personal identity has helped us place this discussion of memory, I will pursue this inquiry without drawing any broader conclusion about persons and personal identity. Locke's discussion yields several principles, including one that I regard as insupportable (that memory is necessary and sufficient for the self's strict, numerical identity through time). But we may appeal to Locke's insight about the relationship between memory and responsibility without adopting his related views about memory and personal identity.

In its emphasis on persons as public identities, Locke's term 'forensic' has other confusing connotations. It threatens to sweep us through to legal and perhaps public-policy conclusions before we have clarified all that may be involved in responsibility ascription. We consider such conclusions in the chapters following this one, and we will also look at the particular senses of 'responsibility' and of 'self' appropriate to therapeutic contexts and purposes. But it will be helpful first to speculate free of the purposes and interests tying responsibility ascription to particular practical contexts.

Memory and Responsibility

For our purposes, Locke's discussion yields the principle that continuity of memory is necessary for ascription of responsibility. Call this *Locke's principle*. Successive selves where total unawareness, or amnesia, entirely prevents self 2 from being aware of the deeds of self 1 most neatly fit the model of memory and responsibility expressed in this principle. Indeed, as we know from the hypothetical examples Locke conjured up to illustrate his conviction, memory disturbances and failures of the kind found in some clinical cases of dissociative disorder are surprisingly close to what he envisioned. Although he apparently did not recognize that such a man might inhabit the realm of the actual rather than the merely possible, his hypothesis that the same man might have "distinct incommunicable consciousnesses" at different times well fits the apparent multiplicity in the description that follows:

> Tom Johnson, a twenty-two-year-old man, came to legal attention following an extortion attempt for which he claimed total amnesia. At intervals for years Johnson had awakened to find unexpected, expensive objects in his room. While surprised at these periodic discoveries, he had made the convenient assumption they were simply unexpected anonymous gifts from well-meaning friends or other unlikely sources. No legal problems had arisen in action with these "unexpected gifts." Johnson presented as a likable, pleasant young man with no prior criminal history.
>
> In this case, the second personality presented himself spontaneously, and the forensic psychiatrist was startled when Johnson abruptly nodded off, apparently in a petit mal seizure. Johnson reopened his eyes as an altogether different character who presented himself as "Ed," a sullen, hostile, verbally aggressive and sarcastic individual who held Tom in the greatest contempt, wished to live as a pimp, and readily described a lengthy series of successful thefts.
>
> Other findings were similarly consistent with the initial impression of a hostile young man versed in the mannerisms and language of a "street tough" who expressed boundless scorn for those who tried to "make it" by ordinary means. When interviewed later ..., the second personality again emerged spontaneously and cooperated with the interview and testing. (French and Shechmeister 1983, 22)

As long as we are persuaded to accept some version of Locke's principle, we seem required to judge that the ignorant and powerless Johnson cannot rightly be held responsible for Ed's misdeeds. This is a start. But this is only one case, and seemingly one of the simplest cases, of multiplicity derived from clinical description. The complex interself epistemology of many multiples and the perspectival shifts undergone through personality change found in other mental disorders not classified as dissociative both stretch and challenge our usual concepts of remembering and forgetting in ways that Johnson's amnesia over Ed's deeds does not. For example, will we concede that the information one self acquires by "listening in" on the thoughts or experience of another counts as memory in the appropriate sense? What of the self whose awareness of the doings of another self is characterized by detachment and disownership? If a later self repudiates ownership and agency in relation to a past action taken during an episode of mental disturbance, would her memory of the event be judged as remembering in the requisite way? It must be determined what sort of remembering is involved in the memory purportedly required for responsibility.[1]

Distinct but equally urgent are questions pressing on the principle's warrant. Locke's principle may be compatible with some of our usual moral responses and our practices. But he offers little argument to defend it. If he is right, and memory of some sort works as a requirement for culpability, why should this be so?

Were memory thought necessary because it is an empirical confirmation of causal guilt—a not implausible interpretation of Locke's tacit view—then it would be profoundly insufficient. Memory is fallible. Not merely the pieced-together narratives of therapeutic reconstruction but even normal memories involve a creative recasting and selection of past experience, and they involve misremembering. Although memory is sometimes pictorial, detailed, and accurate, the remembering mind is not like a file of snapshots. Although the snapshot model is invited by Locke's empiricist epistemology and may be implicit in this kind of justification of responsibility, it is unconvincing.

Moreover, if memory were thought to confirm personal identity, and thus to ensure appropriate responsibility in this way, it would be equally insufficient, as Locke's critics have frequently pointed out. My remembering *now* that I did the deed *then* cannot establish an identity between present rememberer and past doer, for it presupposes one.[2]

Moral Attitudes Attending Responsibility Ascriptions

Our responses to our own deeds and toward others' deeds form an attitudinal nexus around responsibility ascription. These attitudes have cognitive components, and they embody normative judgements, but also, and very important, they have an affective aspect; they are moral *attitudes*, not merely beliefs. (There is also a set of more solely cognitive judgments, such as the causal ones on the basis of which we make ascriptions of moral responsibility, liability, guilt, or accountability, for example, 'The voluntary movement of X's arm holding the axe resulted in the death.' But these cognitive judgments are not to be confused with, although they in part form, the attendant *attitudes* of responsibility ascription themselves.)

These responses, or attitudes, are instances of Peter Strawson's "reactive moral attitudes." For their fitting and accurate ascription, he has argued, certain reactive moral attitudes we adopt toward others, particularly resentment, gratitude, and forgiveness, require that others be regarded as free and responsible agents. On this "expressive theory of responsibility," Strawson asserts that to hold someone responsible *just is* the proneness to react to them in these ways under certain circumstances (Strawson 1968).[3]

In making and even constituting ascriptions of responsibility, moral attitudes and responses may help us grasp the seemingly important yet elusive relation between memory and responsibility, about which answers are sought here. Such attitudes and responses are not always reliable (the guilty man may feel no contrition) or appropriate (there are neurotic guilt feelings and unfounded blame). But without being infallible guides or necessary features, these attitudes and responses nonetheless play a central and significant part in our understanding of personal responsibility. They are much more than the insignificant side effects of responsibility ascription that their role in some discussions of moral theory suggests.

Responsibility, Memory, and the Cognitive Components of Contrition

The cognitive aspect of a moral attitude that ascribes of responsibility to ourselves and to others is something like 'I did it' or 'She did it', respectively. Considered more closely, 'I did it' resolves itself into two cognitive components, one associated with identity in the sense of ownership, the other with action or agency.[4]

The first cognitive component is 'It was *my* action.' This is the belief that the action was done by me, not by another person. This component corresponds loosely to the notion of the actions being indexical for me. But the belief 'It was *my* action' is compatible with the remembered experience of the action remaining nonautobiographical. I may ascribe an action to myself without experiencing that action as having been mine.

A second cognitive component concerns agency and explanation. 'It was my *action*' captures that a particular relationship pertained between what happened, on the one hand, and the totality of my beliefs and desires as they are remembered to have been at the time of the action, on the other. It emphasizes the sense in which not only did the action take place because of me but also I brought it about.

My discussion here is directed toward only one form of remembering. These cognitive components characterize recollection of our own experience, not memory of facts nor remembered skills and capabilities. Moreover, it specifically concerns one form of experiential memory: memory of one's own (or what are purportedly one's own) deeds. Our other experiences and more passive states are also remembered from the inside in this way. But my focus here is on the past *actions* we remember *doing*.

Recollection of our own deeds often and, we may say, characteristically yields the cognitive attitudes, such as contrition and remorse, that we adopt toward our own misdeeds—the ownership and agency components of 'I did it.' It is something less than a logically necessary source for such cognitive states, however. If my memory is unreliable or insufficient—because of temporary amnesia, willful forgetting, or head injury, for example—I may acquire the appropriate belief for contrition ('I did it') from the testimony of others or by a process of inference from facts I observe (perhaps damage wrought or a photographic record of my forgotten past doings). Nonetheless, remembering doing the deed is the most common way normal people come to the cognitive attitudes of contrition and remorse. And there is an uncontroversial sense in which direct, experiential memory of this sort is *as of* our own lives and experience, not others' lives and experiences; it is remembering "from the inside" (Wollheim 1984, Shoemaker 1984).

Such memory is *as of*, if not *of*, our lives and experiences. Remembering doing the deed in this sense is compatible with our being mistaken, with misremembering. I may not have actually done the deed. For this reason, Richard Swinburne (1984) has proposed that we entitle such forms of recollection "apparent memory." But the point I am making here is not one about personal identity. It is about different kinds of memory as we experience them. We may indirectly, nonexperientially remember another person's experience, remembering that it occurred, for example, as we might remember other facts, such as the date of women's emancipation in England.

And on occasion we may even mistakenly or through empathic understanding recollect another's deed or suffering *as if* from the inside. But generally and characteristically, we recollect our own experience with an interiority and, moreover, a fullness and completeness not matched by any "remembering" of another's experience.

Because memory is often the source of the attitudes and responses we adopt toward our own deeds—attitudes whose general possibility may be required for responsibility, even though no given responsibility ascription depends on any one of them—we now see a sense to Locke's conviction that responsibility requires memory. People do not generally remember others' experiences in the same way, or as well, as they do their own.

Thus, to recapitulate, memory is indirectly necessary for responsibility. While not required for it, memory is the typical source of the cognitive aspect of those reactive attitudes (such as contrition) in terms of which we understand responsibility ascription.

When we speak of past deeds, experiential remembering of the kind identified here contains the cognitive components of contrition and remorse. When a person remembers doing an action, then in the normal case, the memory can be expected to contain ownership and agency components: 'It was *my* action' and 'It was my *action*'. This may be termed 'memory of ownership and agency.' Thus *memory of ownership and agency* is apparent experiential memory as of having done a past deed that characteristically contains cognitive components of ownership ('I did it') and of agency ('It was my action').

If memory of ownership and agency is associated with ascriptions of responsibility, systematic failures of such memory might encourage us to withhold those ascriptions. And just such failures as these, we know, are found in the failures, lapses, and distortions of awareness and memory associated with successive selves in abnormal psychology.

Before considering these cases, we must acknowledge another qualification on Locke's principle, at least as it applies to the normal case: forgetting itself is not always blameless. While it may be unjust, as Locke believed, to blame the culprit for the forgotten deed, it may be equally wrong to absolve him of forgetting.

When is forgetting culpable? More technical notions like suppression and denial fail to capture the multitude of ways we put out of mind something we are not eager or willing to remember, the fecundity of our forms of self-deception. We soften, distance, deny, white-wash, and disassociate ourselves from past doings. We obfuscate, distort, select, and shade past memories. And sometimes we thereby succeed in (culpably) forgetting them. The fact that forgetting may be culpable constitutes a serious challenge. When Locke's principle is applied to normal people in everyday situations whose self-deception takes these forms, this fact considerably diminishes the utility of the principle.

Foreseeability and Prevention

Any analysis of responsibility and memory must acknowledge the part played by foreseeability and prevention. Foreseeability and the power to prevent future undesirable outcomes always enter into ascriptions of responsibility. But the moral importance of foreseeability resides in its being, in the normal case, a guide to prevention. A version of the widely accepted commonsense moral conviction captured in the philosophical slogan that 'ought' implies 'can' precludes our casting blame for behavior beyond the subject's control. Without foresight, there cannot be preventability, without preventability, there ought not to be blame or reproach. In Stevenson's tale Dr. Jekyll initially transforms himself into the unrecognizably evil Mr. Hyde by voluntarily taking a potion. When later he is compelled by scientific curiosity to repeat his experiment, Dr. Jekyll finds himself the involuntary subject of these hideous changes. After his first experiment with the potion, Dr. Jekyll might foreseeingly have prevented the evil in advance. Because this is so, we, and Stevenson, hesitate to absolve him of all culpability over Mr. Hyde's actions. Even acknowledging that it was not he but Mr. Hyde whose deeds they were and that at the time of their doing, Dr. Jekyll was both unaware and powerless to effect them, we hold him to account.

Responsibility and the Successive Selves of Abnormal Psychology

The links between memory and responsibility have been sketched here as they seem to present themselves in ordinary people—with the usual ratio of selves to bodies—whose forgetting, we recognize, might itself be culpable. Now we must reflect on how these conclusions apply to cases of successive selves.

First, back to the thief. Johnson is portrayed as lacking the ability to remember many experiences and deeds ascribable to the self (Ed) with which he shared the thief's body. Clinical descriptions regularly suggest that memory disturbance is not within the control of its subject. Indeed, the word 'amnesia' reflects just this feature: amnesia is memory disturbance that the subject cannot control.

Claims about a patient's "nonculpable forgetting" cover distinguishable activities here, notice. Dissociative barriers are not broken through an immediate effort of will, this much seems clear. Merely concentrating or relaxing or appealing to mnemonic devices sometimes permits us to recollect items initially unavailable because of normal forgetting. And Johnson could not readily do this. Nor did he appear to be in immediate control of the "switching" to another self, Ed, who would release the inaccessible memories. We know that one of the goals of therapeutic intervention with multiples has been to develop this capability, however. And to the extent that such a capability was initially present, then the suggestion of culpable forgetting may prevent the protection afforded by Locke's principle. Even to the extent that the possibility of acquiring that capability was known to the subject of memory disturbance resulting from dissociative disorder, which, some claim, it often is, then culpability becomes an issue.[5]

It will be helpful to separate epistemological concerns here. We may have no way of ascertaining whether a given description reveals the absence of control associated with nonculpable forgetting: clinical descriptions are opaque and ambiguous. Moreover, so are human beings, not only to others but also to themselves. We deceive ourselves over our own powers and capabilities, over what is and is not within our voluntary control, as over many other things. Granting these limitations, and the difficulties they will present in making policy decisions, we may nevertheless set aside such limitations while pursuing our inquiry here by casting *Locke's principle as a hypothetical*: if Johnson experienced nonculpable memory loss over Ed's misdeeds, then he could not be rightly held responsible for those deeds.

Because of this epistemological opacity, questions of responsibility will often go unresolved in practice. It may be necessary at times to adopt, as a working maxim for therapy, 'I don't care who did this. I'm holding you responsible!' not only as a pragmatic device for instilling a sense of responsibility, as it is used with children, but also as a default response to our inability to accurately determine responsibility because of the opacity of answers to these control questions.[6]

The complex epistemology of multiples vis-à-vis separate selves' access to one another's mental states cannot be captured entirely by the notion of total unawareness. Some selves are ignorant of the mental states of others, it is true. But other selves are portrayed as able to "observe"—albeit helplessly, disinterestedly, and without identification—the states and actions of other selves as they occur. In this impoverished and distorted way they may afterward recall the facts. Such failures or aberrations of resultant memory suggest that to the extent that these failures are beyond voluntary control, they too might rightly exonerate the subject from responsibility by Locke's principle. Such subjects do not reflect the characteristics important for this principle. They fail to exhibit the beliefs of ownership and agency encapsulated in 'I did it.'

A second group of subjects also appear at risk of suffering diminished memory of ownership and agency of deeds in many instances: those suffering the sequences and rotations of apparently separate selves exhibited in schizophrenia and mood disorders.

Although not amnesia in the usual or clinical understanding of that term, memory disorder is often found in schizophrenia and mood disorder and is likely to affect memory of ownership and agency. Because the role played by this form of memory in our everyday attitudes and responses to our own past deeds is closely tied to normal responsibility ascription, these alterations and distortions of memory may also count to preclude responsibility, on Locke's principle.

To illustrate some of these more problematic instances, let us revisit a case introduced earlier, the manic episode of Mr. M. (see page 62). As the result of manic disorder, Mr. M. a hitherto quiet, happily married postal worker, underwent an extreme personality change. He became incorrigibly optimistic, talkative, gregarious, and energetic. He spent the family's savings on aquaria and other equipment for tropical fish, with the goal of modifying existing equipment so that "Fish won't die anymore ... [and] we'll be millionaires" (Davidson and Neale 1986, 196).

Although this man's excesses are not known to have resulted in crime, the frivolous use of the family's savings likely imposed hardships on his wife and children, for which, were he not mentally disturbed, he would be held morally accountable, at least. Let us project Mr. M. beyond this manic phase. Chastened, returned to his quiet, unenterprising earlier personality, reinstated, let us say, in his humble job, how should he, and how should we, judge the harmful excesses of the manic self? And if we are reluctant to hold the later Mr. M. (self 3) responsible for the misdeeds or omissions perpetrated by the earlier Mr. M. (self 2), does our reluctance somehow rest with failures of memory on his part?

To outsiders, at least, changes in Mr. M.'s behavior and beliefs appear puzzling and beyond the realm of rational, or "intentional," explanation: they often seem to result from physical or organic causes rather than from reasons or reasoning. And after the passage of time or therapeutic intervention, the public perspective, or something close to it, is often adopted by the subject of such changes as well. Restored to his earlier personality and having relinquished the beliefs and desires that motivated his behavior—his conviction, for example, that he could make fish live forever—Mr. M. too would be inclined to see his former behavior as a disease or temporary possession. At this point Mr. M. likely lacked memory of ownership and agency of his earlier deeds.[7]

The cognitive state associated with memory of ownership and agency comprises two elements: one related to ownership (It was *I* who did it) and the other to agency (It was an *act* of mine). But Mr. M.'s later memories, as we have been postulating them, will not always include the cognitive element of agency, even if they do include that of ownership. If not the disowning 'It was not I to whom it happened', which denies both ownership and agency, Mr. M.'s judgment seems likely to have been one that at least denies agency: 'It was I to whom it happened.' Thus Locke's principle—as it has been interpreted here—would seem to apply. Since he remembers his past misdeeds in this meager and distorted way, Mr. M. would not be held responsible for those deeds.

The memory distortion and rearrangement we recognize as likely in Mr. M.'s case may serve to protect Mr. M. from responsibility for his past wrongs by this application of Locke's principle. But they can do so only if we are satisfied that the changes of memory that have taken place were not themselves forms of culpable forgetting, i.e., were not fostered by the self-deceptive stratagems familiar from everyday life experience. It would be naive to suppose this could not happen in cases such as Mr. M.'s. Continuing stigma attaches to episodes of mental disturbance. Moreover, acceptance of traditional identity assumptions encourage and foster such attitudes as embarrassment and shame over our pasts. These attitudes and feelings constitute strong motivation for self-deception. At best, then, we can propound another hypothetical: if such memory failures are not culpable, then Locke's principle should protect Mr. M. from responsibility over his misdeeds.

Before we leave Mr. M., we must acknowledge the force of perspectival considerations here. To their sufferer at or near the time of the episode in question, some of the seemingly abrupt changes of behavior and psychology found in schizophrenia and mood disorders result from normal or rational causes. Because of changes in beliefs and desires, as it seems subjectively, the person comes to adjust his thinking, feeling, and action. Mr. M. is described as spending several nights designing and writing about his invention for tropical fish. He reached the optimistic and seemingly momentous conclusion that he could save fish from death in this way and adapted his behavior appropriately on the basis of reasoning that, while it may have been flawed, broadly resembled the way we ordinarily adopt new ideas and redirect ourselves through time. At worst, we might say, from his own immediate perspective, Mr. M.'s impulsive, wholesale, and rapid transformation resembled the abrupt life changes we associate with ideological conversion.

What can we make of this perspectival quandary? Mr. M. was not *more* responsible closer to the time of the misdeeds associated with his manic excesses, when he understood himself to be their author, than he was later, when memory of ownership and agency was lost. Two responses seem possible. It may be tempting to discount Mr. M.'s immediate subjective perspective. Treating this consequence as a reductio argument would allow us to insist that the more public perspective Mr. M. comes to adopt is to be privileged: it alone can be relied on for the moral answer we seek. But this would be an arbitrary favoring of one perspective over another. Better, we may allow this case to direct us toward another feature of Locke's principle. Appropriate memory connections are not the sole requirement for ascription of responsibility, this quandary makes clear. At best, Locke's principle is proposed as a condition necessary for responsibility ascription; it alone is not sufficient.

The more complex case of Mr. M. revealed additional barriers to an easy interpretation and acceptance of Locke's principle. To those barriers may be added others. The kind of memory distortion discussed here admits variation, in degree and in kind. I may acknowledge my agency concerning one action ('It was an act of mine') with greater and less conviction. Not only are 'It was an act of mine' and 'It happened to me' possible, as we saw; so too are 'I think it happened to me' and 'It happened to me, but it did not feel as if it was me' and 'I did it but it felt dreamlike and unreal' and so on. At different times and phases of these conditions, the quantity and quality of memory failure will vary.

So if it is plausible at all, Locke's principle must be given a guarded formulation: inasmuch as, and to the extent that, memory of ownership and agency was absent, diminished, or weak in these cases—and this want of such memory was not itself culpable—then responsibility will be rightly withheld, we may propose. Call this the *guarded formulation of Locke's principle.*

These observations are a guide, at most, to a case by case approach, our analysis has made clear. And they certainly will not allow us to establish that any particular class of cases, as clinically defined, exhibits responsibility. There are classes here, but they are philosophical, resting on philosophically relevant differences, not clinical ones.

One last qualification to these claims concerns the relation between foresight and the characteristic patterns of recurrence or rotation found in the successive selves of mental disturbance. The repeated emergence and reemergence of each character, we saw, contributed to Dr. Jekyll's culpability, because it was associated with the added anticipation, foreknowledge, and preventive power that Dr. Jekyll was later positioned to enjoy. The parallels between Dr. Jekyll and some of the clinical cases I have been discussing occur closer toward the story's end. It is often not the power to foresee but the power to prevent (the undesirable outcome) that, for example, the multiple appears to lack, just as Dr. Jekyll came to lack later, when transformations from one self to another took place involuntarily. Particular selves of the multiple sometimes have, or through therapy can soon acquire, partial power to foresee (Putnam 1989). But this power of foresight is often radically severed from prevention, at least before effective therapeutic intervention. To the extent that such foreseeability and control are possible, then like Dr. Jekyll in the earliest stages of his duality, the selves comprising the multiple must be held responsible for the misdeeds of other selves with whom they share a body.

Recurrence is also present and is again associated with preventive power in the case of sporadic disorders like schizophrenia and, notably, the cyclical swings of mood disorders. It invites and perhaps morally requires certain forms of advance planning, at least when to do so is to anticipate and prevent causing harm to others. (This issue of responsibility and planning for the care of future selves are explored in chapter 10.)

The conclusion reached here concerning self 1's responsibility over self 2's actions may now be related to a an important contemporary discussion that has grown out of hierarchical analyses of the self and its desires. The following brief introduction of "real selves" theory will allow us to check the conclusions drawn here through an application of Locke's theory against those we might reach through the use of a very different moral framework.

"Real Selves" and Responsibility

The notion of a person who is self-determining in being governed by a "real" or "authentic" self or character is an important one in therapy, where such self-determination is often held as a therapeutic goal or ideal. And it has been propounded by philosophers attempting to analyze the ingredients of responsible action. Relying on hierarchical theories of desire, the moral philosopher Susan Wolf (1990) has developed such a real-self account of responsibility. Only when we are governed by higher-order desires and values, or what Frankfurt has called second-order desires, and thus free to choose and shape ourselves in the light of those desires, are we rightly held responsible for our actions, on this analysis.

The real-self view of responsibility is consonant with much of our thinking about normal psychology and is also applicable to certain forms of mental disturbance. (Impulse disorders, particularly, seem to invite, and perhaps even require, for their understanding hierarchical analyses of the self such as the real-self view propounds.) Thus it will be interesting to notice how contemporary theory complements Locke's when applied to the forms of mental disturbance that display multiplicity. At least in dissociative disorder, this set of ideas also seems to lead us to the conclusion that self 1 is not responsible for self 2's actions. Let us see why.

Any given reigning or presently embodied self at any time may be analyzed into a hierarchy of desires. And in many cases it will be plausible to assert that self-determination, and hence responsibility, prevail: at least for the period of reign, self 1 is guided by second-order desires about her first-order desires.

This analysis extends and runs somewhat contrary to the spirit of the hierarchical real-self theory, admittedly. The real self Wolf portrays is associated with singularity. Yet, unless by fiat, there seems no reason to preclude the possibility of one body housing a succession of several selves, each containing, and during its reign governed by, its own, separate real self. Certainly, theoretically, a separate self may be analyzed into a hierarchy of desires and may exhibit "self"-government by second-order over first-order desires. And in practice, many successfully functioning multiples and many who cycle between different affective phases in mood disorders appear to be as self-governed in this sense as do more unitary persons.

Recognizing that an unqualified real-self view eludes our intuitions about responsibility where the mentally disturbed are concerned, Wolf (1987) has argued that for responsibility, the real self must be determined to be sane by some independent standard of sanity. Wolf herself proposes the standard embodied in traditional legal conceptions of insanity. But applied individually to the separate selves of the multiple, it must be emphasized, this criterion will not prevent us from ascribing responsibility to many multiples. The reigning self in a well-functioning multiple will prove sane, in possession of a real self, and thus, when that real self prevails, responsible for her own actions.

Self 1 will be responsible for her own actions, but what of her responsibility for self 2's actions? If self 1 is sometimes guided by second-order desires about her first-order desires when she is reigning, and self 2 similarly is sometimes guided by *his* second-order desires about his first-order desires when he is reigning, then at least sometimes self 2's actions stem not from self 1's real self but from his own. And thus it cannot be true that self 1 is always responsible for actions executed by self 2 through their shared body. This reasoning is sufficient to allow us to reach the same conclusion we saw invited by Locke's principle, namely, that separate selves are not always responsible for one another's deeds.

In attempting to clarify the moral principles and convictions underlying the vexed questions of multiplicity, memory, and responsibility raised in this chapter, I have avoided several complexities. These must now be acknowledged. Different contexts bring their own distinctive, contextualized purposes, as we will see. And several distinguishable discourses of responsibility ascription require separate analyses.

Purposes and Discourses of Responsibility Ascription

The question of whether one self is responsible for another with which she shares, has shared, or might again share a body invites not one but several answers. Based on Locke's analysis, our discussion thus far has been divorced from any particular context or purposes. When the discussion is so divorced, we have seen, it is plausible to insist that the spatiotemporal person comprises two or more selves or sources of agency, one innocent, and the other guilty, of a past misdeed. But we must now acknowledge the added complexity of some particular spheres in which the issue of responsibility might arise: the therapeutic setting and the more pragmatic contexts of criminal law, inpatient management, and everyday relationships. In addition, we must recognize that there are different discourses involving responsibility ascription, of which that introduced by Locke, with its forensic emphasis on fault, blame, and innocence, is only one. Whether one self is responsible for another will depend not only on the particular contextualized purposes in the light of which the question is raised but also on the notion of responsibility implied. Thus we will see that self 1 may be morally responsible for self 2's care: she may be obliged to avert, if she can, wrongful behavior on the part of self 2. But by dint of this obligation, self 1 is not morally responsible, in the sense of culpable, for self 2's deeds. Moreover, while we may be loathe to hold self 1 morally responsible, in the sense of culpable, for self 2's deeds, for some of the reasons explored in the previous chapter, yet more pragmatic contexts, including the legal one, invite different judgments. The conclusion that the public person comprises both a self who is, and a self who is not, responsible becomes incoherent where discussions of responsibility are interwoven with legal "dispositive" considerations over liability and desert. The person is indivisible for the purposes of punishment, censure, and acquittal.

Only by clearly delimiting and separating these different contexts, purposes, and discourses about responsibility can we understand the question with which we began: whether each self comprising the person is responsible for every voluntary and intentional action perpetrated through his or her body. Yet by so delimiting and separating these different contexts and discourses, we will uncover—not surprisingly—contrary and incompatible answers to this question.

The person possessed of more than one self is not responsible for every voluntary and intentional action perpetrated by his or her body. And some therapeutic and everyday contexts will invite an ascription of divided responsibility and adoption of differential reactive attitudes toward the separate selves involved. What of the whole spatiotemporal person as defendant or plaintiff? For the answer to this question we must turn to the notion of legal responsibility.

Discourses of Culpability and Discourses of Care

The notion of responsibility spans several distinct discourses, including those where we speak of being held responsible, or taking responsibility, for our deeds and those where we are said to take responsibility for others, particularly for others' care, in a more holistic, less formal, and less legalistic way. In everyday life this discourse is pervasive; in theoretical writing it is associated with contemporary feminist theory (Gilligan 1982, 1986; Noddings 1984).

As with liability, accountability, and culpability, responsibility is linked to our own deeds. We are individually held responsible for what we do, together with some of the foreseeable outcomes of what we do, as distinct from what may befall us and, with certain qualifications, from what others do. Also individualistic, for the most part, are the several attendant attitudes and emotions of responsibility ascription: the "reactive attitudes" of blame and reproach, of forgiveness, mercy, absolution, and praise, that we ascribe to others for their doings and the guilt, remorse, regret, contrition and pride we feel for our own.

When we speak of taking responsibility for others' care—typically the young, the infirm, and the very old—the notions of liability, accountability, and culpability enter, if at all, with different emphasis.

Unless some formal authority is involved—that accorded the parent, teacher, military officer or workplace supervisor, for example—we are rarely held accountable for all the deeds and misdeeds of those for whose care we take responsibility. In looking after others, we often seem to commit ourselves to adopting a set of attitudes and to making certain efforts, rather than to taking certain actions. For example, in taking responsibility for others, we commit ourselves to try to ensure their well-being, yet this may not include literally preventing them from undertaking acts of wrongdoing. Moreover, how much fault attaches to our failures, even over these looser goals, will depend on many factors. And our primary shortcomings will often be judged as failures of attitude and effort, not action.

Responsibility for others' care has a singular and important place when we ask questions about self 1's responsibility over self 2's deeds, we will see when we explore notions of responsibility as they reveal themselves in the therapeutic context. It is not only that self 2's deeds regularly affect and bear on self 1's experience, plans, and prospects, which we would expect to give self 1 an interest in them. In addition, the value placed on a unified and continuous self, or "individualism," in our culture—likely enhanced by such caring—may invite a prescription: separate selves perhaps ought to take responsibility for one another's care. Self 1, it can be argued, has pragmatic but also moral responsibility for self 2's care.

Therapeutic Contexts

Our concern here is with differentiating successive or separate selves in moral evaluations related to responsibility. Such differentiation plays a role in a variety of other therapeutic settings as well, however. Some therapists embrace and work with a full cast of inner characters. And although these characters may initially be insufficiently distinguishable, articulate, or self-aware to rank as separate selves, the therapeutic effort is aided by this heuristic. Moreover, such therapeutic techniques sometimes even measure the success of therapy in terms of these characters' fuller differentiation. Thus the psychoanalyst Joyce McDougall observes,

Under optimal conditions the psychoanalytic adventure allows each "I" to bring forth its own Jekyll and Hyde and its own Faust and Mephistopheles, split-off yet vitally necessary parts of every self. Thus love and hate may be reconciled, enabling the subject finally to sign the treaty of many years' silent warfare, which otherwise might lead to exhaustion and death. . . . The many "I"s contained within each patient's official "I" listen to each other. Discovering their paradoxes and contradictions, they can henceforth assume their cohesive identity and their mutual enterprise. (1985, 15)

The separation of "selves" introduced into discussions of moral weakness, ambivalent motivation, and even impulse disorders cannot claim sufficient identifying traits to rank fully as separate selves by the definition of multiplicity adopted here. It is more accurate to refer to these aspects as separate sources of agency, rather than as separate "selves," for it is their agential patterns, at best, that might serve to differentiate them from other persons. Nonetheless, "separate selves" language has also proven a useful heuristic, as the passages quoted earlier from a discussion of overeating graphically indicate (see page 70). Similarly, to help the patient contend with debilitating shame, it has proven useful to emphasize the distance between separate selves or self stages in therapeutic and counseling settings.[1]

It is possible to recognize that the person who houses several selves may be at once guilty and innocent in particular therapeutic contexts. It may even be essential. For certain steps in the therapeutic endeavor, both the therapist and the separate selves may and perhaps must differentiate doer, deed, and innocent "bystanders" in relation to acts of wrongdoing. To do so ineffectually is to run the risk of diminishing a sense of responsibility in the patient by offering a means of escape from it, as some clinicians have noted (Spanos 1983, 1986; Spanos, Weekes, et al. 1985, 1986; Putnam 1989). Nevertheless, effective and successful integrative therapy sometimes requires that these moral discriminations be made. In part, this differentiation can be effected by, and will be reflected in, the adoption of appropriate reactive attitudes such as reproach, blame, forgiveness, and absolution.

Those who, during a bout of extreme mental disturbance, have committed crimes or wrongdoing as a "separate self" will not all require therapeutic attention focused around such differentiation and the adoption of such attitudes, of course. For those who resist identification with a self with a wrongful past, therapeutic endeavor may instead require instilling a sense of individualistic responsibility, the conviction 'I did it' that undergirds contrition, remorse, and penitence. But for others, as for some normal wrongdoers, knowledge of the past wrong brings debilitating guilt, shame, and self-blame. And here something different will be required. Here perhaps only an ascription of divided responsibility (self 1 did wrong; self 2 is innocent, or less culpable) and adoption of differential reactive attitudes toward the separate selves involved will promote healing and self-forgiveness (blame toward self 1, sympathy for self 2, for example). Moreover, toward the past deed, an attitude of what philosophers sometimes distinguish as "agent regret" may be necessary on the part of the patient (Baron 1988).

Agent regret is the attitude appropriate to the perpetrator of unintended harm. Thus if my wrong were accidental, inadvertent, or unintentional, it may be more appropriate for me to experience agent regret than guilt. (What I actually experience is another matter. But our interest here is in the therapeutic relationship, within which the therapist can offer direction and guidance over questions of which feelings are appropriate.) Guilt would be inappropriate in the present case: self 1 deserves reproach; self 2 may not. But equally inappropriate would be indifference: self 2 ought not blame herself for the misdeeds for which she reproaches self 1, yet she ought to acknowledge the causal links by which she is bodily related to the wrongdoing.

These issues arise with force and poignancy in relation to descriptions of dissociative-identity disorder. Thus this general point may be illustrated by appeal to this particular condition and the therapeutic efforts directed at it, which customarily have as a goal an integrated self. (An evaluation of this goal is provided in chapter 13.)

The processes involved in successful resolution or "cure" of dissociative-identity disorder are immensely complex and still little understood. Most perspicuous among the few detailed contemporary discussions of therapeutic technique are those of Kluft and Putnam (Putnam 1989; Kluft 1982, 1983, 1984a, 1984b, 1986, 1987, 1990). From these accounts it is possible to plot the steps and stages through which the more general integrative goals of a unified whole are pursued. These stages are both *analytic* and *synthetic*.

First, the multiple may need aid in acknowledging the diagnosis: she often must learn that she is many, not one. This will require what might be termed analysis: the identification and acknowledgment of separate alters or selves hitherto unacquainted. Such acknowledgement permits efforts at cooperation and reconciliation between separate selves.

Cooperation engenders reconciliation. With an attempt at cooperation, the patient's need for separateness begins to lessen.[2] And cooperation and reconciliation prepare the multiple for the processes of synthesis: the integration, the often dramatic and ritualized denouement of fusion, and the postfusion adjustments of attitude and memory, required for a full sense of personal identity.

Understood in relation to wrongdoers who are multiples, this process contains several steps that appear to require work with reactive attitudes related to responsibility. First, the task of analysis will call upon these attitudes. Reactive attitudes are guides to identity across time (Flanagan 1994). Consider: to experience 'I feel guilty over wrongful deed x' is to recognize 'It was I'. Thus, to acknowledge 'I do not blame myself for x' is to differentiate myself from x's agency ('Helen [self 1] did it; I [self 2] did not').

Later, part of synthesis will involve adopting reactive attitudes. The following passage from Putnam 1989 describes the postfusion attitudinal adjustment required by a multiple whose original fracture traces to early traumatic abuse:

> The patient will still have to come to a new understanding and acceptance of this same trauma following fusion integration. The retrospective viewing of these experiences as a continuous whole, rather than as flashes and fragments of memory, changes the patient's perspective.... While still a multiple, the patient is usually able to maintain sets of contradictory feelings toward the abuser(s) side by side.... The fused state ... forces the patient to face and resolve these very different perceptions. (1989, 318)

Part of filling out and establishing a new unified personal identity, this passage makes clear, involves coming to acknowledge and feel wholeheartedly the appropriate attitudes toward others who have wronged one. In this case, they are felt toward the abuser, and they are rage and blame.

An attitudinal readjustment is also required over past wrong perpetrated by one or another self. Here, though, the newly minted unified self must differentiate finely, as Putnam makes clear in these remarks:

Typically, while a multiple, the patient assumed responsibility for much of the trauma that was inflicted upon him or her, over which the patient actually had little control. Paradoxically, while still a multiple, the patient often ignored responsibility for his or her own hurtful or harmful actions toward others. Following fusion, these discrepancies must be reversed. Accepting responsibility for his or her actions is often extremely painful for the patient to face.... While assuming this responsibility the patient must be consoled and supported by the therapist and helped to understand that he or she was ill and often reflexively inflicted upon others what had originally been done to him or her. (1989, 319)

These remarks may be read to prescribe support of the patient in the sentiment of agent regret. Again, guilt would be inappropriate, so too would indifference. The therapist must foster only the particular attitude suitable to acknowledging a wrong unintentionally committed.

Such illustrations show how reactive attitudes constituting responsibility play a part in therapy with multiples. Next let us examine the proposal that the therapist ought to encourage the multiple's selves to take responsibility for each other's care.

We are familiar with some of the strategies of self-command from less sensational cases of inner heterogeneity in normal people. When ambivalent or weak, we engage in a kind of indirect and "imperfect" rationality (Elster 1984), anticipating and guarding against a future "self" less prudent than our present one. We place the alarm clock beyond reach from the bed, so that in the morning when it rings, we will not be tempted to turn it off and return to sleep. Ulysses blocked the oarsmen's ears so that they would be deaf to the Sirens' song.

Once the multiple recognizes her multiplicity, such strategies of self-command must be her stock in trade. The self-preservation of the composite public identity of the multiple will require it, and it is part of the cooperative engagement between alters or selves that prepares for synthesis and integration (Kluft 1986). But self 1 can learn to anticipate, thwart, or neutralize the effects of the damage other alters or selves might do from motives other than self-preservation. Strategies of self-command not only ease day-to-day living for the composite public identity of the multiple. They are also invited by the communitarian, or corporate, sense of these intimates—the other selves with whom the multiple shares a body and a public life and identity—the sense that they need her care.

This may not be easy. The several selves involved inhabit the same body, thus making the relation among them far more intimate in some respects than that between any two selves or persons of the usual spatiotemporally distinct kind. Yet in other respects, they are more likely than separate persons to be estranged, since the other selves inhabit the body as "pretenders." A particular alter or self may know, understand, and like her best friend much better than she does some of the alters or selves with which she shares her body. The clinical literature abounds with instances where antipathy, scorn, and competitive jealousy mark the relations between the separate selves housed together. Nevertheless, sharing a body entails sharing much else: a life, many interests, perhaps a bank account, a public persona, some mutual memories, and, not least, the possibility of oneness wrought by fusion. This constitutes an intimacy of a particularly intense and pervasive kind. Such intimacy has no close parallels. But we do know that other forms of intimacy are associated with special obligations. So we may hypothesize that perhaps special obligations attach to these relationships. If intimacy brings responsibility for care, then self 1 may have more than self-interested reasons to employ strategies of self-command.

Interestingly, both motivations—moral obligation and self interest—may be required to recover the experience of oneness or unity sought though therapeutic integration. Thus it will aid, and may well be essential to, the therapeutic endeavor that the multiple adopt strategies of self-command to enhance her functional unity. But taking responsibility for other selves' care may also be a means of establishing the identification between selves, and eventual fusion, which the clinical evidence suggests is required for successful, long-term integration (Putnam 1989).

In summary, then, therapeutic goals invite, and perhaps require, that the therapist and the patient or client acknowledge the differences among selves, and a central part of this will be recognizing the different reactive attitudes it is appropriate to adopt toward each over past deeds. With this recognition must come emphasis on how the accused composite public person both is and is not responsible for a deed perpetrated by one self.

Legal Contexts and Purposes

The division between therapeutic and the more pragmatic legal contexts of responsibility ascription reflects the composition of law and legal institutions. Law has a "dispositive" function concerning the legal consequences of actions and states of affairs brought before it (Hohfeld 1923). Something must be done: a legal disposition is required. Thus legal discussions of a concept like responsibility are interwoven with dispositive considerations over punishment and desert: they are wedded to the pragmatic and consequential.

Some of the most helpful writing on multiple selves and the criminal law is Michael Moore's (1984). An analysis that posits divided responsibility, Moore asserts in his discussion, would leave responsibility unacceptably "indeterminate." Thus, he remarks, "the notion of multiple selves would make a hash of the conditions under which we ascribe moral fault, for it would lead to contradiction at every turn. Multiple selves, some of whom are knowledgeable and some of whom are ignorant, would result in actions being both intentional (for the knowing self) and unintentional (for the ignorant self) in every case." This analysis is unacceptable to Moore because "there will be no answer to the overall question, was he (the whole human being) responsible? For . . . he both was and was not" (Moore 1984, 151).

Moore's positive proposal is that for the duration of their condition we accord multiples the status of "suspended personhood." The analogies or models from which support for this view is derived are young children and the mentally ill, whose status of suspended personhood, he says, "is recognized most dramatically in legal and moral spheres: they are not accorded the full panoply of rights held by sane adults, nor held to be proper subjects of responsibility, and not held to be able to calculate their own self-interest." Multiple-personality persons, he concludes, "should be regarded as but a special case of suspended personhood. There was but one person originally, and (if therapy is successful) there will be but one person again. During the time that intervenes, the only answer to the question, How many persons? maybe none" (1984, 406).

Moore's exclusive emphasis on the legal context may encourage misleading overstatement, however. By separating therapeutic contexts and purposes from legal ones, we may successfully avoid asking the "overall question"—indeed, we may recognize that there is no overall question to be asked. To answer the overall question 'Was he responsible?' with 'He both was and was not (responsible)' is to offer an answer that is neither incomprehensible nor inaccurate when it is understood in the terms outlined here. It means simply that the public person comprising both selves was responsible, while the separate selves included one or some who were not responsible. This answer becomes unhelpful and incoherent only in the pragmatic context of a legal system, where such judgments must result in legal consequences.

Moore's failure to envisage *any* purpose for which it may be useful to acknowledge a multiplicity of selves inhabiting the same spatiotemporal body is matched by a comparable oversimplification. French and Shechmeister (1983) have argued that even legal contexts permit us to acknowledge the multiple's multiplicity. Casting the question in terms of the possibility that the multiple may house more than one representable entity, these authors ask, "If one may represent estates and corporations, why should one not represent a personality whose internal coherence and competence has been established?" (1983, 24). And while they concede that public-policy issues may render this unworkable, these authors gesture toward how such representation might be proposed.

On the basis of this analogy with estates and corporations, French and Shechmeister claim there is no legal impediment to treating a second personality as a representable entity. Yet in the pertinent respect identified earlier concerning the law's dispositive function, the analogy with estates and corporations is insufficient. We may dispose of entities greater than one spatiotemporal human body (e.g., corporations) and of collections of nonhuman items (e.g., estates). But a person is different. Persons remain indivisible units for dispositive purposes. It is as wholes that persons are sent to prison or acquitted. It is as wholes they are directed to undergo some psychotherapeutic regimen, even though, as part of that regimen, they may be required to acknowledge their multiplicity.

In contrast to both positions outlined here—Moore's and French and Shechmeister's—it is true neither that the multiple should never be judged as a multiplicity nor that she must always be so judged. Rather, in some contexts and for some purposes, we are free to, and perhaps should, acknowledge the multiplicity present in these cases; in other contexts and for other purposes, we are not free to, and should not.

With this clarification completed, we may turn to responsibility questions arising in the more pragmatic and consequential circumstances associated with the law. Ideally, we would punish the guilty selves when they were reigning and release or acquit the innocent ones during their periods of control of the body, continuing until an appropriately severe, or effective, sentence was completed. But the shifts between different selves do not permit such policy. They are not predictable, either to any self or selves of the multiple or to outside observers. Their rotation and recurrence defy understanding and are apparently unpatterned. Moreover, they are so swift and short-lived, in many cases, as to elude a system, say, of release and reimprisonment, no matter how flexibly such a system were to be designed.

The law has a strong and abiding interest in individualism. There are compelling reasons—alluded to by Moore in the passage quoted above—why the legal notion of responsibility, linked as it is to liability and penalties, presupposes a unified person, as must any concept with practical public-policy implications. For the purposes of punishment, censure, or acquittal, there can be but one person.

The necessity of seeing the defendant as one rather than several where legal responsibility is concerned has been firmly enunciated in the small body of case law involving dissociative-identity disorder as an excuse or defense. In the case of *State v. Grimsley* (1982) from an Ohio appellate court, Grimsley had been previously diagnosed as suffering multiple-personality disorder (dissociative-identity disorder). Her appeal over a drunken driving sentence involved the claim that at the time of the crime, one personality, Robin, had acted unconsciously or involuntarily. Concluding that the evidence did not support her claim of unconscious or involuntary action, the court observed, "There was only one person driving the car and only one person accused of drunken driving." It was not material whether she was in one state of consciousness or another, "so long as in the personality then controlling her behavior, she was conscious and her actions were a product of her volition." Refusing to acknowledge the woman's multiplicity, the court insisted it would not begin to "parcel criminal accountability out among the various inhabitants of the mind" (*State v. Grimsley* 1982, 832). There was a culprit, in other words, and there could only be one.

In the face of these undeniable legal necessities concerning responsibility, we have several options. But we are not free to follow the moral reasoning developed earlier and assert that the legal person embodying several selves both is and is not guilty of past wrongdoing. Only removed from the constraints imposed by the dispositive function of the legal system can such a conclusion be drawn.

Several options acknowledging the legal necessity of treating the public person as one rather than many have been introduced in actual cases involving defendants suffering dissociative disorders. These have included (1) appeal to the legal defense of unconsciousness, as the Grimsley defense (unsuccessfully) employed, (2) some version of the insanity defense, by which the defendant may be found not guilty by reason of insanity,[3] and (3) the concept of "diminished capacity," used until recently in courts in California. To these we may add (4) the status of suspended personhood, proposed by Moore (1984). Finally, there is (5) an acknowledgement of guilt. Some of these options would diminish punishment or delay it, some would substitute a therapeutic regimen for punishment, some would acquit. The last option, (5), would require that we treat multiples in the same way as normal—and normally unified—defendants.[4] While associated with very different dispositions, (1) through (5) each alike requires us to relinquish the complex judgment we saw invited and even required in less pragmatic settings whereby guilt and innocence can be simultaneously attributed to the same public person.

An analysis of the strengths and weaknesses of the arguments entailed in (1) through (5) will be found in the following chapter.

The Therapist's Role

The therapist stands poised between these several contexts for and discourses about responsibility ascription and must acknowledge and partake in each. On the one hand, clinicians necessarily must confront the law when patients with these disorders enter the legal arena. Moreover, where the more pragmatic goals of inpatient management require it, the dispositive constraints here identified with the legal context may be found in therapeutic contexts as well, as those working with multiples in inpatient settings have recognized.[5]

On the other hand, the integrative therapeutic task requires differentiation of guilty selves from innocent "bystanders," and identification and reidentification through use of differential reactive attitudes. Moreover, as we saw earlier, the therapeutic task may, and perhaps should, include instilling responsibility in the sense of concern for other selves' care.

Because the therapist engages in the several contexts and discourses associated with ascription of responsibility, we must clarify the purpose-relative nature of claims about a public person's oneness and multiplicity. As a patient or client in the context of therapy, the multiple may most helpfully be acknowledged to be a multiplicity. As a defendant in court, psychiatry must concede that the public entity is one, indivisible, and as such *wholly* responsible for or innocent of past wrongdoings (although not necessarily *fully* responsible for or innocent of them, since responsibility admits of degree).

Everyday Relationships

Those who embody successive, simultaneous, or rotating selves—both multiples and persons transformed by mental disorder and dysfunction in other ways—are not merely defendants in courts of law and patients in therapeutic contexts. They are also people leading their day-to-day lives; they are colleagues, spouses, mothers, brothers, friends, and acquaintances. What reactive attitudes over issues of responsibility are appropriate in these less formal settings? Stephen Braude has raised such questions in relation to multiples: "Just as the legal community must consider the propriety of punitive measures for multiples who commit a crime, parallel questions arise when a multiple's friend (or spouse) wonders how to deal with the hostile (or insensitive) behavior of a single alter. Is anger appropriate, and if so, toward whom should the anger be directed?" (1991, 19). Other issues of responsibility concerning agreements, promises, and the loyalty due to intimates and loved ones also arise. And they will arise, it should be stressed, as well with the successive selves of other disorders as with those found in the dissociative disorders, which have been the particular focus of much of this chapter. How should we judge the discomfort we feel as we plot with care givers to thwart a brother's manic excesses? Is it betrayal, for which we should feel remorse, necessary but regrettable? Or is it to be dismissed as an inappropriate scruple over a marauding stranger?

Legal questions about sexual consent have arisen over multiples. (Does 'rape' describe the act of sex with one self based on the consent of another?) And so must questions of consent arise in any union, sexual or otherwise, involving multiples, and in any relationship deep enough to involve cooperative endeavor.

Some of the ways in which we relate to the disunified selves we know outside the formal bounds of legal or therapeutic contexts will reflect the same pragmatic constraints required by legal and inpatient management. I must treat my multiple colleague, spouse, mother, brother, friend, or acquaintance as a unity for many practical purposes. But other purposes may be compatible with, and may even require, the more nuanced acknowledgment of moral difference permitted in the context of the therapeutic relationship. If my friendship with self 2 is strong and abiding, then it behooves me to understand and perhaps even share the shame she feels over the harm wrought by self 1, with whom she shares her body. Sympathizing with self 1 is inappropriate; so too is blaming self 2. Shame must be the response.

When questions of responsibility do not immediately arise, informal contexts and purposes in which differentiation may be appropriate are not difficult to resolve. In handing out Christmas gifts, planning a meal, or choosing a topic of conversation, to use Braude's examples, we naturally would, and perhaps should, acknowledge the individuality of the separate selves. When responsibility is involved, however, these judgments are more difficult. These relationships elude simple rules of conduct or appropriateness. Attitudes held about the presumption of organicity, beliefs about the degree of culpability associated with foresight and preventability, and convictions that pragmatic advantages are to be derived from holding others responsible for their deeds, whether or not they were responsible for them, might each affect our judgment over the individual self's responsibility. In the present discussion we may hope at best to draw attention to the moral complexity involved and to emphasize that the issue is an important one deserving consideration by theorists.

If we discover a morally and philosophically innocent "bystander" among the several selves making up the public person, it follows neither that the composite person including a culprit should be, nor that he or she should not be, censured, blamed, or punished in the legal sphere. Because the separate selves share a body, we still have to determine the judgment suitable for the composite person on the stand in a court of law.

Multiplicity and Legal Culpability

Does the possession of more than one self serve as an exculpating factor in the legal context? Should it? Which sense of self is forensic here? Thus far my emphasis has been on the similarities between the several disorders, dissociative and nondissociative, suggesting separate selves. But now we must acknowledge their dissimilarities, which point toward different answers for these questions. Because our traditional convictions and beliefs about mental disturbance as an exculpating factor are not focused on multiplicity or derived from dissociative conditions, there is little support in the legal tradition to treat dissociative-identity disorder as an exculpating factor. Other, nondissociative disorders exhibiting successive selves fare better, because they receive protection through the insanity defense. I will first consider the factors influencing legal judgments about fault when the wrongdoer is mentally disturbed in these other ways suggestive of multiplicity, and this will lead to an analysis of whether dissociative-identity disorder might to be regarded as an exculpating factor in the legal context.

Within the terms associated with the legal tradition, wrongdoers suffering from nondissociative disorders not defined in terms of the multiplicity they sometimes reveal are protected by the traditions surrounding and embodied in the insanity defense. In contrast, those wrongdoers suffering from dissociative disorders defined as successive selves will not find exculpation, because our traditional understanding of the conditions that excuse do not fit the peculiar traits distinguishing these disorders. Is this to punish the innocent, it must be asked? It is arguable that it is not, this chapter will show, so long as such a question is understood within the retributivist frame of reference.

Mental Disturbance and Criminal Law: Retributivist Presuppositions

To set the stage, we must delimit the legal area captured in the discussion that follows and frame the retributivist notions underlying our criminal-justice system. The criminal law engages with those who are mentally disturbed at three separable "moments." Acknowledging a distinction between accountability and responsibility will help us here. Person X is *accountable* for action A, let us say, just when there being reason to believe X did A entitles us to an explanation and justification of A. X is *responsible* for A just when it is appropriate to blame X for A. At the first moment, the person's competence to stand trial is at issue, and thus the question of his or her accountability. Sometimes the degree of amnesia suffered by the multiple may preclude a trial. A self ignorant and powerless at the time of the crime may now reign. And this self may so lack understanding of the proceedings, and the charge brought, as to be unable to cooperate with his or her defense. In law, amnesia generally has not been sufficient to count as excluding the kind of competence outlined in common law and legislative tests for competence to stand trial. Nonetheless, this challenge has been brought, and it has served to protect some multiples from trial proceedings at least temporarily. I will not further deal with this moment, judgment of accountability to stand trial, because the questions raised are distinct from those surrounding the defendant's *responsibility* or culpability for the crime.

The trial focuses on the defendant's culpability and ushers in the second and central moment. At issue now is whether or not, at the time of the crime, the defendant was criminally responsible for its commission. The insanity defense enters at this second moment and has been important here in protecting from ascriptions of criminal responsibility and guilt the defendant who was mentally disturbed at the time of the crime.

Separable from this process, at least theoretically, is sentencing. The disposition of those found guilty is the third moment. Again, the guilty person's mental disturbance, as currently assessed, may be brought to bear. Some courts, acknowledging the usefulness of this distinction between evaluation of criminal responsibility and sentencing, have introduced sentencing that reflects the guilty person's mental state.

It is particularly important to distinguish these separate moments when we deal with mentally disturbed defendants, because of the changes those defendants may undergo through time. A defendant may be legally sane at the time of trial and sentencing, while insane at the time of the crime, or mentally disturbed at the outset of legal proceedings and temporarily unfit to stand trial, although sane at the time of both the crime and sentencing. A defendant may be mentally disturbed only at the time of sentencing.

At each of these moments, our criminal-justice system presupposes tenets of retributivism, the deontological theory of justice that undergirds English common law and its descendent, the Anglo-American legal system. Except in rare extenuating circumstances or on account of particular excusing conditions or because of the absence of *mens rea*, those causally responsible for crimes are taken to be culpable, criminally responsible for their wrongdoing, and are rightly blamed and punished for it. The purpose of punishment is the imposition of just deserts on the guilty.

This thinking runs counter to much that is propounded by modern psychologists and embraced by modern psychiatrists and therapists. Psychologists and psychiatrists would find it easier to accept an alternative, utilitarian or consequentialist notion of the purpose of punishment, where sentencing serves rehabilitative goals more suited to the professional ends of psychiatry and psychotherapy. But such notions contravene the principles underlying the legal tradition within which this discussion takes place and must be set aside in the context of contemporary legal realities, or at best raised to soften and mitigate at the point of sentencing.

Legal Guilt and the Successive Selves of Nondissociative Disorders

The structures and retributivist assumptions in our criminal law serve more effectively to protect those with separate and successive selves resulting from other psychiatric conditions than the dissociative disorders. In schizophrenia and the mood disorders, the recurrence and rotation observable on a successive-selves analysis are not in general as mercurial as the apparent switches between the several selves of the multiple. The phases of disorder and recovery, of depression and mania, are better understood and more readily predicted. Indeed, part of the careful procedure of the criminal-justice system outlined earlier has grown out of familiarity with such disorders and the explicit impulse to protect those suffering from them. It reflects an appreciation of the changeability of these conditions through time. The pretrial inquiry into fitness to stand trial, for example, is shaped to prevent injustice to the mentally disturbed self at the time of the trial, regardless of the mental state of the self that committed the crime. But shaped as they are by the time frame of other disorders, these fail to accomonodate the mercurial changes of dissociative disorder. Changes lasting a few weeks such procedural protection can accommodate; changes lasting seconds, like the multiple's switching, it cannot.

In addition, familiarity with schizophrenia and mood disorders, which are counted among the "major mental illnesses," has shaped the tests for criminal insanity, the interpretations to which they have been subject, and the role played by the insanity defense. In forming our notions of the kinds of madness and mental disability that should exculpate, jurists have taken account of the symptoms of these conditions in the formal procedures designed to protect those who suffer from them. Traditionally, legal tests of criminal insanity have acknowledged kinds of disability or incapacity affecting thought processes, or cognition. (Some later and lesser recognition was also given to disabilities affecting will or volition.) These categories grew and developed in response to observation of severe conditions where the ability to distinguish shared reality from private fantasy seemed to rob the sufferer of knowledge of right from wrong, and thus of any inner guide to right conduct. The thought disorder, hallucination, and delusion associated with such states best fit the cognitive elements in the defense.

Contributing to the exculpatory force of the schizophrenia and mood disorders that exhibit these symptoms is that they are more subject to the presumption of organicity in both medical and lay thinking than are dissociative disorders. Though their origin is unknown, schizophrenia and mood disorders are often believed to result from some organic cause. When they are treated as excuses, then, it will often be in part because of the conviction—widely held—that diseases excuse.

The successive selves and multiplicity associated with nondissociative disorders do not serve to exculpate as such. It is not because defendant *X* (self 2) (competent to stand trial) is judged to be a different person from the one who committed the crime (self 1) that he is found not guilty by reason of insanity. Rather, it is that if not as self 2, then at least as self 1, defendant *X* was not responsible for his actions due to insanity.

The traditional incapacities and deficits of cognition (and to a lesser extent volition), in terms of which tests of criminal insanity have usually been cast, do not equally successfully capture the symptoms of the several different nondissociative disorders categorized together thus far. The insanity defense serves to protect sufferers from the mood disorders less fully than it does those with schizophrenia. Nevertheless, it protects them with more success than it does those with dissociative disorders, as we will now see.

Dissociative-Identity Disorder and Legal Culpability

There are several options for treating dissociative-identity disorder as a legal excuse, each acknowledging the pragmatic, dispositive necessity of treating the public person as one rather than many. Some of these have been introduced in actual cases involving defendants suffering dissociative disorders, others are merely theoretical proposals. First is the insanity defense, under which the defendant may be found not guilty by reason of insanity. A second option involves appeal to the legal defense of unconsciousness. A third introduces the concept of "diminished capacity." A fourth, proposed by Moore (1984) in his writing on these issues, allows us to accord the status of suspended personhood to the multiple. A final option is to acknowledge guilt. Our general understanding of multiplicity will be enhanced by a closer look at how these five options fail to capture or correspond to the features that distinguish dissociative-identity disorder. So I will examine these options in turn, each in relation to the hypothetical case seemingly most supportive of a defendant's innocence: self 1 committed a crime that self 2 was not only powerless to prevent but was also ignorant of.[1] Each option has weaknesses, making it less than fully appropriate to the multiple, I will show, including the last. Whether we appeal to diminished cognitive or volitional powers (through the insanity defense), to absence of consciousness (the defense of unconsciousness), to lessened capacity (diminished capacity), or to lack of self-interested calculation (as Moore's category of suspended personhood suggests), the self who committed the crime is not exactly wanting or incapable in the appropriate respect. Instead, we almost wish to say that the multiple's problem is one of excess, not of incapacity or insufficiency at all. And it is not excess of a trait or particular disposition so much as too much self, or identity.

Before examining the particular approaches to exculpation that have been proposed or tried for dissociative-identity disorder, let us remember one further point that affects any such efforts: the role played by dissociative amnesia in these cases. There is a body of legal opinion about amnesia, and amnesia is critical, of course, to the present discussion, both as a defining feature of dissociative disorders and because there appear to be important links between remembering and responsibility. Rather than upholding the conclusions drawn thus far about the part played by memory in ascriptions of responsibility, however, the law has shown itself skeptical about granting an exculpating role to amnesia (Hermann 1986a, 1986b; Roesch and Golding 1986; Rubinsky and Brandt 1986). In seeking to use legal doctrine to show why dissociative-identity disorder should excuse, we must acknowledge this formidable impediment.

It is primarily because of the difficulty of distinguishing fraudulent from real amnesia that amnesia by itself has not served to excuse in criminal law. There being no way to distinguish genuine amnesia is commonly cited both to explain why amnesia does not stand in the way of competency to stand trial and to show that it fails to excuse. This difficulty may have been exaggerated. Methods have been devised for differentiating genuine from fraudulent or simulated amnesia.[2] But the issue seems to be one of appearance in part. As long as there remains the widespread belief that amnesia may be simulated, it will and perhaps should stand in the way of an easy acceptance of the defense of dissociative-identity disorder. If they are to fulfill the educative and deterrent role widely accorded to them, the proceedings and penalties of criminal justice must not only avoid being lenient but must also *appear* to avoid being lenient.

A second difficulty associated with amnesia noted in legal commentary is that it is commonly present after the commission of serious crime in those who are not otherwise mentally disturbed. Following rape, murder, or aggravated assault, the perpetrator frequently experiences a genuine blackout and loss of conscious memory of the act. It has been estimated that as many as 45 percent of murderers undergo such subsequent amnesia.[3] This too explains the failure of amnesia to excuse. In the traditional retributivism underlying our criminal law, excuses necessarily apply in few cases.

The Insanity Defense

The multiple may be judged not responsible by reason of insanity. Dissociative disorders have not regularly been accorded the special protection of the insanity defense in law, nor, in my view, are they often likely to be. There have been some notable exceptions to this claim, however. One example is the case of the man known publicly as Billy Milligan, charged with robbery and rape. In finding Milligan not guilty by reason of insanity, the court noted, "The respondent is a mentally ill person in that his condition represents a substantial disorder of thought, mood, perception, orientation and memory that grossly impairs his judgement, behavior and capacity to recognize reality. . . . The respondent's mental illness is a condition diagnosed as multiple personality" (quoted in Keyes 1982, 364).[4]

Such an example and such reasoning aside, several historical and clinical factors explain the reluctance to extend the insanity defense to cover this group of defendants. First, whether rightly or wrongly, the insanity defense has been limited in its application to the major mental illnesses, those conditions thought to severely affect functioning. As their classification with other personality or character disorders attests, dissociative disorders, such as dissociative-identity disorder, were not traditionally regarded as severe enough to require or deserve the special protection afforded by the insanity defense. It may be, as some claim, that the severity (and prevalence) of dissociative-identity disorder was until recently disguised by misdiagnosis, this in turn being a product of the diagnostic challenge multiples present (Rosenbaum 1980). But whatever mistakes have been made are now law and constitute part of a daunting body of legal opinion over the proper scope of the insanity defense. Second, as we saw, legal tests of criminal insanity have acknowledged only two kinds of specific disability or incapacity: those affecting thought processes, or cognition, and those affecting will, or volition. But the defect or disability associated with dissociative-identity disorder seems to fit into neither category. Irrespective of which self reigned at the time of the crime, there is no reason to suppose that self to be impaired in any of the obvious cognitive and volitional ways captured by a standard reading of such tests. The impairment from which the multiple suffers primarily involves memory, time, and identity. Only indirectly and secondarily can these be seen to limit cognition and volition. The thought disorder, hallucination, and delusion associated with conditions like schizophrenia, we saw, best fit the cognitive elements in the defense; the legally less developed volitional elements of the defense are found in impulse disorders. As a symptom, the multiple exhibits neither kind of defect. Like many multiples, the defendant Billy Milligan suffered additional psychiatric symptoms, several of them, as the court recognized, being factors that regularly serve to exculpate. These additional symptoms, not the dissociative tendencies characterizing the disorder, are what did and would invite the protection provided by the insanity defense in this and similar cases, despite the somewhat misleading wording of the opinion in the Milligan case, quoted earlier. Were a court to adopt tests for criminal insanity identifying cognitive incapacities, such as are embodied in McNaughten's rule (*Regina v. McNaghten* 1843), or the Bonnie rule (Bonnie 1983) now favored by the American Psychiatric Association, or were it to accept tests of cognitive and volitional failings such as are found in the definition of criminal insanity of the American Law Institute Model Penal Code (ALI 1955), then on the basis of the symptoms by which the diagnosis of dissociative-identity disorder is attributed, it is unlikely that a defendant suffering dissociative-identity disorder would or should be found to lack criminal responsibility.

Third, rightly or wrongly, the presumption of organicity is absent or weak in clinical and lay understanding of dissociative disorder. There are different tests for criminal insanity and differing interpretations of those tests, it is true, and some place greater emphasis on the specific incapacity or incapacities affected than on any underlying disease state. Nonetheless, all the tests currently in use explicitly name a purported origin of the psychological disturbance with phrases like 'disease or defect of the mind' (McNaghten's rule), 'mental disease'

(Bonnie rule), and 'mental disease or defect' (ALI test). Because and to the extent that dissociative-identity disorder is less strongly associated with this presumption, it must be less protected under the insanity defense as traditionally understood.[5]

Finally, problems arise for jurisprudence because of the similarity of dissociative disorders to states experienced by all or most people in situations of stress, such as those surrounding serious crime. In the retributivist terms that define criminal law, excuses or defenses must protect only a small minority or subset of defendants.

Considerations such as the foregoing would seem to discourage the use of the insanity defense with these cases unless, in addition to the symptomatology associated with their dissociative-identity disorder, the defendants show evidence of other psychiatric conditions. Severe depression and other symptoms of the major mental illnesses that are the primary locus of the insanity defense can often be found in these patients, alongside or even resulting from the dissociative symptoms making up their disorder. Naturally, such defendants should be protected by the insanity defense.

Two options are closed to us, then. From a legal perspective, we are not free to declare the multiple at once guilty and innocent of the wrongdoing; such reasoning, it has been shown, is at odds with the dispositive purposes of the law. Nor may we plausibly support the position that this defendant is not guilty by reason of insanity, at least as that notion usually and traditionally has been understood in the criminal law. Several options remain: the defense of unconsciousness, suspended personhood, diminished capacity, and guilt.

The Defense of Unconsciousness

As in the case of the woman who claimed unconsciousness in appealing a drunken-driving sentence (see page 119), this defense has already been introduced for defendants who are multiples. It is appealing in part because it makes no presupposition of organicity. Unconsciousness has traditionally counted as an excuse in criminal law, and although unconsciousness brought about by mental disease or defect is not precluded, the excuse has more typically been associated with nonmedical, nonorganic occurrences, such as somnambulism. If a person commits an act of wrongdoing during sleep, her unconsciousness may serve to fully exculpate her (*State v. Grimsley* 1982).[6] The unconsciousness defense seems particularly suited to dissociative disorder too because it so neatly captures the central feature of this condition. At least typically, the self or selves without control at the time of the crime's commission are not only powerless but also unaware of the deed.

The parallel between somnambulism and dissociative-identity disorder has been explored by several theorists (French and Shechmeister 1983, Abrams 1983). Impressed by the seeming fit of this defense, these advocates have pressed the analogy further than it will comfortably stretch, however. In so doing, they expose the limitation of the unconsciousness defense for the defendants in whom we are interested.

Self 2 is unaware of what occurs while self 1 commits a crime in the case of the thief, introduced earlier (see page 94). A 22-year-old man whose public identity was that of Tom Johnson came to legal attention following an extortion attempt for which he claimed total amnesia. Subsequent analysis found him to comprise Johnson, a likeable, law-abiding individual, and Ed, a sullen, hostile, verbally aggressive character who held Tom in the greatest contempt, and readily described a lengthy series of successful thefts committed without Tom's knowledge. About this case French and Shechmeister remark that because the defendant, a multiple, "worked [sic] to make himself unconscious at the time of the commission of the offense," serious consideration should be given to raising the defense of unconsciousness. These authors go on to acknowledge the temptation "to give this problem short shrift by holding the body responsible if *any* of its various minds are culpable" (my emphasis). But at the same time, they add, "it is important to remember that somnambulism for example is a well-recognized example of the defense of unconsciousness, and it raises similar issues of mind and body" (French and Shechmeister 1983, 22).

The issues of mind and body raised by somnambulism are less complex than those raised by dissociative-identity disorder, however, and significantly different from those introduced by the case of the thief. The sleepwalker appears to have but one mind or self, unconscious at the time of the action. It is still puzzling how, on a kind of "automatic pilot," the unconscious somnambulist effects complex physical action. Nevertheless, we are not tempted to elevate that "pilot" to the status of a separate mind or self. It has neither a separate and distinguishable personality nor identifiable motivational patterns, for example (none, that is, that persist through stretches of time). In contrast, the thief comprises Johnson, unconscious at the time of the crime, and Ed, who is fully conscious at that time. If the constraints of the legal setting require us to treat the defendant as one person, then there is a culprit: the conscious Ed.

Recall that this was precisely the reasoning of the court in *State v. Grimsley* (see pages 119–120) in response to an attempt to introduce the defense of unconsciousness. So long as the personality in charge of driving the car was conscious, i.e., someone was conscious, then the composite woman was guilty of drunk driving, it was concluded.

Again, to return to the thief, we seem to encounter not impairment or insufficiency but something else. Ed's consciousness at the time of the crime was undiminished. And the lurking presence of the unconscious Johnson reflects an excess related not so much to consciousness as to selves.

In defense of the position they support, French and Shechmeister may charge that the analysis offered here arbitrarily elevates conscious Ed at the expense of unconscious Johnson. Why, they might ask, should we acknowledge the capabilities of Ed merely because he is conscious, and give credit to Ed's consciousness merely because Johnson has been temporarily eclipsed? In answer, we might say, Why not? For to elevate Johnson over Ed is equally arbitrary. At best, such a complaint would leave the application of the unconsciousness defense moot and unresolved. Neither this question nor the alleged analogy with somnambulism can advance the case these authors wish to make.

So while the defense of unconsciousness apparently succeeds in capturing something central about the multiples in which we are interested, their amnesia, this option has deceptive plausibility.

Suspended Personhood

Following Moore's suggestion, we may relegate the multiple to a state of "suspended personhood" for the duration of his or her condition.

This is compatible with, but also a fruitful development on, some of the moral convictions undergirding the uses of the insanity defense.

One might helpfully choose to view multiples, Moore asserts, in the same way as we regard others who are mentally ill. They have the status of suspended personhood. Like young children and the mentally ill, he recommends that we recognize that multiples are not complete persons, even though they may in the future become persons. At least temporarily, they are not proper subjects of responsibility and not able to calculate their own self-interests. Until they regain full personhood, he concludes, "the only answer to the question, How many persons? may be none" (Moore 1984, 406).

Moore's notion looks promising, but it is deeply counterintuitive in some respects. While we may appreciate the sense in which very young children and some mentally disturbed adults are not fully persons, i.e., exhibit a dearth of the qualities we associate with personhood (such as the ability, cited by Moore, to calculate their own self interests), multiples are very different. Rather than being short on personhood, we might say that they are overly endowed with it. Similarly, rather than being incapable of calculating their own self-interests, they comprise a group of selves each zealously, even dangerously, proficient at calculating self-interests. Part of therapeutic integration of multiples requires that some of this talent for self-interest be dulled and lessened (Putnam 1989, Braude, in press). Young children and some of the severely mentally ill (and those suffering certain forms of retardation and neurological damage) clearly present problems of incapacity. But with multiples, the problems seem more to do with counting.

The set of analogies that Moore invites us to embrace in extending the concept of suspended personhood, then, is questionable. Finally, and even more important, we know from history the dangers of withdrawing the status of personhood to any group. As Herbert Morris has eloquently shown in his discussion of persons and punishment (1968), no matter the humane spirit in which such withdrawals are proposed, personhood affords its own kind of protection.

If deficits they are, the deficits of multiples are not quite those isolated by the insanity defense, the defense of unconsciousness, or Moore's concept of personhood, then. One last attempt to capture the abnormalities that mark the defendant suffering from dissociative-identity disorder leads us to the defense of diminished capacity, used for a time in Californian courts.[7]

Diminished Capacity

As it was worded in the California statute, the incapacity in question was free of any presumption as to origin. It was an "abnormal mental or physical condition *however caused*" (my emphasis). And its exact nature was unspecified, except in terms of its effects. Such an incapacity would prevent the defendant from forming "the special intent or mental state essential to constitute the crime or degree of crime with which he was charged" (Calif. Penal Code, p. 35). In these two respects, the defense of diminished capacity looks flexible enough to serve our purposes. Agnosticism as to causation is helpful where the presumption of organicity is as weak as in dissociative-identity disorder. And an incapacity defined in terms of its effects (absence of intent) allows for some dysfunction not captured in the faculty psychological categories associated with the insanity defense. Neither cognition nor will, we have seen, exactly corresponds to the disturbances of memory and identity present here. Yet, finally, the notion of diminished capacity will not prove equal to the challenge of explaining and warranting exculpation with this group of defendants.

Let us see why. The definition of diminished capacity above posits an unspecified mental state or condition necessary for full legal culpability. In the case of the thief, it is true, one self (Johnson) could be said to have lacked the special intent or mental state required. This is precisely what was meant by earlier reference to that self as innocent. But no lack of intent or knowing mental state is evident in Ed. He was fully equipped to form the intentions to commit his crimes and then knowingly to carry them out. Thus we seem to reach a puzzle similar to the one outlined for the defense of unconsciousness: from the perspective of affording a means of defense for the composite person who is the defendant, we must allow, at worst, that the culprit (Ed) exhibits no diminished capacity; at best, that we have no nonarbitrary way to choose between the several selves comprising the composite, public person of the thief, one part of whom may have suffered an incapacity but another part of whom did not, and thus that this criterion is impossible to apply. We saw earlier that the cognitive and volitional incapacities associated with the insanity defense missed the mark, since if 'incapacity' were the correct term, afflicting the multiple would be disturbances or incapacities of time, memory, and identity—not any insufficiency associated with cognition or volition.

But are the multiple's disturbances of time, memory, and identity rightly construed as incapacities? Or are they better regarded as something close to "opportunity costs"? When a person is treated as an indivisible whole corresponding to the publicly observable spatiotemporal bodily whole, the notion of incapacity finds a grip. Viewed as one person, the multiple is severely disadvantaged by these unusual epistemological traits. The composite, unitary "he" has lapses and gaps in his time sequence, and thus his experiential memory. He often does not know who he is, in the sense of being capable of self-awareness and self-ascription for extended stretches of time. However, when the composite identity is construed as a pair (or collection) of individuals—as multiples must each subjectively experience themselves—the picture alters, and this seeming incapacity falls away. Neither Johnson nor Ed has gaps in his own time sequence. While he is Johnson, Johnson's memory and experience are his and available to him, just as while he is Ed, Ed's memory and experience are *his* and available to *him*. It is only when and inasmuch as they are not theirs that the memory and experience attributed to either Johnson or Ed can be said to exhibit failure or disability.

An analogy with normal and normally separate persons, who are spatiotemporarily distinct, may be helpful here and will serve to emphasize the distinction between incapacities and costs. To catch sight of the tall ships entering the bay, you and I must share a telescope, waiting our turn to act, perceive, control. This feature of the situation (there is only one telescope) must limit and diminish the sum total of my possible experiences and memories. I miss the sight of the Russian ship passing the Bird Island Light because you have the telescope at that moment. Subsequently my memories of the experience are patchy and interrupted as the result of your turns.

There are what might be called 'costs' in both cases, whether they are understood as a diminution of the sum total of my experiences (these are "opportunity costs" in the economist's sense, but of time and experience) or as resulting discontinuities and incoherences in my memory sequence. But these costs would not be construed as incapacities or disabilities. Rather, they are features of the situation—inconvenient, costly, and regrettable ("Would that I might have caught a glimpse of the Russian ship passing the light")—but nothing more.

Just as features of the situation and of one person's experience and memory need not be seen as another's incapacity or disability in these cases, so it may be with multiples. Treating the separate sub-selves as separate prevents, or at least strongly deters, us from construing their problem as disability or incapacity rather than cost. True, we have chosen to adopt a particular perspective in developing this analysis. Had we instead treated the multiple as a single entity, we could have shown grounds to use the language of incapacitation. But in relation to the defense of unconsciousness, we saw, it was apparently an arbitrary choice whether to judge from Ed's or from Johnson's stance. And it seems comparably difficult to find nonarbitrary reasons for adopting or privileging the unified perspective over the multiple perspective so that these limitations of memory reflect incapacities rather than mere costs. To conclude, then, the diminished-capacity defense would force us to adopt one stance or perspective rather than another on the question of the defendant's multiplicity. Unlike the pragmatic constraints that require us to see the defendant as one for dispositive purposes, this must be an arbitrary decision, and it thus leaves the defense as an unworkable one.

Because of the difficulties that emerge with each of the options considered thus far, it is time to turn to an alternative solution. The notions of ignorance and compulsion embedded in the insanity defense, of unconsciousness, of the impaired rational calculation associated with personhood, and finally, of diminished capacity each fails to capture exactly the peculiar abnormalities and excesses of memory and identity marking the multiple. A final option would acknowledge the guilt of the multiple.

Guilty

In the absence of other psychiatric problems, when there is sufficient proof to establish that the multiple was the perpetrator of the crime, it is arguable that he or she may be held, without serious injustice, as culpable as a normal and better integrated person would be. In the pragmatic legal contexts where they must be judged and disposed of as single entities, multiples committing wrongdoing perhaps ought to be found guilty and treated in the same way as normally unified defendants. Certainly, therapeutic help ought to be provided as part of the sentence for these persons, just as it should for all immature and mentally disturbed criminals, of whom there are a multitude. Through such therapy and after the eventual integration of the multiple's separate selves, one would hope that each self might come to acknowledge and know of the crime for which the multiple is enduring punishment.[8]

Punishing the Innocent?

The most obvious objection to this policy involves just this last point. It concerns the innocence of the unknowing selves who did not participate in, and in some cases were not even aware of, the crime. Is the punishment endured wrongful punishment of the innocent? If it is such, then our judgment is clear. While we may have a culprit (Ed, for example) we also have an innocent "bystander" or victim (Johnson). The priorities of our system are unequivocal. It is better to let the innocent go free, even if to do so prevents our punishing the guilty.

Certainly, we can understand why such punishment might be thought to be a case of punishing the innocent. Because the innocent selves share a body with the guilty self, they too must submit to the hardship and deprivation of imprisonment. They share a bank account and must bear the material costs imposed. They share a public identity and must endure the shame. They share a life of finite span and must suffer the loss of opportunity and fulfillment. But are such hardships punishment, except in an extended and loose sense? Outside of the retributivist terms that define our system of criminal justice, they would likely be judged so. Such hardships and costs, to a utilitarian, for example, are punishment indeed, regardless of their moral meaning. Yet within the circle of deontological concepts and distinctions defining retributivism, such hardship may not so readily be judged as punishment.

Legal punishment often places costs and hardships on other persons as well as those for whom it is designed. The families of criminals who are incarcerated, for example, often suffer, materially and emotionally. They may suffer more than the person punished. Yet we do not usually speak of this suffering as punishment. Thus within our system and the circle of its terms, it is generally supposed that the mandate to punish the guilty overrides any adverse effects it might have on those who are close or related to the guilty. This is an application of what philosophers call the "doctrine of double effect." As the system is structured, punishing a person who has been found guilty of wrongdoing has as its sole intended effect the allocation of just deserts. Any additional, undeserved suffering or hardship endured by others as the result of this administration of justice is morally insignificant, a mere side effect to be disregarded.

Such a doctrine and attitude may prevent us from arguing that the hardship endured by the "innocent" selves sharing a body with the guilty self is a form of punishment of the innocent and contrary to the principles of justice. I do not mean to insist on the ultimate justice of this appeal to the doctrine of double effect. But it is strongly entrenched in the moral principles underlying criminal law and penal practice, and is applicable to the case in question. On this analogy, it is implausible to argue that there are legal or moral grounds to refrain from imposing penalties on public persons who suffer from dissociative disorder and are guilty of wrongdoing, because they comprise selves who are not guilty.

If we could, of course, we would only punish the multiple's guilty self. But the inexplicable and mercurial shifts between different selves do not permit such a policy. What is the next best thing? In an attempt to limit the harm imposed on the other, innocent selves, we might suppose it right to choose the least restrictive sentence compatible with the more pragmatic goals of criminal punishment. In doing so, we would seek a balance between the rights of the innocent self or selves and the guilty culprit's just deserts.

Is dissociative-identity disorder an exculpating factor in the legal context? Within the dispositive constraints, the discourse of responsibility, and the retributivist presuppositions imposed by that setting, the answer, it seems, is that it is not.

The notion of responsibility at work in discussions of legal culpability concerns past wrongful deeds. Further legal and policy-related questions are raised in the two chapters that follow, but they take us outside the criminal-law context to mental-health settings. The moral question framing the discussion now becomes, Who should have responsibility for decisions concerning a mental patient's care and treatment?

Paternalistic Intervention

The aim of this chapter and the next is to clarify some of the implications for, and underlying theory of, the self involved in discussions about paternalistic therapeutic intervention. The justifications for such intervention reviewed here deserve close attention because they each invite, and have in some cases received, interpretations seemingly contrary to traditional identity presumptions.

Under the broad title of 'paternalistic intervention' I will discuss therapeutic recommendations derived from two sources. First are those made by others: guardians, caregivers, or proxy decision makers, often medical personnel or family members. Second are those issued by the mental patient at some earlier time concerning the care or treatment he or she wishes to receive in the future. (These are instances of "advance directives.")

Paternalistic intervention requires justification, even when the mental patient's current disposition is disregarded in favor of a care or treatment plan previously expressed by that patient. But the burden of justification rests more heavily on those interfering for the patient's good *without* such a guide. Two purported justifications for this kind of interference are examined here, each seemingly contrary to identity presuppositions captured in the "one to a customer" rule. Of these two, the restoration of authenticity proves problematic and insufficient as a justification for interference. The critique of proxy decision making, which follows, draws attention to some of the complexities underlying the notion of substituted judgment.

Paternalism and Treatment Refusals

The terms 'paternalism' and 'paternalistic' convey a range of different connotations. At one extreme, paternalism is treated as a necessary and desirable form of assistance for those less fortunate or able; at the other extreme, it is an unwarranted and undesirable interference with others' rightful exercise of self-determination. In choosing the terms 'paternalism' and 'paternalistic' to capture the forms of interference with mental patients' immediate wishes that I discuss here, I intend something in between these two extremes of interpretation.

Recommendations for care that in any way contravene the patient's current disposition, while they may be morally justified and even desirable or obligatory, at least require some justification.[1] Indeed, any sort of intervention against the immediate wishes of a patient who is not dangerous calls for moral justification, since it contravenes a presumption of freedom guaranteed by the U.S. Constitution and by our liberal tradition. Even the imposition of advance care directives issued by the patient herself at an earlier time requires some justification when they are not in accord with her current wishes. So, to a stronger degree, do all recommendations for a patient's treatment made by other people—guardians, family members, and caregivers—whose intent is to approximate the patient's own competent decisions or to interpret and ensure the best interests of the patient.

There is one context in which issues of justification arise with special emphasis and force: treatment refusals. Many different kinds of justification have been offered by those who would impose therapeutic measures against the mental patient's current wishes, of which two will be examined here. The first, which while it may not presuppose an analysis of successive selves, at least strongly suggests one, claims that the enforced treatment of mental patients is warranted because it restores an "authentic" self—a self that has been lost to us as the result of mental disturbance. A second justification is supported by appeal to the proxy decision maker's or guardian's substituted judgement. Here the proxy decides what the patient would have wanted in a phase of greater competence. When this decision runs contrary to the present expressed wishes of the patient, it is proffered as a justification for paternalistic intervention, and here too we may be tempted to postulate an underlying theory of successive selves at work. The proposal that the patient's previously established advance care directives be honored even when they conflict with the patient's present wishes is a third justification for interference, which I will deal with in the following chapter (chapter 10). It too is hospitable to, and has received, a successive-selves interpretation.

One point must be emphasized at the outset. With each kind of paternalistic intervention, our understanding is that the patient involved poses no threat to other people. Thus these recommendations are paternalistic in the sense also of being directed toward the patient's *own* protection and/or improvement, rather than toward ensuring the safety of others. Of the therapeutic and custodial intervention necessary when a patient is dangerous and poses a threat to other people's safety, nothing will be said in this book. In practice, the distinction between those patients who are dangerous to others and those who are not has proven itself immensely difficult to establish. Nevertheless, the theoretical and moral separation is immediately apparent, and is profound. Therapeutic (and other) intervention with dangerous patients is permitted by the liberal "harm principle" (Mill 1859). It neither requires comparable justification nor presupposes such complex theories of self.

Who Decides and How?

Who should make treatment decisions for a patient, and how should such decisions be made? An answer to the 'who' question might include a disjunctive set, we have seen: medical personnel, family members, a guardian or legal proxy appointed to decide for the patient, the patient at an earlier time in anticipation of her mental disturbance, the patient herself at the time of her mental disturbance, and, in the case of dissociative-identity disorder, any given self, while reigning. There is no reason to expect unanimity among proposed treatment plans from each of these sources.

In answer to the 'how' question, we may be able to distinguish decisions judged by others to be in the patient's best interests from those made by the patient directly or aimed at approximating what the patient would have wanted, would want were she competent, or would want at some future time. While not yielding results that are mutually exclusive, these two strategies ("best interests" and "would have wanted") may also be expected to lead, on occasion, to contrary and even conflicting decisions.

The value of freedom, on the one hand, and the recognition that the self presently embodied has certain moral priorities by dint of that embodiment, on the other, will be shown to suggest an order for the two sets of possibilities enumerated in response to the 'who' and 'how' questions. There will be a presumption, at least, favoring the wishes of the self over those of other spatiotemporarily distinct persons (family members, care givers, medical personnel, and guardians). There will also be a presumption favoring the decisions of the patient at the time of treatment (or the presently embodied self) over those expressed in advance directives issued by the patient at some earlier time (issued, we might say, by previous selves). Finally, there will be a presumption favoring the express wishes of the reigning self over other selves in the case of dissociative-identity disorder. These contrasts, the arguments surrounding these presumptions, and the qualifications they may require determine the limits and focus of this discussion. Before we examine these arguments and the theoretically complex forms of justification for paternalistic intervention, it will be useful to clarify two further notions: responsibility and incompetence.

Responsibility and Incompetence

As well as entering different contexts, the notion of responsibility, we have seen, spans several discourses, including the one where we are said to take responsibility for others, particularly for their care. And this kind of caring relationship seems possible and even desirable between selves that share a body (whether successively, simultaneously, or sequentially), just as it is in the more normal case between two persons whose bodies are spatiotemporally distinct.

When we take responsibility for others in the normal case, we direct ourselves to their nurture, protection, and care, acknowledging them with special attention and aid. Taking responsibility for others' care is closely associated with those who are young, old, or infirm. Each of these conditions—infancy, youth, advanced age, and infirmity—render the individual less than fully competent, either in some specific respect or generally. These are states in which people are in need of others for care, special attention, and aid.

This need is recognized as central in a set of moral convictions widely accepted in our culture that concern self-determination, consent, and incompetence. What I will call the *incompetence/consent proviso* often seems definitive: unless others have such a specific or generalized incompetence or offer special consent, we believe, we rarely should take responsibility for them. And we rarely do. Others who are competent do not require our care. It is both possible and desirable for them to take responsibility for themselves. Taking responsibility for oneself is valued. Thus in most cases we take responsibility for apparently competent others only with their explicit consent; to do otherwise would be viewed as a violating their self-determination.

This picture may need qualification. Recently developed ethics of care (Noddings 1984, Held 1990, Hoagland 1991) have revealed that the bare legalistic language of this formulation of our convictions about self-determination, consent, and incompetence fails to capture something of the human caring response (which is emotional and spontaneous) and of the role it plays in benevolent action. Nevertheless, the incompetence/consent proviso gives some guide to the moral limits on paternalistic intervention.

As the centrality of the incompetence/consent proviso indicates, incompetence is an important ingredient in any discussion about paternalistic intervention. But the notion of incompetence is elusive and unresolved, particularly as it concerns the shifting and varied forms of disability associated with mental disturbance. If the nature of competence itself were clearer, then some of our moral questions about justifications for paternalistic intervention against the patient's expressed current contrary wishes would be unnecessary. Were there an easily discerned and agreed upon measure of competence available to us, for example, then the incompetence/consent proviso would permit paternalistically motivated treatment and care just when, according to this standard, we determine that there is incompetence. Again, if most mental patients were clearly and obviously either competent or incompetent, and each consistently so, then we would have a means of distinguishing unwarranted intervention that violates self-determination. Or finally, were competence construed as a concept admitting of degree, then we could recognize at least relative distinctions. Even if each met some minimal-competence threshold, the mentally well-balanced advance-care planner would likely be more competent than the disturbed patient who changes her mind.

In reality, however, the notion of competence is deeply unresolved in clinical contexts, and it belies each of these three characterizations. First, controversy surrounds the formal standards of competence. Varying concepts of and tests for competence can be found in writings on medical ethics or derived from statute and case law (Roth, Meisel, and Lidz 1977; Reatig 1981; VanDeVeer 1986; Thompson 1987; Buchanan and Brock 1989; Sternberg and Kolligian 1990). Some of these, the least stringent, require merely that the patient be able to express a preference. More stringent standards dictate the decision's outcome or content. One rules that the choice be a reasonable one, for example, or be what other reasonable or rational persons would choose. Other standards emphasize the reasoning process by which the decision is reached and the level of competence exhibited in the patient's understanding and reasoning capacities. Moreover, recent clinical opinion emphasizes that there may be "affective" as well as cognitive forms of incompetence (Bursztajn, Harding, Gutheil, and Brodsky 1991; Bursztajn, Scherr, and Brodsky 1994).

Second, determinations of competence are normative judgments, which we choose and decide on, not discoveries of empirical fact, as these disagreements indicate. Because the definition of competence rests on a normative decision and not an empirical inquiry, our intuitive reactions to and construal of actual cases could influence and help shape its outcome. But these intuitive reactions too remain ambiguous and opaque when we confront the incompetence of mental disturbance, in part because of the shifting and elusive patterns it exhibits. Mental patients cross and recross the borderland between competence and incompetence with the ebb and flow of their condition. (In contrast, victims of degenerative diseases like Alzheimer's all eventually reach (and, tragically, maintain) a degree of incompetence over which there can be little intuitive disagreement.)

Some form of impaired judgment is a characteristic feature of mental disorder, and some mental patients, it is true, will sometimes become unequivocally and incontrovertibly incompetent by any standard and any intuitive assessment whatsoever. Where there is extreme disintegration of the personality, as in some psychotic reactions, or where there is apparent discontinuation of all but autonomic functioning, as found in catatonic reaction, it is clear that incompetence prevails. But few who succumb to periodic bouts of mental disturbance are robbed of all judgment and mental capacity. Often they fall between clear and indisputable competence, on the one hand, and unmistakable incompetence, on the other. On some understandings of competence, both formal and intuitive, they are competent to decide, and on others they are not.

Finally, competence is not safely construed as a concept admitting of degree. Competence tests only admit of one judgment: competent or not, and rightly so in an opinion widely voiced in contemporary medical ethics (Buchanan and Brock 1989). Several considerations seem to dictate that competence be interpreted this way. The autonomy and rationality of mental patients and those with a psychiatric history tend to be assessed against the higher standard of autonomy and rationality construed as ideals, instead of against the approximations to those ideals exhibited by ordinary, imperfect reasoners and agents; the dangers of discrimination attached to this temptation and tendency are clear. Moreover, the range of competence found in psychologically normal reasoners requires that competence be treated as a threshold concept, not a relative one, in these contexts. Also adding to the difficulty and danger associated with attributing competence in cases of mental disturbance is another temptation: an observed tendency to underestimate the mental patient's competence. A presumption of global incompetence fails to acknowledge the often limited disabilities involved as when, for example, flaws of reasoning and decision making affect only particular, discrete ideas or responses.

Incompetence, then, is a *contested* concept, whose application introduces normative judgments, over which there is continuing controversy. The conditions suffered by mental patients regularly place them in the uncertain area where notions of incompetence remain unresolved and unresolvable. Because of the continuing dispute over the competence of the mentally disturbed, there will be many cases of arguably competent mental patients about whose treatment refusals we must raise the moral issues of justification introduced above. In the face of resistance on the part of the disturbed patient, is it right to interfere paternalistically with his or her wishes?

Restoring the Authentic Self

In some philosophical writing, rule by the "real" self, or character, is associated with responsible action (Wolf 1980, 1986, 1987, 1990).[2] And the "real" or "authentic" self is widely honored in our culture. Not surprisingly, then, the restoration of an earlier more "authentic," "real," or "characteristic" self arises in several mental-health contexts. Sometimes it is understood as a goal of therapy and a justification for therapeutic procedures willingly embraced by the patient or client, both earlier and during treatment or therapy. But in the situation under consideration here, the claim that therapy can restore an earlier and/or more authentic self is pressed into service as a justification for intervention against the patient's expressed wishes. This justification has been put forward by Ruth Macklin (1982), as well as others, and because her account remains one of the most closely argued, it deserves our attention. Macklin approaches authenticity indirectly, proposing that being the author of one's own beliefs, desires, and actions, being "self-directed," presupposes the idea of an authentic self, "a self that has a continuity of traits over time." Macklin justifies forced treatment for mental patients to return them to this authentic self, by appeal to the purported relationship between authenticity and autonomy. Valuing autonomy, we should recognize, she insists, that it "may be lost by a patient's refusal of psychiatric treatment—treatment that might have prevented deterioration, humiliation and decline" (Macklin 1982, 333).

She introduces examples to illustrate the costs just outlined:

A colleague of mine who is a psychiatrist described some cases to me. In some instances, those who underwent manic episodes engaged in public behavior that threatened their careers, their reputation, their family's well-being and perhaps even their own self-respect.... In most cases, those who were victims of hypomania expressed overwhelming gratitude—once they returned to "normalcy"—to psychiatrists, family members, and others who had intervened, even over their protests. In all these cases, those who exhibit such behavior act uncharacteristically.

They ... depart from their *own* established character. They are not their *true selves*, they lack continuity with their typical or normal or characteristic personality.... If there is a reasonable likelihood that their autonomy can be preserved or restored by medication, then forced treatment of such patients is warranted. (Macklin 1982, 339–340)

This argument is of particular interest to us because Macklin's use of terms like 'authentic', 'true', and 'characteristic' strongly suggests a successive-selves analysis. Such an analysis introduces a notion of self that attributes identity and reidentifiability on the basis of psychological traits, not spatiotemporal continuity. Spatiotemporally, there can be no warrant for separating the earlier and later selves this way: space-time identity—linking the earlier mentally well, and the later mentally disturbed, person or self stages—leaves no room for the duality suggested by the term 'authentic' and its contrast 'inauthentic'.

We may resist this view, insisting that dissimilar though they are, the earlier and later "self stages" of these patients remain part of the same person. If so, we will want either to question the argument's coherence or else to construe Macklin's language as entirely figurative. The language of successive selves is often used figuratively, we know. But it is not often introduced into a context with such weighty practical and moral consequences as decisions over treatment refusal. To rest an argument of such practical moment on so flimsy a base seems unacceptable.

Further difficulties are to be found in this argument. If selves succeed one another within a single body, why should the earlier self restored through treatment be preferred to the subsequent self that prevails during mental disturbance? Macklin offers two claims to show why. The earlier self is more authentic, and it exhibits more autonomy. These desiderata are themselves separable, however.[3] A chronic sufferer from schizophrenia may be characteristicly herself in her withdrawal and passivity yet may lack self-direction or autonomy. Also, mental illness may produce major changes in motivation, beliefs, values, and reasons for action without significantly altering the quotient of self-direction or autonomy exhibited. Some mental disorders are characterized by a singleness of purpose and a self-direction that closely approach the ideal of autonomy from which Macklin's notion is derived. The single-mindedness with which Mr. M. pursued his eccentric vision as he worked to develop aquarium equipment to keep fish alive forever reflects an extraordinary degree of self-direction by any normal standard. Yet it was a self-direction that was uncharacteristic, and thus inauthentic, for him.

Macklin's several discussions of this theme propose rather different accounts of the relationship between these two desiderata. One implies that authenticity entails autonomy; another that autonomy is to be identified with authenticity. Because authenticity and autonomy are apparently separable traits, not even correlated with any regularity in mental disorder itself, neither account is entirely satisfactory. Moreover, because they are separable, we must question whether they are separately or only jointly sufficient to justify intervention against the patient's current wishes.

As a desideratum, authenticity suffers additional weaknesses. Macklin's choice of cases places exclusive emphasis on unauthentic selves that are short-lived, discrete, and readily distinguishable from the states and personality making up the desired authentic self. But this is a distortion. Personality may change as the result of conditions that arise as early as adolescence and last a lifetime. A person who has had an "inauthentic" personality—let us say a depressed one—may have had it for many years. After a time her depressed personality surely must be ranked as authentic for her. In subsequent writing (1983) Macklin has come to recognize this weakness in her appeal to authenticity. But the example casts doubt on any use of authenticity as a desideratum. If authenticity were valued, it would have a paradoxical result in a case like the one of the woman with lifelong depression. Paternalistic intervention would be warranted early in the woman's life but not later. And an arbitrary judgement would determine the point where a customary personality is sufficiently authentic, or characteristic, for further therapy to be declared unwarranted. Some might be prepared to adopt this policy. Particularly if the entrenched traits are stable, and meet certain functional standards, we may accept 'Let well enough alone' in the case of the long-term sufferer of depression. But whatever its overall effectiveness as a policy, such an approach cannot avoid the criticism of arbitrariness.

A more general question arises here. Authenticity (like autonomy) admits of degree. Those attempting to justify paternalistic intervention by these outcomes must provide an account of how little authenticity warrants interference. How inauthentic is inauthentic enough? Partial similarity to the original authentic self, similarity in some respects, may be insufficient. A phase of mental illness will be unlikely to leave any character entirely unchanged, however, so it will be unrealistic to demand an identical character. Somewhere between these two, an arbitrary ruling must be made.[4]

One defense that might be made of Macklin's preference for the therapeutically restored "authentic" self draws attention to the nature of the personality change that has occurred. The earlier self should be restored, it may be argued, because the subsequent disturbed self is the product of an illness, an infliction over whose presence the subject has no control or understanding. Unlike the changes wrought by some form of rational persuasion, even the radical and unexpected ones resulting in ideological conversion, how the mentally disturbed self is brought about disqualifies it from equal status with the earlier favored self.

This is an interesting argument, one that is found intimated and suggested in many discussions that, like Macklin's, make appeal to the restoration of authenticity as a therapeutic goal. Before embracing such an argument, however, we should recognize two problems. The first concerns the perspective from which we make judgments about the causation involved. From the more detached perspective of the public observer, a change may seem to have been brought about by nonrational causation. But the same change may seem to its subject in every way naturally or rationally caused, brought about by alterations in belief and desire voluntarily and knowingly embraced. By choosing to privilege the perspective of the detached public stance, we are not reporting from a perspectiveless and thus "objective" viewpoint. There may be reasons to make such a choice and to prefer the public perspective. But it is a choice and must be evaluated on the strength of those reasons; it is not simply a discovery of empirical fact to be adopted without defense.

The a second difficulty lies with the setting of "treatment refusals" in which we are offered this argument (the disturbed self is a product of illness). The restoration of authenticity and its accompanying set of assumptions are often appealed to as a therapeutic goal, as we saw. But this is where such therapy is voluntarily sought. For justifying the paternalistic intervention involved when treatment refusals are overridden, in contrast, such an argument can have little use. Forced treatment also produces change in a way that is contrary to the model of rational persuasion. This will be entirely so when drugs, psychosurgery, or other physical therapies are imposed, and true to a lesser extent when the therapeutic regimen involves some form of psychotherapy. It may be doubted whether psychotherapy, unwillingly sought, could be successful at all. If effective, however, it can hardly be said to change the patient's character through rational persuasion as we usually know it, since such change is of its nature freely sought.

In summary, restoration of authenticity strongly suggests a notion of the self that takes us beyond the customary identity presuppositions of the "one to a customer" rule. Whether it derives from a metaphysical theory of successive selves or is merely figurative usage, however, as a desideratum the restoration of authenticity seems insufficiently clear or compelling to justify forced treatment.

Like the argument just examined, justifications of intervention based on proxy and substituted judgment also rely, in some formulations, on presuppositions seemingly contrary to traditional identity claims, and these will be the subject of the remainder of this chapter.

The Proxy and Substituted Judgments of Guardians

Guardians and other proxy decision makers take the place of the patient at the point, and for the duration, of incompetence. Here too, then, difficulties arise over the standard for competence and determinations of this standard, although I will not pursue them further. With guardianship and the appointment of other proxy decisions makers, we find intimations of the problems that arise over advance care directives issued by patients themselves. The question of whether the substituted judgment of the proxy is to be preferred over the patient's current expressed wishes, when these two conflict, parallels exactly that of whether directives issued in advance by the patient herself should be given preference over her current wishes.

The moral dangers of proxy and substituted judgments are more transparent, however. Unlike the patient at an earlier time (or as an earlier "self"), the proxy decision maker is a separate spatiotemporal person. If the decision of the proxy is preferred to the current wishes of the patient with borderline competence, the wrong risked would involve coercion or slavery, quite literally understood. Because of the ambiguity and controversy surrounding the concept of competence and the frequency of these borderline cases, such risks are enormous, and this enormity can hardly go unrecognized.

Several frameworks within which proxy and substituted judgment may be construed are distinguishable here, each with its separate presuppositions.

"Best Interests" Reasoning

Even in cases where the patient's want of competence is incontestable, several issues require clarification. One concerns the understanding on which proxy decisions are made and the roles this understanding presupposes. Sometimes guardians adopt "best interests" reasoning on behalf of their incompetent charge, taking upon themselves the task of ascertaining and presenting the decisions most likely to further the patient's future, long-term good. But as the notion of a proxy suggests, this decision-making role is often understood more intimately. It is taken as an attempt to reach the judgment that the person would want, that is, would have reached had she been competent (or had she "been herself," colloquially speaking).[5]

Since the patient's current wishes, however expressed, can no longer guide us as to her hypothetical disposition, an elaborate and implicative determination is now required on the part of the proxy: ascertaining what the patient would have wanted.

"Would Have Wanted" Reasoning

The phrase 'what the patient would have wanted' reads ambiguously. In ascertaining the patient's wishes, the proxy may be understood to seek two logically separable judgments: one, the wish of the patient before she became ill (i.e., what she would have wanted previous to the onset of her condition); the other, what she would now want were she not ill. While logically distinct, these two judgments could be expected to coincide in many cases. But opinions and wishes alter with the passage of time; people have second thoughts and changes their minds. Normal and normally accepted change must lead us to expect occasional divergence; again, the task arises of determining whether to privilege the earlier, over the present, hypothetical dispositions.

Efforts have been made to adjudicate between the "best interests" and the "would have wanted," or "proxy," approaches to the guardian's role. Thomas Gutheil and Paul Appelbaum (1985) have urged a return to the "best interests" model because of the difficulties in interpreting and deciding what the patient would have wanted; their concern is epistemological.

Allan Buchanan and Dan Brock (1989), on the other hand, have emphasized the role played by normative issues, arguing that if we value self-determination, a strong case may be made for preferring a "would have wanted" approach (see also Thompson 1987). To this may be added two further reasons that seem to discourage us from adopting the "best interests" approach. The first derives from John Stuart Mill's (1859) well-known counter to paternalism: as fillers of our own shoes we are likely the best judge of our own interests. If this is so, we may suppose, then, that "would have wanted" will lead to one's best interests, accurately understood. A careful determination of what we would have wanted is likely to be closer to our best interests than what others decide for us.

A second reason against adopting the "best interests" approach is suggested by the disorder and havoc wrought by recurrent mental disturbance in peoples' lives. The notion of best interests appears to presuppose a degree of stability, consistency, and order among an individual's values and goals; a linearity and sequence to their lived experience; and a sense of self too often belied by the actual experience and chaotic lives common to many sufferers of mental disturbance. For such a life, defining best interests must involve additional challenges.

Other considerations supporting a "would have wanted," or "proxy," role for guardians are more personal. However irrational, it might be supposed, a judgment reflecting of one's own beliefs and values, even one's admitted whims and foibles, would be preferable for many to an impersonal calculation of one's interests. A decision reflective of one's life as a whole or one's established character may well diverge from what comports with a "best interests" calculation. By adopting a "would have wanted" role, the guardian may attempt to acknowledge and honor these personal and idiosyncratic visions.

No theory of successive selves is implied or presupposed on the "best interests" understanding of the substitute decision maker's role. Interesting and important for general discussions of paternalism in this area as it must be, we may set it aside for our purposes and focus instead on the proxy's role in "would have wanted" decisions.

"Will Want" Reasoning and "Thank You" Theory

The period of incompetence associated with mental disturbance is often limited. Thus the proxy's role is also understood to encompass more than what the patient would have wanted (a) at some earlier time and/or (b) had he or she not been so afflicted. In addition, the proxy's role is to seek the decision the person would later reach and—when later restored to mental health—would share and even thank one for. The proxy decision maker hopes to decide what the patient *would* have wanted and *will want* (Thompson 1987).

The quest for an unambiguous indication of the incompetent patient's wishes understood in any of the ways distinguished above will be full of difficulties, however. In a close analysis of how such a quest might unfold in real life settings, Gutheil and Appelbaum (1985) have shown that paradox and ambiguity surround the notion of what the patient would have wanted (and perhaps the notion of what the patient will want) because of the inevitable ambiguity of human behavior. By applying to her present circumstances decision principles derived from an interpretation of the patient's past behavior, these authors have demonstrated that the proxy decision maker has an unworkable degree of discretion.

Such problems are significant. But even setting them aside, some important theoretical and value issues may arise when guardians adopt proxy roles in this way. The judgement that what a patient would have wanted—and perhaps will want—is usefully distinguished from what she now wants. Such a judgment may presuppose that the disturbed, incompetent self is not her earlier self. It may not. Distinguishing and, when the wishes in question are in conflict, privileging what a person would have wanted at t_1 from what she wants at t_2 are compatible with traditional identity presuppositions. An acknowledgment of this set of distinctions is at best entirely compatible with a theory of separate and successive selves.

Whether or not such a theory or metaphysics is implied, the successive-selves analysis helps us recognize the extent to which positions we adopt in the area of proxy decision making rest on *decisions*.

Why should the substitute decision maker favor the earlier wishes expressed at t_1—and perhaps the subsequent ones expressed at t_3—over those expressed during the phase of mental disturbance (t_2)?

When the patient is in a state of borderline or contested competence, this question requires an answer. The proxy model's focus on satisfying initial or subsequent wishes at the expense of wishes expressed during the phase of disturbance may be presumed to be warranted by the superior competence, autonomy, and perhaps authenticity of the self at t_1 (the earlier self). The same considerations, we saw, encouraged Macklin (1982, 1983) to endorse the restoration of the "authentic" self through involuntary treatment. Yet none of these merits can be accepted without question. In cases of contested or borderline competence, to claim superior competence for an earlier self is to risk violating the decision to treat competence as a threshold concept. Authenticity, we saw, is an uncertain and ill-defined value requiring further defense if it is to justify forced treatment or care. And autonomy alone may not be sufficient when we are proposing interference that would violate presumptions of liberty.

Moreover, the fact that the proxy decision maker's judgment may concur with that of the patient at some future time (or with that of some future self) by itself is not sufficient to justify this preference. Nor is the fact that a 'thank you' may later be expressed. (This is the claim of what has been called "Thank you" theory.[6]) Overwhelming gratitude may later be directed toward those psychiatrists, family members, and others who intervened, as Macklin claimed for her cases. Yet it still may be wrong to have interfered. In Brian Clark's play *Whose Life Is It Anyway?* (1980), a physically disabled man, who judges his life to be valueless, insists on his right to decide to end it now. He does so even while he acknowledges that, as his therapist insists, he would later be grateful to those who take the choice out of his hands, were they to do so. That a person would be changed at a later time (t_2) to a point where he would be grateful then is compatible with his right to have respected his present wish at t_1 to die: this the play makes clear. But if this conviction seems plausible, then the fact that the proxy decision concurs with the judgment we predict that the person would subsequently prefer at t_2 is by itself not sufficient to warrant adopting the proxy decision at the present time. After all, many things we do now may violate the wishes and even physical well-being of what we might, or might have, become. Although such concurrence is perhaps grounds to offer advice, persuasion, and caution, it does not usually constitute a reason to prevent a person from acting as he or she would.

There is one important qualification to this claim, we will see in the next chapter. When there is rotation or recurrence of selves, the multiplicity associated with dissociative-identity disorder or with a recurrent mental disorder like manic-depression makes it appropriate to understand the future self as a past self *returning* or *recurring* at some future time. Only then is there reason to defer to the wishes of the future self. But in the normal case, like that illustrated in Clark's play, such recurrence is not assumed. In the normal case, what we will become, to which "Thank you" theory accords priority, is yet unformed. Were he prevented from achieving the satisfaction of his wish to die, the protagonist of Clark's play would in time become another self. But the future self, whose life it then (at t_2) would be, is as yet "unborn." To privilege this future self's interests over the express wishes of the presently embodied self appears at least arbitrary.

This critique of proxy decision making does not imply that the wishes of the mentally disturbed self should always be preferred to those of the proxy, even in cases of contested competence, however. Its aim was merely to draw attention to some of the complexities underlying the notion of substituted judgment.

Examined here were some of the justifications offered for paternalistically directed intervention when it is contrary to a patient's immediate wishes concerning treatment. In the chapter that follows we turn to an often analogous justification for interference: the patient's previously established advance care directives.

Responsibilities over Oneself in the Future or One's Future Selves

By issuing an advance directive, we bind ourselves in advance to some course of action or treatment. When Ulysses directed his sailors to ignore the entreaties he predicted he would later express, he issued a kind of advance directive. A living will is another kind. Here a person conveys instructions about the medical treatment she wishes to receive, or about the proxy in whose hands that decision will rest, when she is no longer capable of deciding because of some form of incompetence or incapacity. We issue less momentous advance directives as well ('Wake me up at seven if I seem to sleep through my alarm'). Different as they are, these instructions about future treatment are loosely linked. When there is reason to predict that our usual exercise of autonomy will be impaired or interfered with—due to temptation (as in Ulysses' case), physically induced incapacitation (as in the case of the living will), or unconsciousness resulting from sleep (as in the last example)—we exercise Elster's "imperfect rationality" (1984) to ensure that, through the cooperation of others, our autonomy and rationality will be expressed or sustained.

Informal advance directives issued to friends, relations, and care givers have always played a role in the lives of those who were, or who anticipated becoming, mentally disturbed as they struggled to shape and direct their unruly destinies, interrupted plans, and thwarted long-term goals. Recently, with increasing emphasis on patient autonomy throughout medicine and the development of legal means for recognizing advance care directives in nonpsychiatric areas, formal advance care planning for potential mental patients has also been proposed (Buchanan and Brock 1989, Hackler 1989).

Whether formal or informal, such psychiatric advance directives enter into a discussion of paternalistic intervention in two ways. As we saw in the last chapter, they are appealed to in overriding a patient's immediate wishes, and they will require and justify intervention on the part of other people (family, medical personnel, or care givers). Explored here is a second, less obvious "paternalism." Adopting a successive-selves analysis, we may contrast the self whose wishes are expressed in the advance directive at an earlier time with the currently embodied later self who may oppose or question those wishes. In so doing, we may recognize a sense in which to honor the advance directive requires that we permit the paternalistic imposition of the wishes of the earlier self (self 1) on the subsequent one (self 2). To explore the moral force of advance directives thus construed, we have to revisit our convictions concerning responsibility, incompetence, and consent, outlined previously.

We may show the moral dangers of advance directives by appeal to successive-selves analyses in several ways. Interpretations hospitable to the notion of successive selves reveal morally abhorrent features of this form of binding oneself in advance, features purportedly avoided by maintaining traditional identity or singularity presuppositions. A more conservative analysis may avoid the conclusion that advance directives reflect an unfair favoring of the *wishes* of one self over another self. But such an analysis cannot avoid the conclusion they reflect the unfair favoring of earlier over later wishes. In addition, whether by rejecting a metaphysics of successive selves or by interpreting it conservatively, such conservative analyses expose a different set of concerns over the moral authority of these contracts.

The everyday ways in which we decide when to honor the promises and resolves we make concerning our own future seem to cast doubt on many of these contracts and to challenge any general policy of according moral authority to advance directives. There is one exception. A successive-selves metaphysics, together with the application of a liberal harm principle (we may override a person's wishes just when those wishes are likely to harm another), will ensure the moral authority of such directives when they seek to prevent self-destructive behavior. But this will only be so with particular kinds of mental disorder: extreme dissociative disorder and nondissociative conditions like schizophrenia and mood disorders, whose origins are not fully understood.

Advance Directives or Ulysses Contracts in Psychiatry

In the so-called "psychiatric wills" or "Ulysses contracts"[1] proposed for use in the mental-health field, which will be our concern in this discussion, the prospective mental patient expresses instructions about treatment and care in anticipation of future mental disorder. Unlike a living will, the Ulysses contract established by a mental patient, or someone with grounds to believe he or she will become one, is usually designed to circumvent temporary, rather than permanent, incapacitation. With conditions whose causes remain unknown, such as schizophrenic and mood disorders, the desire and hope for recovery will always be present, indeed. A person whose history of mental disturbance leads her to expect a future disabling condition, or one who expects a current condition to worsen, plans for the later occurrence, recurrence, or worsening of her disorder.

Often the contract focuses on therapeutic interventions, requesting, or requesting exemption from, a therapeutic regimen. Typically, the Ulysses contractor may have been warned, or will remember from past experience, that with the occurrence or return of her disorder, her condition will affect her judgment and prevent her from evaluating her situation and interests at that time as well as she is able to now. She predicts, moreover, that she may do and say things she might subsequently regret. She may also predict costs: without medication she is likely to languish for months, perhaps years, unable to live a full or productive life. Alternatively, with medication, she will undergo debilitating side effects. She may fear being a source of distress or a financial burden to others.

Part of the composite case portrayed here suggests Ulysses' struggle: like Ulysses, the mental patient expects poor judgment to prevail. In part this case is like the living will: the patient attributes her predicted incapacitation to an undesired and undesirable condition of her brain or body (Ulysses willingly sought his temptation, however, while she does not seek her mental disturbance). In part the case is like the mundane advance directive for a wake-up call in the morning: The break between sleeping and waking states, robbing a sleeper of awareness of her earlier wish (to rise at seven), corresponds in a loose way to the break that the prospective mental patient often seems to anticipate. She is unfamiliar with the person she predicts she will become. She cannot rely on the normal continuity of desires and intentions, which would ensure the carrying through of earlier established goals.

The idea of using advance directives in the mental-health field has received support from many in medical ethics, although their application, at a practical level, has not proven easy (Gutheil and Appelbaum 1985). But practical difficulties aside, these advance directives introduce certain moral issues that need to be resolved. Are Ulysses contracts morally binding? Do they warrant interfering with a mental patient's right to refuse some form of care or treatment, for example?

One way in which the doubts generating these moral questions may be viewed introduces issues about the person's purported singularity through time and the notion of successive selves. With the onset or recurrence of severe mental disturbance, a mental patient often undergoes a dramatic personality change. Particularly when this change is so radical, it naturally invites a language of successive selves. If this language is grounded in a successive-selves metaphysics, these advance directives would look morally questionable. Allowing an earlier advance directive to override the wishes of the disturbed self looks like allowing the initiator of the advance directive (self 1) to oppress the disturbed and radically altered self into which she has been transformed (self 2).

Not Enslavement but Unfairness

An important contribution to the discussion of the relation between personal identity and advance directives has been offered by Buchanan and Brock (Buchanan 1988, Buchanan and Brock 1989). These authors have gone so far as to suggest that if successive and separate persons or selves are involved and the later self (self 2) is subject to the advance directives of an earlier one (self 1), then we may speak of the unjust "enslavement" of the later by the earlier. Buchanan and Brock eventually propose a counter to their own enslavement criticism of the moral authority of advance directives. Moreover, their term 'enslavement' only inexactly captures the wrong risked here. When a person is enslaved, she is subjugated by another person who has no rightful access to her psychological or bodily parts or capabilities. (At least from the moral perspective of our present culture and liberal tradition, it seems true to say that no enslaver enjoys such rights or such access, regardless of contractual arrangements.) Because the successive selves with which we are concerned here each have rights over the same body, the analogy between the enslavement of persons and the power one self exerts over another with which she shares a body seems strained. A more accurate portrayal of the purported wrong here would instead stress the unfairness of honoring the wishes of one self rather than those of another. But Buchanan and Brock's 'enslavement' language at least graphically serves to illustrate the problem. If we are dealing with successive selves or persons, by what right can one dictate the treatment meted out to the next?

In discussing advance directives advocated for patients suffering severe and irreversible neurological damage, Buchanan and Brock have argued that no troubling moral issues of this kind would ever arise. On standard criteria for personhood, no subsequent person or self can be said to have succeeded the initial contractor issuing the advance directive (self 1) in such cases. The patient is transformed not from one self or person to another but from one self or person to a state where no self or personhood can be attributed to her. For the degenerative diseases these authors describe, this conclusion appears unexceptional. Intuitively, it does seem appropriate to accord moral authority to this kind of advance directive. Moreover, the transition from personhood to nonpersonhood portrayed by Buchanan and Brock does seem to eliminate concern that these advance directives could be described as the wrongful subjugation of one person over another.[2]

Unlike the advance directives associated with degenerative disease, however, with advance directives in the mental-health setting, this clarity and certainty quickly disappear. Neither our particular preanalytic intuitions about the rightfulness of according moral authority in actual cases nor our concepts of personhood and identity allow an easy and unequivocal conclusion.

Attempts to Rebut the Moral Challenge

Buchanan and Brock's (1989) discussion is one of two sustained attempts to overcome the kind of challenge to the moral authority of advance directives highlighted by a successive-selves analysis; the other is offered by Joel Feinberg (1986). Feinberg's argument is designed to show we must reject a successive-selves analysis. Buchanan and Brock aim to show how a successive-selves analysis, construed in an identity-conserving way, allows us to honor advance directives. Neither argument, in my view, proves sufficient. I will discuss them in turn to show why.

The central value underlying Feinberg's proposals is individual autonomy: the freedom to choose for oneself without interference by others. In determining whether to honor her advance directives in the face of a disturbed patient's expression of a contrary wish, Feinberg appeals to the standard of voluntary decision and action. Whether issued at an earlier or later time, the more voluntary decision is the one that should be respected. When the decisions and wishes of the earlier and later selves appear equally voluntary, he concludes, then on the assumption that explicit instructions to disregard later requests were built into the earlier self's advance directive, the wishes of the earlier self should be honored.

Why? At the heart of the autonomy we so value lies a capability, Feinberg believes: we are able to bind ourselves in advance. And this capability in turn presupposes, he believes, that we treat the earlier and later "selves" as one person at different times and embrace the traditional ratio of one person or self to a bodily lifetime. With this reasoning, Feinberg resolutely discounts a successive-selves analysis.

Feinberg appears to have overstated his argument here, however. True, the capacity to bind oneself in advance is a reflection of our autonomy. But an equally central expression of autonomy seems to lie in one's ability to change one's mind in the light of new evidence, changed values, and an altered situation (Radden 1994). So Feinberg's argument is insufficient to justify privileging an earlier wish over a later one, even without a successive-selves metaphysics.

Unlike Feinberg, Buchanan and Brock do not preclude the possibility of a successive-selves analysis, but they attempt to avoid its implications. Adopting a metaphysics that admits of successive selves, these authors insist, does not force us to acknowledge advance directives to be morally objectionable. For whether advance directives reflect this particular kind of unfairness or injustice (between separate selves) will depend, in part at least, on the degree of personal change required for us to determine that one self has succeeded another. In asking whether the person issuing an advance directive should be seen as the same person as the disabled one she will presently become, Buchanan and Brock acknowledge that they may be asking how close the interconnections among a person's psychological states and dispositions must be to support an ascription of psychological continuity sufficient for personal identity. Their answer: even limited continuity should count as sufficient to warrant our speaking of the same person from one time to another.

Theories of personal identity have been shown to be flexible. But are they as flexible as Buchanan and Brock seem to suppose? Must we conclude that such directives are to be honored if we adopt a strong singularity position and are not to be honored if we do not? By interpreting the contrary wishes (expressed at t_1 and t_2) as expressions of the same self or person at different times, we do not resolve concerns over the moral authority of advance directives, as Buchanan and Brock assert.

Weakness of Will, Changes of Mind, Promises, and Resolves

In determining whether to honor commitments and resolves of any kind, we must begin by acknowledging that commitments are broken in different ways and for different reasons. Sometimes there is felt inner struggle. Here we remain of divided mind, still holding the principles, the beliefs, ideas, and values that prompted the resolve but finding ourselves incapable of adhering to them. At other times, in contrast, we change our minds, making and then breaking agreements, decisions, and resolves as the result of a change in our beliefs, values, or attitudes. In this case we are consistent in our mental attitude: no divisions or heterogeneities, subjectively apprehended or publicly attributable, fracture the unity of purpose we have achieved. Ulysses' advance directive to his sailors, which has always been accorded moral authority, conforms more closely to the first of these cases. The sailors were entitled to ignore their captain's subsequent entreaties. As Homer encourages us to understand it, Ulysses' "contract" with the oarsmen was based on his recognition of the nature of temptation. Ulysses knew that when he heard the sirens sing, he would be of a divided mind. His desire to avoid the dangers presented by the sirens would persist, but it would coexist with, and likely be overridden or nullified by, the enchantment of their song and the perilous desire to go to them.

Next we must distinguish decisions that affect and are known to others and whose revocation is likely to affect those others adversely, from resolves and commitments that affect and are known to ourselves alone. These are *promises* and *resolves*, respectively. We do describe as promises vows made to and affecting ourselves alone, and as resolves those affecting others, so these terms only roughly correspond to the way we customarily speak, I must caution.

A good part of what makes promises binding concerns their effects on other people. When promises are not kept, others may be expected to suffer adverse consequences. Because their revocation is likely to affect others adversely, promises as a general class are widely treated as binding, except in very special situations. An overriding obligation might force us to break such a promise, for example, the duty to relieve others' distress in a crisis (Ross 1930). In general, however, the explanation for our breaking promises—whether, as is sometimes so, it is moral weakness or forgetfulness, or because the promise rests on a belief we have come to disavow—is rarely sufficient to absolve. (It may serve partially to excuse.) And aiding another in promise breaking is regarded as equally unjustified. Usually, it is wrong to break promises for whatever reason.

As they are understood here, resolves have a different moral structure. We are usually not judged to have wrongfully broken a commitment when we fail to follow through with a resolve because we have thought better of our initial decision. We are permitted to change our minds. Only when there is evidence of a disqualifying factor, such as weakness, is the resolve treated as having been binding, in the sense that our breaking it brings disapprobation. The person who fails to live up to her private vow due to moral weakness—sloth, greed, or bodily appetite, for example—is ill judged for breaking her resolve. But when the broken vow results from altered beliefs, a change of values, or a change of mind, one is not so judged. Genuine personal development; change voluntarily and knowingly sought, or acknowledged in the light of new information; and a spirit of openness to ideological and spiritual revision are each too central to our notion of character formation for us to disallow the freedom to change one's mind.

Many, if not most, of the cases of Ulysses contracts we are interested in here are actually unlike Ulysses' case because they involve not weakness but a change of mind or something that feels like a change of mind. If we narrow our focus to the particular case of treatment refusals, for example, the patient with a divided mind like Ulysses' is not the most common one. Believing the medicine will do her good while dreading its uncomfortable side effects, a patient may struggle with whether to accept treatment. Anecdotal and clinical evidence indicate, though, that more often patients feel wholehearted in their refusal. And if we remember the considerations involved here, this does not seem untoward. Often there are motives that are strong enough to leave little room for ambivalence. The person undergoing an elevated mood—the excitement and high energy level associated with manic and hypomanic responses, for example—understandably wishes to have the condition continue unchecked. Moreover, some awareness of the uncertain success and medical risks posed by many forms of psychiatric treatment, together with grounds for the patient to believe her condition likely to be of temporary duration, might also suffice to produce a wholehearted refusal of treatment. So, finally, might beliefs about the spiritual and emotional value of a certain kind of intense experience. If such metaphysical and religious convictions have a weight comparable to that accorded them in normal people, then these too will likely count as sufficient reasons.

Some mental patients will be unlike Ulysses in a second respect: their earlier commitments will be like resolves, not promises, in that they affect none but the patient herself. If so, there may not be warrant for enforcing them. By breaking his promise to take medication during a manic phase, a patient may bankrupt his needy family. Here his advance directive has the form of a promise and is clearly to be honored because of the potential costs to others involved by its revocation. But another patient, without dependents and of ample financial means, may reject her previously established treatment plan with impunity. Her change of mind would prolong her hospitalization by several months, let us say. It will thus affect others, though not adversely. Yet it is close enough to a resolve that—again, given borderline or contested competence—her change of mind should probably be respected.

The perspectival quandaries noted throughout this book are intensified here. A resolve broken through a change of mind and one broken through weakness of will have different moral significance. We must know, then, from what perspective the resolve was broken. A broken resolve may feel like a change of mind from the perspective of the disturbed patient. From the more detached perspective of an observer, on the other hand, it will likely be figured as closer to temporary interference, or even "possession": the body is beset by an alien autonomous system that issues unfamiliar decisions and wishes. When these perspectival differences arise, the subjective perspective of the patient may be alone in showing the moral authority of the advance directive to be doubtful.

It is true that the conditions for changing one's mind are interpersonal and intersubjective. The liberty to change one's mind, as Annette Baier has emphasized, requires validation and confirmation from others, resting on "membership in a community where there is mutual recognition, [a community] which trains its members in some conventions" and has the practice of "second-thinking" an individual's judgment (1985a, 66). Like the psychologically normal reasoners Baier describes, the mental patient too will have been schooled in such a community to learn second-thinking. But as Baier herself admits, the skill, once acquired, becomes autonomous. The mental patient's changes of mind, subjectively understood, are no less changes of mind even though they are not consonant with the beliefs and desires of the community in which she finds herself.

The several perspectives from which a patient's decision can be viewed are not exhausted when we have distinguished the self's subjective experience of itself from others' public apprehension of that self. The subjective perspective is temporally bounded. Not only the potential patient, who at t_1 issues the advance directive, but the subsequent treated and restored ex-patient, who looks back on the mental disorder that beset her at t_2 from the detached perspective of t_3, may share the more public view of the broken resolve. Indeed, the potential patient anticipates her future instability from the public stance. At the time of issuing any advance directive concerning care during subsequent mental disturbance, the person almost certainly believes the anticipated state of mind will bring at least temporary clouding or interference with her initial judgment—if she did not, the advance directive would likely not be required. Newly restored to mental health at t_3, the ex-patient sometimes experiences having recovered her oneness with the initial potential patient. She remembers the ascendancy of the mentally disturbed patient at t_2 very much as an observer portrays it: as an alien possession.

Which perspective should be favored? It is arguable that we should respect the subjective account of the presently embodied self. As we saw earlier, this self's present embodiment is a kind of privileged relationship. The case can also be made that the perspective we should privilege is the more considered public one, which is more likely to be associated with a steady and sustained view of the person's long-term interests. As Thomas Schelling (1984, 91) has shown, in sensitive and acute writing on perspectival questions of this kind, such a public judgment too reflects a standpoint. The moral to draw here, Schelling helps us see, is not that one or the other perspective is preferable so much as that there is no "objective," perspectiveless point of view. Without such a viewpoint, however, we are without a way to resolve this question over whether the patient's resistance to earlier plans should be understood as a changed mind or not.

The particular set of perspectival quandaries explored here seems to add to earlier doubts over the moral authority of advance directives. Certainly there are conditions that allow us to honor the kind of advance planning involved in Ulysses contracts. When the patient is clearly and unequivocally incompetent, when the earlier commitment affects, and/or involves an agreement with, other people and is thus binding in the manner of a promise, when weakness of will rather than a change of mind seems to account for the altered attitude, even from the subjective and immediate perspective of the disturbed person herself—in these cases it may well be right to honor an advance directive over the changed wishes of the disturbed patient.

The foregoing discussion shows the ways in which we decide when ordinary promises and resolves should be honored. These ways, with all their complexity, will often be applicable with advance care planning for mental disorder, whether, with Feinberg, we choose to reject a metaphysics of successive selves or, with Buchanan and Brock, we interpret such a metaphysics in a way that is identity-conserving.

Two efforts to support the moral authority of advance directives have been reviewed here, neither one sufficient to encourage us in accepting that authority. However, advance directives of one particular sort find special justification in an argument unrelated to those examined thus far. These are advance directives aimed at preventing future self-destructive behavior.

Self-Destructive Wishes

To get our bearings in this exotic region before we turn to the successive selves found in abnormal psychology, let us begin by considering normal people and the sometimes radical changes they undergo through time. Later transformations of our selves regularly violate the wishes, goals, and even solemn vows of those selves we once were. We often find this prospect disappointing and—when we observe it reflected in others' inconsistencies, recalcitrance, and backsliding—regrettable. But unless the vows were promises, made to or affecting others, or unless the later dishonoring of an earlier embodiment was particularly flagrant, we in general do not find this retrospective thwarting of an earlier self's will morally objectionable, in ourselves or in others. Yet we often do find it objectionably when a later self is bound by an earlier self's plan for her future with which she now disagrees. The later self is embodied *at the time* of the allegedly unjustified subjection. She it is who must most immediately suffer the pain and enjoy the pleasure resulting from "her" decisions made at and concerning the present time. And only she—or some future self as yet unformed—can be affected by her decisions concerning the future. For the later self's wishes to be overridden by the directive of an earlier self is in certain respects worse than a later self's betrayal of an earlier self's plan or dream.

Here lies a significant difference between the normal case and the abnormal ones, to which we now turn. In the normal case, progression is inexorable. The earlier self will never be embodied again: at least some of its stake in the composite person's future is extinguished by time and change. (How much we ought to relinquish that stake is itself a philosophical question, as Parfit [1984] has recognized. But the modest assertion made here seems unassailable: knowing that I may return to this body requires me to care about this body in ways in which I would not were I leaving it without prospect of return.) In contrast, the successive selves associated with mental disorder are recurrent, and in dissociative-identity disorder, contemporaneous. Even where change seems irreversible, with all disorders whose causation is not fully understood, the chance and hope remains that something approximating self 1 will return.

Sharing a body has additional significance in our cases, then. The successive selves resulting from maturation or ideological conversion may be seen to inhabit the same body merely sequentially. (This will also be true, notice, of the successive selves resulting from irreversible disease or damage to the brain, like the two selves of Phineas Gage. There was no hope that the earlier Gage would return: the brain damage was irreversible. Thus on a separate-selves analysis, the old Gage could have little stake in the doings of the self resulting from the accident.)

The author of the advance directive, it might be supposed, is taking responsibility for the self she will later become. In our culture we place great value on autonomy, in the sense of taking responsibility for oneself. Because this is so, taking responsibility for another spatiotemporally distinct person is only warranted, when she represents a danger to others, when she exhibits some particular or general incompetence or when she explicitly consents to such intervention. Let us consider in turn these three factors—consent, competence, and danger to others—in light of the extra significance that sharing a body takes on for the successive selves we encounter in abnormal psychology.

Neither future selves nor those now reigning among the coexisting selves of the multiple can (now) provide consent. Nor would they be inclined to consent were it logically possible. The problem arises because they *resist* the earlier directive. Moreover, as we have seen, their competence or incompetence is often precisely what is in question. So the incompetence part of the incompetence/consent proviso will not be helpful in determining a decision in these cases. We are left with the liberal *harm principle* in such instances: we may override a person's wishes just when those wishes are likely to harm another (Mill 1859).

The context of this discussion is that dangerousness to spatiotemporally distinct other persons is not at issue. But left unaccounted are self-destructive impulses. The peculiar way in which the interests of those sharing a body are entwined means that self 2's suicidal or otherwise physically self-destructive impulses (for example, the wish to cut or mutilate oneself) do pose an immediate danger to self 1, with whom she shares a body. On a successive-selves analysis, then, we may be entitled to honor the advance directives seeking to prevent self-destructive behavior. But this would not be because such self-destructive behavior endangered the presently reigning self. Rather, it would be because such behavior endangered other selves with strong claims on the shared body and because they were likely to return. The force of this kind of argument has been recognized by VanDeVeer (1986) in an extended discussion of the moral bounds of benevolence. And Parfit too has acknowledged the general point, remarking that we ought to prevent anyone from doing "to his future self what it would be wrong to do to other people" (1984, 321).

Only the presence of incompetence permits interference to prevent suicide when the more traditional singularity-conserving metaphysics associated with individualism and liberalism is buttressed by the harm principle. Unless those who are suicidal show a want of reason, they must be left free to destroy themselves. And incompetence is notoriously difficult to establish with those who are suicidal. This has been demonstrated by many in the liberal tradition, who are uncomfortable with this implication of the harm principle (see, e.g., Feinberg 1986, 360). In contrast to the traditional identity-conserving metaphysics of liberalism, a successive-selves metaphysics would seem to readily accommodate the impulse to prevent self-harm. Self 1 may be supported in her advance directive for preventing self 2 from acting on self-destructive, and in particular, suicidal, impulses.

VanDeVeer's concern is with the limits of paternalism. Prohibitions on self-destructive behavior to prevent the harm of successor selves, he stresses, are not paternalistic grounds for interference; instead, they are most closely analogous to ordinary interpersonal cases in which we interfere with A to protect B (VanDeVeer 1986, 161).

Yet VanDeVeer's argument endorses prohibition—whether or not it is paternalistic, strictly speaking—of a wider range of potentially self-destructive action than does the argument developed here. By treating potential successor selves on analogy with actual other persons, VanDeVeer's application of the harm principle would warrant, or require, the prevention of all self-destructive action. My claim, in contrast, is that such interference undertaken on the part of potential future persons is generally thought not justified. In the case of the group of mentally disturbed patients we are concerned with, the special feature of past embodiment and potential recurrence (a past self has been an actual person and is likely to become one again) makes this an unusual exception to the standard permissive liberal position on self-harm.

Here too moral intuitions and convictions meet and challenge theory. We have a choice: Only if we adopt a successive-selves metaphysics need we concede to these consequences of the harm principle. On an identity-conserving metaphysics, interference in self-destructive behavior would remain inadmissably paternalistic. Without consulting our moral intuitions and responses to these cases, it is difficult to imagine how we should decide. And unless we consult these moral intuitions and responses, it is difficult to imagine we can rest content with our metaphysical decision.

Choosing physically self-destructive impulses to illustrate this argument allows us to avoid a perennial problem: the definition and limits of harm. We know from the more standard context of its application to groups of spatiotemporarily distinct persons that the simplicity and plausibility of the harm principle is matched by profound difficulties of application. What kind of harm? What degree of harm? What risk of harm? Each difficulty is separate and fraught questions when we seek a warrant for interference to protect others. And none of these questions is easier to resolve in the context of intrapersonal harm.

We cannot hope to achieve policy recommendations in this area without resolution and decision on these points of definition, and such resolution will not be pursued further here. But what does seem apparent is that answers to each question (What kind of harm? What degree? What risk?) are no harder to resolve in the intrapersonal case than in the more standard interpersonal case. Moreover, their resolution in the intrapersonal case will require no additional considerations. Depriving another of opportunities by undertaking short-sighted or imprudent action, for example, would generally be insufficient to rank as harming the other, whether in the interpersonal case or in the intrapersonal case. Acting so as to likely injure another person physically would be sufficient. And somewhere in the contested area between these two extremes the line must be drawn.

Other limitations are perhaps clearer. There are cases in which one self may be seen to follow sequentially upon another in the same body: maturational change, ideological conversion, and personality change resulting from irreversible brain disease or damage, as beset Phineas Gage. But the application of some version of the harm principle to the successive selves associated with mental disorder is tied to the distinctive way these successive selves have been seen to share a single body. Thus other instances of sequential selves will not fall under the rubric of the harm principle in the same way. Because of ideological conversion, for example, self 2 may be expected to succeed and endanger a body now inhabited by self 1, which he will inherit. But the harm the principle will not permit us to honor self 1's advance directive limiting self 2's predicted behavior in this case, as it would, we saw earlier, with the recurrent selves of mental disorder.

Also excluded from an application of the harm principle to successive selves is the person with recurrent and regular weakness of will over some appetite, or one whose "impulse disorder" invites a description of duality, for example, the alcoholic, the compulsive eater, or the smoker. Both in therapeutic and in less formal understanding, we see a tendency to figure the source of the willful, impulsive, "thirsty," or "hungry" agency as one self and the source of the more prudent agency as another. Nonetheless, these locutions must be regarded as metaphorical and potentially misleading. A good case can be made that the recurrence and/or coexistence of these behavior patterns should be seen as distinct and contrary sources of agency. But they are not full selves, deserving the protection provided to others by the harm principle. It may be that the advance directive of the smoker who asks for others' help in resisting or thwarting an impulse to buy cigarettes ought to be honored. But if so, it is not because we can appeal to a successive-selves metaphysics and the harm principle.

We may acknowledge an application of the harm principle in explaining why certain advance directives ought to be honored, then, but only when the notion of successive selves is sufficiently circumscribed and not extended beyond the central cases identified here.

Where recurrence is absent and self 1's advance directive does not serve to protect the shared body from harm wrought by self 2, we have seen that the decision to honor advance directives figures as an unjust favoring of the wishes of an earlier self, or an earlier decision by the same self or person, over those of a later self, or a later decision. Whichever metaphysics we adopt and whichever interpretation we accept, we may remain suspicious of Ulysses contracts when they extend beyond proscribing self-destructive behavior.

Although most advance directives lack moral authority, might one self nonetheless have obligations toward the other selves with which she shares a body? This question requires us to consider the relation of care between earlier and later selves or self stages.

Responsibilities Over Oneself or One's Selves

When it concerns spatiotemporally distinct persons, we saw, paternalistic intervention in the lives of those providing no danger to others is held in check by the incompetence/consent proviso. This proviso reflects the fear that some exercises of paternalism permit unwarranted interference in others' lives, and particularly in others' rightful exercise of autonomy. Now we must consider how much difference sharing a body makes and whether such a formulation can be helpful when we enter the realm inhabited by successive and multiple selves.

The perspective summed up by the incompetence/consent proviso is one grounded in individualism and in the traditional individualistic metaphysics of one self to a body or a bodily lifetime. In applying this view to the case of responsibility where one self is required to take care of another sharing the same body, then, we are crossing over from one set of metaphysical assumptions to another. Most notable among the disanalogies to which we must be sensitive are those related to the entwining of interests between selves sharing a body. There is a strong, indeed unique, sense in which we must understand sharing a body when such sharing is attributed to the recurrent or potentially recurrent selves in disorders such as manic-depression, or to the contemporaneous selves in dissociative-identity disorder. The formulation sketched above presupposes the frame outlined at the start of this discussion in the previous chapter, where the actions of one person are unlikely to endanger or harm others. Yet when we turn to the relationship between successive or contemporaneous selves sharing a body, this frame cannot easily be maintained. These selves share, rather than sequentially inhabit, a body. They must literally live with the effects of each other's decisions, then, in ways differing from, and having few parallels with, the relationships between distinct adult persons, however those persons may be entwined. (The exception is perhaps the fetus and its host, but the disparallels here are evident and extensive.)

So the moral constraints on responsibility for care of other selves sharing one's body do not take quite the form that caring for others does when 'others' refers to other spatiotemporally distinct persons. These disanalogies duly noted, it seems arguable nonetheless that one self ought to take responsibility for another's care. To the extent that this is possible, as we have seen, and within constraints something like those expressed in the incompetence/consent proviso, self 1 ought to be encouraged to concern herself over self 2's welfare and well-being. The earlier self anticipating future incapacitating mental disorder is in certain respects well placed to issue a Ulysses contract or psychiatric will, and taking responsibility in this way seems like a good idea. In a society where the nuclear family is valued, it would be reasonable to foster responsibility for one's incompetent siblings. So a society, like ours, that values individualism in the sense of honoring the ratio of one person to one body might see a person's taking responsibility for the care of the less competent parts of him- or herself housed in the same body as socially desirable.

What is the prescriptive force of the claim that self 1 ought to take responsibility for self 2's care? Ethics of care have often been juxtaposed to ethics of obligation, so it may be quite weak. Thus while not something we owe to ourselves, or our selves, taking responsibility for other selves' care is certainly morally permissible and may be, perhaps, a practice to be encouraged.

An argument based on the relationship among selves sharing a body might also invite something stronger: an *obligation* to take responsibility. The closeness or even, we might say, "intimacy" of the relationship between self 1 and self 2 seems to invite some obligations. Sharing a body and what this entails—sharing a public life and even, when we speak of the coexisting multiple selves of dissociative-identity disorder, sharing the possibility of a unified future—constitutes intimacy of the most profound kind, and this intimacy seems likely, if anything does, to bring its own special obligations.

Taking responsibility for intimates in this way may not be easy, we have seen. Attitudes of abhorrence and alienation, not fondness or felt closeness, may characterize my relationship with my other self, which expels me from my body during phases of my cyclical disorder or with which I alternate reign and control in dissociative-identity disorder (Putnam 1989). Nevertheless, if there are responsibilities of care toward intimates that we cannot as easily relinquish as those we have toward strangers, then they would seem to have application here, however much they challenge natural inclination. The exception to this prescription, we saw, must be when the earlier self seems likely to endanger the future self through self-destructive action.

I have undertaken a review of moral and policy-related issues in this and the last four chapters aimed at clarifying our value presuppositions about multiplicity and reponsibility in particular real-life contexts. By providing some answers to the question with which we began concerning how to treat people who change radically as the result of visitations like mental disturbance, these discussions should have advanced the central goal of this essay. But they had to do so at several levels. Guidance and direction over particular questions, such as the moral authority of advance directives, will find immediate, concrete application. In addition, however, these practical discussions about multiplicity and responsibility must contribute in a different way. We saw that in determining how to understand the language of successive selves and whether to embrace a metaphysics involving successive selves, we have to engage in a delicate circling exercise, wherein moral responses shaped theory and theory in turn curbed and directed these responses. This process of reflective equilibrium now requires that we return to theory and examine more fully the theoretical context within which a metaphysics of successive selves finds its place.

III

Successive Selves and Individualism

A Metaphysics of Successive Selves

Despite the informal language of successive selves, we more commonly speak as if the self were one, not many: speech reflects customary identity assumptions. Is this merely a convenience, a *façon de parler*, or must we see and speak of the self thus? The theoretical constraints that might oblige, permit, or deter us from so speaking are explored in this chapter. These are metaphysical questions, suggested by philosophers' attention to issues of personal and self identity, identification and reidentification, and individuation in a long tradition that was introduced earlier with the theory of John Locke and will be intercepted here, first, in the theory of self put forward by Hume in the eighteenth century. Several philosophers—including William James and more recently the contemporary thinkers H. P. Grice, Derek Parfit, and Sydney Shoemaker—form part of this tradition, amplifying and completing the theory of the self's singularity through time as it was sketched by the empiricists Locke and Hume (James 1890; Grice 1941; Parfit 1971, 1973, 1984; Shoemaker 1963, 1968, 1970, 1979, 1984).

This tradition is metaphysical in the sense that it is conducted at such a level of generality as to claim to speak of what is universally true.[1] Hume and the other philosophers discussed here have put forth theories that, if they are true at all, are true for all selves, regardless of the particularities by which those selves are severally and socially identified. Metaphysics seeks universalities.[2]

Pursuing Hume's notion of the self's continuity through time as it is filled out by James and contemporary philosophers, we will see that it is flexible and open to interpretation. While permitting us to maintain one aspect of traditional metaphysical notions—the ratio of one self to one body through that body's lifetime—this analysis also allows us to maintain the more radical notion of a possible multiplicity of selves housed in the same body. We are permitted, but not forced, to acknowledge for the self a continuity through time linking earlier and later self "stages" into a unified and continuous whole. Decisions and judgments are required of us as we determine when to acknowledge the force of the language and the truth of the metaphysics of successive selves.

Empiricist Theories of Personal Identity

It was Locke's view, we saw, that a continuity of memory and consciousness provides the basis for personal identity, the judgment that the self (or "person") remains singular and unvarying through time. Locke's was an ambitious claim: he held that a relation of strictest numerical identity links earlier and later person stages. Like Locke, Hume attributed the singularity and invariance of the self through time to the continuity between earlier and later psychological states. But for Hume, this was an artificial singularity and a *relatively unvarying* nature.[3]

The well-known conclusions that Hume drew from his fruitless pursuit of the self as an object of experience may be understood to explode certain beliefs about the self's putative identity. Rather than a simple, united whole comprising the *res cogitans* of Cartesian tradition, Hume described an untidy bundle of heterogeneous and ever-changing impressions. Instead of a strict and perfect identity intrinsic to the self and associated with its continuation through time, by which it was thought to be changeless, Hume pictured an imperfect and "imaginary," or "fictional," identity, imposed from without for the convenience of the observer.

Hume was not denying some loose singularity and invariance to the self; he was not countenancing radical discontinuity or fracture, let alone successive selves sharing the same body. Nor yet was he questioning the self's unity; he was not acknowledging radically divided minds. Rather, he was denying the basis for making claims about unity and continuity: the Cartesian notion that underlying these two unities, singularity and invariance, stood a metaphysical subject of experiences. This Cartesian subject or self, for which Hume notoriously searched in vain, was thought to encompass a unifying principle. It linked items in the imagination at a given time and, remaining unaltered through time, provided the continuity of perfect identity persisting throughout the individual's life. If, as Hume proposed, there was no subject of experiences, then both unifying functions would be lost. Yet the unity of experience, ensured by the imagination, remained. Based on the relations of contiguity (by which Hume meant proximity or closeness), resemblance, and causation, a loose and relative continuity, misnamed 'identity', linked earlier and later experience stages in a way sufficient for us to speak of the person as remaining the same through time. Hume, then, still had a theory of self; he still spoke, for the most part, as if the self were a thing. But his is a reductionist theory for all that: our references to the self reduce to, are nothing but talk about, a bundle of experiences—just as, we might say, curtains may be seen to reduce to, or be nothing but, yards of fabric cut and sewn in particular ways. Their spatio-temporal continuity accounts for our tendency to speak of curtains as remaining singular through time. And if we speak of selves as one at a particular time and through time, it must be due to the rough empirical cohesion among, and continuities between, parts of the self—ensured, Hume believed, by the imagination.

In the philosophical tradition since Hume, attempts have been made to extend and develop his empirical explanations of our tendency to speak as if the self were one—continuous, or at least relatively unchanging—through time. His analysis (with which he was himself almost immediately dissatisfied) has also been countered and challenged, most notably by his contemporary Immanuel Kant (1781, 1787). But because, in the present century, scientific and psychological thinking about the self's identity or sameness through time has for the most part followed the bare, empirical path of Hume's analysis, my discussion of the self's identity will draw on those philosophers who may be seen to have adopted and refined that analysis, especially James and Parfit. Although a fuller explanation of the self's seeming identity may require us to appeal to transcendental claims, I follow Hume and James in supposing that our tendency to speak of persons as singular and invariant can be understood without appeal to nonempirical posits.

The Role of the Imagination

Can we account for our common tendency to speak of the self as one through time by appeal to the relations of continuity, causation, and resemblance linking the earlier and later bundles of a person's experience, as Hume thought? One thinker who supposed this to be so was James. Having paid obeisance to the transcendental subject (the Knower), James proceeds to undermine its purported numerical identity through time. The "metaphysical" self's supposed identity as "the permanent, abiding principle of spiritual activity identical with itself wherever found" must be questioned. A loose, empirical "identity" that James calls "functional" links the passing states of consciousness (James 1890, 202). This "functional identity," he asserts, seems really to be the only sort of identity in the thinker that the facts (the empirical facts) "require us to suppose" (1890, 202).

What is this functional identity? With characteristic facility, James describes the feeling of the link between past and present experiences. Nascent thought has a "trick," he observes, of immediately taking up the expiring thought and "adopting" it—a process that leads to the appropriation of "most of the remoter constituents of the self." Who owns the last self, as he puts it, owns the self before the last, for "what possesses the possessor possesses the possessed" (James 1890, 205). The stream of consciousness is made up of thoughts, each different yet each possessing the last, each "at each moment different from the last moment but appropriative of the latter, together with all that the latter calls its own" (James 1892, 82). Each successive part of the stream of consciousness thus "should know, and knowing, hug to itself and adopt, all those that went before—thus standing as a *representative* of an entire past stream with which it is in no wise to be identified" (James 1890, 205).[4]

James's account is reminiscent of Hume's references to the unifying role of the imagination, and we know that, like Hume, James regards empirical "identity" as loose and relative, requiring no more than a rough approximation of sameness. Yet James's description of the appropriative function of thought and imagination suggests an introspectable oneness and invariance between past and present states, or stages, of consciousness at odds with what we know of the ragged incompleteness of much memory. After all, few remotely past experiences seem to linger in present awareness in any form. In an often quoted example, we would be reluctant to say of a man that he was not the same person throughout his life, although he might change from being a boy to a young officer, and again to being a general, and, as a general, not remember incidents from his boyhood. (The example is Reid's [1785].) While, as a young officer, he may have remembered being beaten for robbing an orchard as a boy, his apparent identity must withstand the fact that later as a general he had entirely forgotten the incident, although he remembered capturing the standard (flag) as a young officer. James's account of the way nascent thought "adopts" and "appropriates" expiring thought fails to explain such lapses through time.

To amplify and fill out James's account at this point, where it is least complete, we may now introduce other contemporary theories attempting to offer empirical accounts of the self's seeming (though rough) singularity and invariance though time. Like those of Hume and James, these accounts appeal to something observable and non-transcendental that, because it remains relatively unchanged through time, provides an anchor and warrant for our talk about selves as unities. Also like those of Hume and James, these theories point to psychological states as the source of this warrant.

Psychological Forms of Continuity

If the self is experienced as relatively continuous through time, this may be because we are disposed to remember, we have seen, albeit we do not remember perfectly. H. P. Grice (1941) has sketched a memory theory of personal identity that acknowledges that we do not always remember all we experience, by treating memory as an overlapping series. He introduces the concept of a *total temporary state* (TTS), which is a set of simultaneous experiences of a single person, and argues that a sequence of TTSs comprise parts of the same person (and thus constitute an identity) when a certain relation obtains between them: each (TTS) is disposed to remember at least one experience contained in the last, or contains an experience of which the next contains a memory. A single person's TTSs thus form an *interlocking series*, defined by Grice as a series in which no subset of members is independent of all the rest. Memory is understood dispositionally here. A TTS is *memorable* when it contains as an element some experience, and given certain conditions, a memory of this experience occurs as an element in some subsequent TTS. A TTS is *memorative* when, given certain conditions, it contains as an element a memory of some experience contained in a previous TTS.

To ensure singularity, Grice's analysis calls for a very modest continuity, illustrated by the case of the general who forgot his boyhood spanking. Though almost everything else changed, one shared memory between two self stages may be sufficient for us to speak of those stages as earlier and later parts of the same person. Grice's account is thus a relatively conservative, i.e., singularity-conserving, theory. In all but the most extreme cases of discontinuity, it allows us to maintain traditional identity presumptions, such as the ratio of one body to one self.

A feature of the thesis that some kind of memory continuity could explain our identity language and presuppositions is that memory is intimately dependent on the person's internal life, at least when we understand memory in the customary way as a mental occurrence of which we are aware.[5] Making some degree of memory continuity the basis for judgments about the self's singularity and invariance through time presupposes subjective confirmation and introspective report. In this respect, at least, the memory criterion for personal identity differs from the continuity of personality traits.

Personality theories—focused on the individuating function of much language about the self and built on the notion of trait clusters—promise another way to explain our use of identity language for selves. We know this from the appeal to personality and agent traits as criteria for separate selves, which were suggested by the story of Dr. Jekyll and Mr. Hyde and were developed in our analysis of multiplicity. The presence of separate personalities (motivations, styles, tastes, and capabilities), such as are found in multiples, seems to incline us to judge these cases, at least, as showing several selves inhabiting the same body.

Psychological Continuity and Connectedness

Parfit's influential empirical-continuity argument (1971, 1973, 1984) is much more encompassing than Grice's, since it accommodates both memory and personality continuity. On Parfit's analysis, the "psychological states" whose continuity explains language suggestive of a singular and invariant self include behavioral traits and tendencies as well as occurrent mental items dateable to a particular moment—not only memories, dispositions, and personality traits but also other, more general capabilities, like how to speak or swim. Since psychological states include many publicly discernable behavioral dispositions among the psychological continuities and no privileged place is offered to those items known through introspection, such as memories, we can see that Parfit's account favors, in certain respects, the detached perspective of the external observer. Parfit's primary concern seems to be the singularity and invariance judgments made by and about others. Certainly his theory enables others to establish identity claims with ease.

Like Grice, Parfit uses the notion of an overlapping or interlocking series. Earlier and later self stages housed in a single body at different times have *continuity* when and to the extent that they overlap. Should psychological states *a* and *b* overlap in this way between t_1 and t_3, then there is *connection* between *a* and *b* at t_2. Parfit has also introduced the notion of survival. If person *P* remains the same between t_1 and t_3 because of such overlapping connection, then *P survives* as one between t_1 and t_3.[6] In speaking of change and continuity of psychological attributes, Parfit makes appeal to a quantitative principle: the more traits are continuous, the more survival there will be. So connections admit of, and can hold, to any degree:

Between *X* today and *Y* yesterday there might be several thousand direct psychological connections, or only a single connection.... Since connectedness is a matter of degree, we cannot plausibly define precisely what counts as enough. But we can claim that there is enough connectedness if the number of connections over any day, is *at least half* the number of direct connections that hold, over every day, in the lives of nearly every actual person." (Parfit 1984, 206)

Its strongly quantitative emphasis may be reason to quarrel with this formulation, but it is clear enough: if between t_1 and t_3 person *P*'s connected traits numbered 100 and person *Q*'s numbered 50, we could conclude that between t_1 and t_3 person *P* survived more fully than person *Q*, since there was greater continuity between *P*'s earlier and later person phases. Survival stands in contrast to identity in this respect, I must emphasize.[7] Leibniz's law ensures that entities either remain identical through time or they do not.[8] P may survive between t_1 and t_3 more or less fully than Q, but P may not be more or less identical between t_1 and t_3 than Q.

Parfit's psychological-continuity analysis permits a broad set of traits to determine survival. A person in whom brain injury has brought about total amnesia concerning her past life, together with radical personality change, may have retained no trait of memory and personality entitling us to judge her to be the same person after, as before, her injury. But while there remain some overlapping traits—she can still knit and swim, let us say—we may speak of survival on Parfit's account. After her transforming brain injury, this person may be judged to have remained one, not several, albeit marginally. Thus Parfit's theory offers two features allowing us to overcome the insufficiencies of actual memory that seem to beset James's account of psychological continuity (or "functional identity"): the notion of an interlocking series and the range of psychological states and dispositions sufficient for continuity.[9]

The notion of a disposition, as we saw earlier, is a causal one. This means that the continuity provided by interconnected dispositions is what Shoemaker has called "causally grounded continuity" (1984, 90). This causal basis of psychological dispositions has been particularly emphasized by Shoemaker, who regards the continuity of persons through time as an instance of the more general continuity of "continuants" (things that we treat as the same through apparent change). Direct psychological connection between earlier and later stages of a person, he points out, is guaranteed by the later stage's being appropriately causally dependent on a state contained in the earlier stage (Shoemaker 1984, 83).

The question of whether survival or singularity requires that these chains of psychological continuity and connectedness result from normal causal processes is one with which philosophers struggle (see, for example, Parfit 1984, Shoemaker 1984, White 1991). (Would 'survival' rightly describe my acquisition of artificially created "quasi memories" otherwise bearing the appropriate relation to my current states?) But it is one that, eschewing science fiction for clinical fact, we may leave to them.

More generally, since the normal person has continuity of several kinds (memory, personality, psychological traits), how do psychological-continuity theorists such as Parfit proceed to establish their claims? Typically (we might even say 'traditionally', since the practice has been a central feature of philosophical discussion of personal identity since Locke), the philosopher engages in a thought experiment to imaginarily eliminate the other continuities. We are then asked to consult our intuitions or impressions and allow convictions based on these to determine whether we would attribute sameness. If we would, then the basis of our judgment must be the single continuity represented. The findings from these various thought experiments will not be evaluated here. There are problems with this method that make any choice among their outcomes less than conclusive (see chapter 5).

Interpreting the Criteria of Survival or Singularity

How much variance of psychological traits through time ranks as sufficient for us to speak of multiplicity, or to conclude that one self has replaced (or joined) another in a single body, will depend on context and the purposes and interests we bring to the decision. (Parfit, of course, recognizes this.[10])

The decision to accept a certain degree of psychological continuity as constituting survival or singularity will not be an arbitrary choice. But it is a decision and is not determined by the facts to the extent that a discovery might be said to be. Normative considerations, reasons to favor regarding the self as singular through time, are several and weighty. For this reason many would balk at adopting a particular level of overlap between psychological traits that are compatible with speaking of the same body as housing a succession of selves through time, at least in the everyday continuities we encounter outside abnormal psychology. And by allowing for differing thresholds, Parfit's psychological-continuity criterion for survival or singularity will permit easy identity-conserving conclusions. Perhaps even Dr. Jekyll and Mr. Hyde, who shared little but abilities and general knowledge, are best seen as aspects of the same self.

It was not Parfit's intention to assert a metaphysics of successive selves. His analysis concerns normal, not abnormal, psychology and at least within this limited sphere, the language of successive selves is understood to be a *façon de parler*, at most. Yet theories such as Parfit's are hospitable to a metaphysics of successive selves. They permit us to adopt such a metaphysics without requiring us to. This flexibility in Parfit's model is a feature of his theory that has not received the attention it deserves. Once he has set in place the notion that survival admits of degree, no particular threshold can be seen as binding or absolute. We may choose to adopt any degree of overlap between psychological states as sufficient for survival, whether it be extremely, moderately, or weakly singularity-conserving.

Refining the Language of Successive Selves

Our customary and common language of selves reflects the presuppositions of traditional theories of identity: persons and selves remain the same through stretches of time; a ratio of one self to a body prevails (the "one to a customer" rule). It has been shown here how Humean and neoempiricist theories of self, such as Grice's and Parfit's, are sufficient to explain why we continue to speak that customary language. Although our traditional language and presuppositions of personal identity reflect a deep and natural tendency to attribute unity to the self and are historically associated with the unifying principle of the Cartesian subject of experiences, such language and presuppositions are compatible with the empirically observable continuities emphasized by these analyses so long as they are subject to fairly conservative (singularity-conserving) interpretation. On the other hand, these same theories also encourage us to countenance a language of successive selves.

An attempt to link the neoempiricist theories of personal identity or survival introduced here with our informal language of successive selves will benefit from some refinements and qualifications. It may not have been the intended purpose of these philosophical theories to reflect the natural language.[11] Yet the marked similarities between the two discourses (the theoretical language of successive selves permitted by Grice's and Parfit's theories and the language derived from naturally occurring locutions such as 'She's a new person') suggest it may be worthwhile to attempt to adjust and restate the theories so as not to alter their substance in any respect yet reduce the differences between their formal description and the ways of everyday speech.

First, on Grice's analysis, TTSs (total temporary states) are said to remember experiences. But since we more naturally attribute the ability to remember to people than to states, let us reword his definition so that TTSs make up the same person when each TTS *contains a memory of* at least one experience contained in the last TTS or contains an experience of which the next TTS will contain a memory.

Second, to accord with natural language, each of these accounts (Grice's and Parfit's) must be understood to avoid an oversimplified, overly quantitative analysis in which psychological traits are represented as transferable, commensurable, aggregative items whose particular details are unimportant to the grand calculation by which psychological continuity, and hence survival, is reckoned. In acknowledgment of this point Parfit is careful to speak of the number and *strength* of psychological traits to be counted. The natural language of sameness and change suggests that some traits elude quantitative analysis, that salience allows us to discount or double-count certain traits, and that context and normative issues affect weighing. (If a person's self-concept and public persona are shaped around her skills as a comic, then her losing her sense of humor—because, let us say, of neurological damage or ideological conversion—will more likely prompt the judgment that she has become another person than the loss of half a dozen other traits and capabilities less closely linked to her "identity" in this richer sense of the term.) In short, while judging identity may be a broadly quantitative enterprise, it is not as simple as the arithmetic suggested by some of these descriptions (such as that quoted on page 189).

Another issue of quantification attached to certain psychological traits calls for further decisions. Consider sight. The ability to see is necessary for being able to ride a bicycle. Between t_1 and t_3 I may acquire and then lose my ability to ride a bicycle without any change in my ability to see. Do we judge this as the loss of one capability, or the loss of half of one, or the maintenance of one and the loss of the other? While nothing significant appears to hang on how we decide to count such complex dispositions, it must be remembered that *most* psychological dispositions and general capacities exhibit this same complexity. So the overlapping links in the continuity/discontinuity chain will be far different from the simplified models offered by the theories. A related point is that unlike the ability to ride a bicycle—a cluster of subcapabilities that, with some disentangling, could be specified (sight, balance, muscular strength, sense of direction for steering, etc.)—the traits associated with personality seem to be open-ended and indefinite, defying specification. To possess the trait of generosity, for example, may be to possess an indefinite number of situationally dependent tendencies and may call on an agreeing in-definite set of capabilities.

Objections to Psychological-Continuity Theories

Psychological-continuity theories, such as Parfit offers, are vulnerable to a number of different kinds of objections. As we saw earlier, some theorists insist on bodily continuity as a criterion for personal identity, arguing that only the continuity of the body through time permits us to identify and reidentify persons uniquely. They marshal elaborate constructed examples of fusion and branching, brain transplant, and mistaken identity in support of these conclusions. Psychological-continuity theories have been subject to a rather different challenge. Serious normative costs are purported to be associated with the em-pirical self that explains identity language and presuppositions with-out resort to a numerically identical subject and that countenances several selves possibly coexisting or succeeding one another within a bodily lifetime. The effect of Parfit's work in particular has been a marshalling of the reasons to value the unified and numerically iden-tical self associated with individualism and a rehearsal of the norma-tive costs of rejecting it. The case for preserving these goods, as well as their alleged incompatibility with metaphysical theories such as Parfit's, will be the subject of the next chapter.

The Normative Tug of Individualism

Postmodernist trends lead away from the unified "modern self," speaking even of, and speaking out for, its dissolution (Henriques 1984, Flax 1990, Nicholson 1990, Schemen 1994). But multifarious "modernist" voices are raised in support of maintaining identity presuppositions and personal pronouns, of speaking as if there were a self and as if that self comprised a unity or individual at a given time and through time. Emphasis on the singularity of the self forms one of the strands of modern individualism.

Another strand of individualism, not endorsed here and discussed only briefly at the end of this chapter, is the idea that the self is separate—a socially and emotionally isolated agent deciding and acting without interference—and alone. The ideal of the isolated, autonomous individual is now widely judged to be unrealistic and undesirable. In contrast, the newly applauded relational self of object-relations psychology, communitarian political theory, and feminist thought reveals a self not only indebted to relationships for its formation but understood as constituted, once formed, in social relation. The individualism whose tug I consider here rests on the less controversial notion of the unitary self, not of the socially isolated self.

Modernist voices supporting individualism are heard from those who, like the neo-Kantian thinker Christine Korsgaard, would regard the unity of the self as metaphysically secure (Korsgaard 1989, Scheffler 1982, Darwall 1982). But they are also heard from those—both philosophers and the constructivists of social psychology—for whom the unitary self is an illusion, albeit a useful illusion (James 1984). Shared by many of these thinkers and perspectives is the view that some instrumental value or values inhere in the concept of a unitary self, although over what that value or those values may be, the champions of a unitary self hardly speak with one voice.

What is our particular interest in the individualism associated with the self's oneness? What are the substantive goods so valued and so dependent on the notion of a unitary self? The answers to these questions constitute the normative considerations for maintaining the traditionally accepted understanding of self. Allegedly, only the notion of a unitary self will permit us to preserve the concepts and distinctions surrounding our sense of ourselves as voluntary agents, planners, and goal-directed actors. Although these concepts may be only local, characteristic of our particular context and culture, rather than universal, we similarly believe that some of our central moral notions—notion like responsibility, obligation, culpability, promise keeping, and rights—depend on this individualistic conception of the self. Several related emotional attitudes and responses also have been held to presuppose a unified and continuous self: pride, gratitude, shame, regret, guilt, remorse, shame, and other time-spanning emotions that involve "self-assessment" (Taylor 1985). Trust is another attitude that seems to require a sense of others as invariant through time, and the development and judicious exercise of such trust has been implicated in the moral life and in epistemological practices. Self-knowledge and self-understanding too, it has been proposed, rest on this individualistic sense of self. A further link connects the self's sameness or invariance and the conception of character (and character traits) essential to our society's moral notions of vice and virtue, and to its reliance on virtue-based ethical systems, I will presently show.

The argument is appealing: if we value the sense of ourselves as autonomous agents, as responsible, as fit citizens for a democracy, as knowers of the world around us and of ourselves, if we acknowledge that we possess characters and virtues, then we may indeed have reason to resist talk of fractured or successive selves. In evaluating these blandishments, however, we must keep two things in mind. First, appealing as they are, these normative considerations are less than logically compelling. If we do not value the senses of our selves enumerated above, it may be possible to relinquish the traditional view of selves as persisting unchanged through time. Its very links with agency, rationality, and causal concepts, we must remember, accounts for some postmodernist thinkers' rejection of the modern self and its connotations of unity. Second, the normative argument may rest on false or misleading connections. If the relationship between certain traditional conceptions of the self and the goods desired has been misrepresented, it may be possible to relinquish our notion of the self as absolutely unitary without endangering our value system. Normative considerations may tug us toward seeing the self as one rather than a multiplicity without requiring the lifelong identity of the "one to a customer" rule to preserve these values. There are strong reasons to avoid adopting a successive-selves metaphysics, which would permit a new self to arise every minute or day, and an infinite number of selves to succeed one another in the same body, but some loosening of traditional identity-conserving presuppositions may be possible without enormous normative costs.

The purpose of this chapter is to examine the various expressions of this kind of normative defense of individualism. They may have been misleadingly overstated, but taken together, these assorted normative considerations constitute compelling reasons to maintain a notion of the self as at least relatively unchanged throughout the lifetime of the body to which it is attached.

Does Continuity Matter?

The goods to be enumerated here allegedly depend on the singularity of the self through time and are related to it as ends to instrument. Yet our cherishing these goods only in part explains the value placed in this culture on lifelong singularity or identity. Sameness is cherished and honored for itself alone, and not merely because it is seen as presupposed by these other goods.

So too are change and discontinuity, however, and this coexistence of seemingly conflicting values suggests tension. As well as constancy and continuity, personal growth and development are also prized—indeed, prized as highly as sameness. Even in modern liberal society, whose individualism is so closely linked with the notion of the unitary self, there runs an ameliorative strain (Gray 1986, x). The faith that only through change can people (and society as a whole) improve is equally an expression of modern liberalism. Because of this, a life of long-term, even lifelong, projects is not judged superior to one filled with shorter-term projects. Our heroes, whose lives we hold up for praise and emulation, include both kinds: those who have striven after a single goal and those whose lives—ruptured and divided by contrasting themes and projects—reflect a discontinuous succession of self phases. Rather than threatening the notion of agency allegedly at stake here, ideological conversions of various kinds, and the radical changes of goal and interruptions of continuity that such conversions imply, are admired as its finest flowering. Moments occasioning radical character change, such as Augustine's conversion, stand at the center of our celebration of individualistic agency.

On a Cartesian metaphysical analysis of the self's identity, this tension was more apparent than real. The invariant and identical self, or subject, provided the frame within which these transformations were seen to take place. Change was contained by sameness. Stripped of such a metaphysical frame, however, the value of change would seem to challenge and oppose that value of sameness and invariance. Because the ideals of change and constancy are each values we hold dear, perhaps neither can be said to be absolute or paramount.

As well as the intrinsic value vested in the sameness and continuity of the self, singularity of this kind is judged as an instrumental good, necessary to other states and conditions we hold to be worthwhile. The several goods thus valued and thought to depend on the self's singularity or self-sameness through time will be introduced in turn. Each forms a dependency thesis, pointing to concepts and categories we value that seem to depend on the self's individuality and constancy through time.

Moral Categories

The first recognition of the thesis that there are moral and conceptual priorities embedded in the aspect of individualism that posits a singular self came in eighteenth century from the same Thomas Reid we have encountered before in this essay. Agency has a time-spanning nature, Reid (1785) argued. Moreover, unlike the identity we ascribe to bodies, which admits of degree, the personal identity required for agency is the notion of identity associated with the Cartesian subject of experiences. This subject remains invariant and numerically identical, one and the same for its possessor's lifetime. Such a self is required for the categories we customarily employ to portray the moral life: rights, obligation, and accountability. Identity when applied to persons, as Reid says, "has no ambiguity, admits not of degrees, or more and less." "It is the foundation of all rights and obligations, and of all accountableness" (Reid 1785, 112).

The argument that these moral notions depend on the self's identity has been widely rehearsed and is often made by appeal to the deeply individualistic features of our notion of responsibility (Haksar 1979, Madell 1981, Korsgaard 1989). We find such reasoning in Nietzsche 1967, for example, as well as in the modernists of today. In taking on obligations (from which, in turn, are generated rights), we embrace a prospective self and bind it in advance; in holding ourselves or others to account for past deeds, we refer to a past subject or self who was the author of those deeds. To hold another to account for deeds of *mine*, or to bind in advance without its consent or knowledge a self not identical with mine, would be wrong. This is thought to be because of what, we saw earlier, has the status of an unassailable conviction of commonsense moral intuition: I alone am responsible for my deeds (together with some of their foreseeable consequences); others alone for theirs.

Some champions of the normative considerations favoring individualism focus more strongly on how the self's oneness is presupposed by our emotions, reactions, and attitudes, rather than on these broader categories. These arguments are not unconnected: By establishing that appropriate ascriptions of blame and forgiveness presuppose a unitary self, we are capturing the moral categories of accountability and culpability, since such reactions and attitudes are usually understood to be rightly ascribed only when accountability and culpability are present. Similarly, by focusing on subjective states and reactions like guilt, contrition, and remorse, which seem to presuppose identity between past and present self stages, we also presuppose the culpability believed to be required for appropriate experience of such states. Despite these undeniable links, however, some thinkers have emphasized affective responses, or attitudes, rather than the moral categories with which they are usually associated, and these must be examined separately.

Time-Spanning Emotions of Self-Assessment

Recent attempts to defend more traditional notions of the self's identity against a metaphysical theory hospitable to successive selves, such as Parfit's, have proceeded along the lines just sketched, appealing to common emotions and outlining their dependency on the notion of a unitary self (Williams 1973, Madell 1981, Korsgaard 1989). A conception of persons as comprising a succession of "person phases" (Madell 1981, 116) would deprive our ordinary moral attitudes of their ground, it has been argued, and we would fail to make sense of a whole range of ordinary attitudes. It is unthinkable to suppose we could ever dispense with attitudes such as fear, praise, blame, gratitude, pride, remorse, shame, and guilt. Why should I fear pain? Why should I experience pride over an achievement? Why should I feel shame and guilt about my transgressions? These questions, the argument insists, have only one answer: because the pain, the achievement, the transgressions are *mine*.

Arguments such as these parallel Strawson's (1968) claim that the "reactive attitudes" we adopt toward others presuppose for their appropriate ascription that we see others as fully responsible agents. An argument of this kind does not always claim that the decision to relinquish some particular conceptual scheme results in incoherence. Rather, it may aim to show the cost of giving up the category in question in conceptual and linguistic terms, and in experiential richness.

While potentially compelling, this argument requires restatement. Several of these reactive attitudes are entirely compatible with the possibility that more than one self might inhabit the same body through time (Radden 1995). The breadth of pride and shame, for example, allows us feel these responses over the doings of others, as well as our selves. No barrier can thus stand in the way of our extending such attitudes to earlier or later self stages attached to the same body, however different they may be. One set of reactive attitudes, in contrast, are deeply recalcitrant to any but an individualistic notion of the self that has at least some span and continuity through time. These are remorse and contrition. We cannot rightly be said to suffer remorse or contrition over the deeds of another, i.e., a self attached to another spatiotemporal person. This makes it problematic, at the very least, to extend such attitudes to earlier or later selves inhabiting one's own body. Such reactive attitudes seem to depend on traditional identity presuppositions about the self. To the moral concepts and categories, such as responsibility and culpability, then, must be added these reactive attitudes that depend on the self's identity through time: remorse and contrition.

The Concept and Acknowledgment of Agency

Similar arguments have been mounted to show that not only the moral category of the agent but any concept of agency presupposes that there is a unitary self. Only because there are links between the antecedent (for example, a plan or intention I form) and the consequent (its being carried out by *me*) do I have reason to proceed from the one to the other, it has been argued (Reid 1785, Korsgaard 1989). Not only would the ascription of responsibility be lost with the loss of self identity, so too would any distinction between purposive and nonpurposive behavior. One philosopher, Christine Korsgaard, has put the point thus:

In order to make deliberative choices, your present self must identify with something from which you will derive your reasons, but not necessarily with something present. The sort of thing you identify yourself with may carry you automatically into the future and ... this will very likely be the case. Indeed, the choice of any action, no matter how trivial, takes you some way into the future. And to the extent that you regulate your choices by identifying yourself as the one who is implementing something like a particular plan of life, you need to identify with your future in order to be *what you are even now.* When the person is viewed as an agent, no clear content can be given to the idea of a merely present self. (Korsgaard 1989, 113–114)

Korsgaard offers several arguments in her important discussion of the self's unity, including some that speak more to the "pragmatic" necessity of our understanding the self as unified at a given time. The passage quoted captures a major argument for the self's oneness through time, or singularity. A merely present self cannot encompass or match the instigator of life plans and actions, whose perspective spans more than the present moment. The very notion of a self is of an entity we can view from some distance in time, looking not only backwards but forward as well.

The unitary self, it has been argued, is required for emotional reactions and attitudes and for moral categories. Now as the self emerges in Korsgaard's remarks, this argument construes the unitary self as necessary for agency understood in the barest and broadest sense. Any rational or purposive activity, decision, or action fundamentally requires temporal stretch, and this temporal stretch takes us some way into the future, as Korsgaard puts it.

It is not only our moral concepts and categories that seem to depend on the unitary self. More general features of our epistemological framework, such as extending judicious trust, also have been seen to call for something like a traditional conception of the self.

Judicious Trust

The presence of trust has been recognized by philosophers as a special kind of instrumental good, a precondition for both moral and epistemological practices and possibilities we value and rely upon. Annette Baier (1986, 1991) has demonstrated how the moral life and other moral concepts are grounded on attitudes of trust between persons and on the expectations those attitudes bring (see also Govier 1992, 1993). More recently, exploring the interdependence between persons required to yield knowledge, another philosopher, Lorraine Code (1991), has shown the role played by trust in this complex epistemic process. For most of what we know, Code argues, we depend on others. This requires that we know others and can trust them. It is as important for a would-be knower to be able to recognize when *someone else* knows and can be trusted, this argument insists, as it is for the knower to be able to demonstrate that she herself is knowledgeable. In fact, "the issue of establishing and relying on authority and expertise, morally, politically, and epistemologically, turns on questions about how to be appropriately judicious and circumspect in granting and withholding trust" (Code 1991, 182).

We trust in several different ways. We trust others not to change, to remain recognizable and reliable through time. In trusting them with our secrets and vulnerability, in trusting enough to believe what they say, promise, and do, we also depend on others' invariance, their sameness through time. And central to trusting others in these several ways is the other's actual, and not merely perceived, oneness. When these forms of trust are not injudiciously or blindly extended—when we are entitled to trust, that is—there needs to be, it seems, the one-ness between the other's earlier and later self stages captured in the notion of character.

If judiciously conferred trust depends on a unitary self in the way suggested, this is a compelling reason to maintain traditional notions of the self. It may even be more. Trust is a ubiquitous good, so pervasive as often to go unremarked. We inhabit a climate of trust, as Baier has observed, "as we inhabit an atmosphere" (1986, 234). Because trust is the fabric of social practices and everyday life, the specter of intercourse without it seems well-nigh incomprehensible.

Self-Understanding

Another good that allegedly depends on the self's oneness, and par-ticularly significant in discussions of therapeutic practice, is self-understanding, self-knowledge, or, as it is sometimes known, insight. This case has been put by Charles Taylor (1989) in the context of a strong endorsement of the self understood as one through time, not many.

Taylor's general thesis is that we cannot think of human persons without a certain "space" of value questions. The subject of such questions "generally and characteristically" is "the shape of my life *as a whole*." Self-understanding necessarily has temporal depth and in-corporates narrative, because my sense of myself is of a being who is growing and becoming, and in the very nature of things, "this cannot be instantaneous."

> It is not only that I need time and many incidents to sort out what is rela-tively fixed and stable in my character, temperament, and desires from what is variable and changing. . . . It is also that as a being who grows and becomes I can only know myself through the history of my maturations and regres-sions, overcomings and defeats. (Taylor 1989, 50)

If we accept Taylor's notion, self-understanding, that characteristi-cally human art and practice that stands at the center of much psy-chotherapeutic endeavor, requires that there be but one self to be understood.

A last normative consideration has not received the same atten-tion as the goods enumerated thus far. To these must be added a further variation: a unitary self is presupposed by any understanding of the moral life in terms of character, vices and virtues.

Vices and Virtues, and Their Moral Framework

The current revival of interest in ethical theories based on the virtues by philosophers like Annette Baier (1985b, 1986) Alastair MacIntyre (1981), and Michael Slote (1983) has emphasized the several significant respects in which a virtue-based morality is inimical to the rights-based deontological system associated with individualism. Yet virtue-based morality too is in its own way deeply individualistic. It presupposes and requires a notion of the self or person as (at least relatively) invariant through time. This is because, like personality theories of psychology, it involves dispositional analyses. To ascribe vices and virtues to a character, to understand as the proper subject of moral evaluation character and disposition rather than—or at least as well as—particular right or wrong actions is to acknowledge the presence of at least relatively stable and predictable states of the self. Pride, kindness, generosity, constancy, mendacity, selfishness, and a sense of justice are all dispositions, as is character itself. For those who value a virtue-based approach to the moral life or acknowledge the extent to which such an approach still enriches our present liberal, democratic culture, here is another normative consideration inviting us to speak as if there were a unitary self.

Earlier eras and other cultures, for instance, eighteenth-century western Europe, have embraced more fully than we do now a virtue-based approach to the moral life.[1] Twentieth-century moral thinking may place less emphasis than that of the eighteenth century on the understanding of the moral life expressed in talk of vices and virtues precisely because of the relative disunity and discontinuities of the self acknowledged in the twentieth century. Indeed, such thinking may have been partially responsible for this retreat from virtue-based systems.[2] Nevertheless, in the sphere of "private" morality, references may still be found to virtues and vices and to the other categories these concepts presuppose, such as character. Consider the eighteenth-century virtue of constancy, manifested in none other than the preservation of that continuity of self about which I have been speaking. And consider too integrity, embedded in which is the ideal of a self that is one and indivisible, as its derivation from the Latin *integritas*, for wholeness, attests.[3] We may no longer use the term 'constancy', but the kind of moral steadiness 'constancy' implies is still striven for and honored in others. And integrity remains respected and valued.[4]

In conclusion, then, vices and virtues, and character, constitute another sort of dependent good: concepts and categories that purportedly presuppose a unitary self.

Dependency Theses: Clinical Confirmation

The states and conditions associated with the radical fragmentation of self seem to provide some empirical confirmation of the alleged dependencies outlined here. The effects of severe brain damage or disease, and of extreme forms of mental disorder produce behavior that seems to bear no relation to the subject's mental life, and these present challenges to our usual notions of autonomy, responsibility, trust, and self-understanding. As our criminal law attests, the moral categories of guilt, culpability, and responsibility break down when we encounter serious mental disintegration of this kind, so mental illness is judged as an excusing condition, for example. The same seems broadly true, moreover, of emotional attitudes and of the virtues. Where we can speak of a self lost to extreme fragmentation, in the sense outlined, ascribing guilt, remorse, or gratitude seems to be a doubtful exercise. So too, indeed, does according moral virtues like integrity or courage to such a "person." Character ascriptions such as these presuppose much about the beliefs and desires of the individual; with severe fragmentation, such presuppositions seem unwarranted.

These illustrations from psychiatry serve to confirm at least one version of the dependency thesis: where all unity is absent, the concepts and categories enumerated here (moral categories; the time-spanning emotions, attitudes, and concepts of self-assessment, agency, judicious trust, self-understanding, vices, and virtues; and their moral theory) can gain no hold and must have no meaning. These concepts seem to require for their application at least a relatively united and coherent person. How united and coherent I try to establish in chapter 14.

Dependent "Goods": Are They Good?

The force of the general normative argument under consideration rests, I pointed out earlier, on a traditional evaluation of the "goods" enumerated above. As we have seen, virtues and vices and the notion of character, while they endure as a complement to other moral frameworks, are no longer as central to all moral understanding as in other cultures. This alone is a loss. But their elimination would diminish vastly our experience and understanding. Similarly, our lives and experience would be immeasurably impoverished without our concepts of responsibility, culpability, and accountability, along with the reactive attitudes that accompany them: praise, blame, contrition, guilt, and remorse. Not everyone would agree, however, and accept as unalloyed goods each moral category or emotion in this network of categories and concepts surrounding our ascriptions of responsibility. For example, Sarah Hoagland (1991), in undertaking a reconstruction of ethics and a new "ethic of intelligibility," has proposed that we renounce moral praise and blame, and relinquish the emphasis on justification and guilt that now attach to our notion of agency.[5]

Those prepared to relinquish or recast such categories as blame and guilt might yet hesitate before attempting to jettison the less moral and moralistic categories among the goods depending on a unified self. Whether or not it would be desirable, sacrificing the moral concepts and categories associated with responsibility seems comprehensible and within our imaginative capability. Some idea of what life without responsibility concepts would be like, it is sometimes suggested, may be derived from social-scientific writing and from the ostensibly neutral categories and concepts associated with modern-day psychotherapeutic theory and practice (though psychotherapeutic exercises are themselves deeply normative, as the next chapter will reveal).

It is considerably harder to comprehend how we might manage to do without the general categories, at once more neutral and more encompassing, of purposive action and judiciously conferred trust. Everyday life and psychotherapeutic practice in particular would be diminished without self-knowledge. But shorn of the categories of human action and judicious trust, life and psychotherapeutic practice may each be unintelligible.

In my view, maintaining of our traditional notion of the self's singularity through time is a small price to pay to avoid losing any of the dependent goods enumerated here. Such loss is a daunting prospect, and the sacrifice of these concepts and categories is one many would be unprepared to make. Yet the specter of this loss and sacrifice is one whose terror may have been somewhat exaggerated.

The goods enumerated here that depend on certain strands of individualism find elaboration in the goals adopted in therapeutic endeavor. To the extent that our valued concepts and categories depend on the unified self of individualism, so must these therapeutic goals. These goals must be explored more fully, and to this task I now turn.

13
Therapeutic Goals for a Liberal Culture

Our cultural allegiance to individualism can be found in much relating to the policies and practice of psychotherapy, but its clearest reflection is in the goals—explicit and implicit—that guide the course of therapy. These will be the subject of the present chapter. From a close-grained perspective, the goals of therapy probably match or exceed in number the patients and therapists who seek them. Moreover, these goals may differ even in a therapist-client conjunct among those attributable to the therapist and those attributable the client. Inasmuch as all therapy is interactive and personal to some degree, each of these ends presupposes a concept or concepts of the self and of personal or self identity. But of concern here are the proposed goals or ends of therapy that introduce individualistic notions of the self and self identity. The three broad goals examined here are each a recognizable reflection of the individualism that marks our liberal traditions: self-unity, self-knowledge or self-understanding, and self-determination or autonomy.

Normative tenets of individualism are reflected in central goals associated with therapeutic practice. Self-unity or integration, self-understanding or insight, and self-determination or autonomy, we will see, not only explicitly value unity over disunity but rest on a set of preconceptions and presuppositions about the self that seem to reject radical multiplicity.

The stage at which we intercept the therapeutic endeavor will affect what we see of the adoption of, and adherence to, these goals. The goals and sense or senses of self at play early and late in even short therapeutic engagements may well shift and develop with alterations in the client's needs, circumstances, and conception of the project. Another factor affecting the adoption of these goals is the severity of the mental condition involved. When therapy is offered to more disturbed patients, the most immediate and pragmatic goals are usually sought: reducing mental suffering or self-destructive behavior, increasing practical capabilities related to day to day living. Taken at face value, functional criteria like these are compatible with a number of different theories of self. Ostensibly functional criteria are not always simply functional, though. Sometimes they are nested in more theoretically ambitious ends, like the goal of increasing client self-determination or autonomy. Nor are functional goals only sought in therapy with more severely disturbed patients: in seeking to maximize their potential in love and work, less disturbed clients desire such ends too. But these clients are searching for improved versions of themselves, while the aspirations of the disturbed are often more modest: a return to an earlier state of functioning.

I introduced several of the more theoretically weighty desiderata of the therapeutic endeavor in my discussion of paternalistic intervention. Alleged reasons to override the immediate wishes of a mentally disturbed person include self-determination, autonomy, and enhanced authenticity achieved through a return of the patient to an earlier state. A rather different set of goals are found in so-called "insight therapies," where self-knowledge or self-understanding are sought. Alternatively, we may distinguish integration as a separable goal: the idea that the parts, phases, or aspects of a person may be woven together into a whole that is more coherent or unified than before.[1]

The popularity of these three goals is a reflection of the normative tug of individualism. The self we value in our individualistic culture is one, not many. It is defined by and celebrated for its freedom and autonomy. And finally, a tradition we can trace to the Socratic source of our Western cultural and philosophical heritage requires of us that we seek self-knowledge, and self-understanding. To have identified as goals or ends self-unity, self-knowledge and self-determination, then, is not to have named universal values or ends. These goals are particularly fitting for, and perhaps in some cases peculiar to, our late twentieth-century, English-speaking liberal culture. They may not travel widely beyond this context, either metaphysically or normatively. Other cultures have relied and continue to rely on differing notions of the self. They also embrace different values.

As they are encountered in clinical practice, these three goals are more closely entwined than their enumeration here suggests. The patient hopes both to be given self-knowledge and to be more closely integrated (she hopes, indeed, for almost everything).[2] Moreover, these goods are judged to be related as instruments to an end. Through enhanced self-determination comes the realization of both pragmatic goals related to day-to-day living skills and more lofty and abstract improvements.

Notions like integration, self-determination, and self-knowledge or insight are loose and vague, and the relationships between them multistranded and complex. Each of the goals identified here will be analyzed in the context of particular therapeutic practices and theory. Integration finds its starkest contrast in those suffering some of the most literal disintegration: multiples. Psychoanalytic practice directs itself most persistently and wholeheartedly to the goal of self-understanding or insight. And we will examine self-determination in the context of therapeutic intervention with those engaging in self-defeating or self-destructive behavior patterns.

A normative question arises with the introduction of these goals: are these values worth having? Inasmuch as integration and self-knowledge each entails valuing greater self unity, they may be seen to draw appeal from the normative enticements of individualism introduced earlier. Some degree of unity and continuity is believed to be necessary for states and ends we normally prize in our culture. At least traditional concepts of responsibility and the attendant attitudes and ascriptions of blame, forgiveness, reproach, and praise, together with concepts of agency, trust, character, and virtue, seem to call for a degree of psychological continuity incompatible with the fragmentary and disconnected self phases of the untreated multiple. Thus, more practical and functional advantages aside, some therapy may be judged to be desirable for these other reasons. However, a fuller analysis of the worth of each of these goals, and the normative issues embedded in their use in practice, is beyond the scope of this book.

A critical further question concerning professional ethics, of course, intrudes on any discussion of the goal of treatment—will the treatment achieve the goal desired? This question is not necessarily obviated once it is understood that the patient or client undertook the therapy willingly and knowingly. It does not go away even if there was complete "informed consent." Regardless of the client's attitude, it is at least arguable that the therapist's obligations will or should be affected by his or her own understanding of the likely outcomes of therapy. This ethical concern is important and complex because of the difficulty of proving what the outcome(s) of therapy are. However, it is an empirical issue that we will put aside here.[3]

Seeking Integration in the Dissociative Disorders

Unity and integration are much-voiced ends, shared by a number of different kinds of therapeutic endeavor. Standing as they do at the center of the individualism that marks our culture and its institutions, they convey many things, all desirable. Speaking of the yield of successful psychoanalysis, Roy Schafer has described a "more unified, subjective self." Such a self, he explains, would have "more room in it for undisguised pleasure, but also for control, delay, decisive renunciation, remorse, mourning, memories, anticipation, ideals, moral standards, and more room too for a keen sense of real challenges, dangers and rewards in one's current existence" (Schafer 1976, 33).

The more unified subjective self is, for Schafer, the expansive autonomous self, the self of passion and vitality—a paragon of human experiencing. I will focus discussion here, however, on the treatment offered a rather different patient or client group than those whom Schafer assists in their quest for self unity: the sufferers of dissociative identity disorder. Because dissociation, separation, disunity, and fracture constitute the defining traits of these patients' condition, closer integration is not just one, but often the central and even sole, goal of the therapeutic endeavors undertaken with them. In these general terms, we may say that treatment approaches have differed little since Prince's efforts to discover, integrate, and elevate the real Miss Beauchamp (see pages 50–51). Moreover, the modest unity and integration that therapists seek on behalf of multiples—then and now—retains clear, literal, and descriptive meaning. The urgent task of therapy, it is widely agreed, must be the integration of the separate personality elements into one transparent self.[4] Therapy must be directed toward making available to "the entire system of personalities the knowledge and secrets held by specific alter personalities," as one authority has it (Putnam 1989, 115).

As a goal for therapy with multiples, integration is often justified in terms of the improved function it yields. Just as concern over social and occupational dysfunction most commonly brings the multiple to seek help, so achieving these practical goals is most commonly appealed to in descriptions of successful treatment.[5] Less often in these cases, perhaps, is integration justified as lessening psychic pain and suffering. (It is not clear that it always does, at least in the short term (Putnam 1989).

The desired integration or "fusion" must serve to bring together the different personality elements at a time and through time.[6] First consider this goal as it may be understood at a given moment. Integration effects a kind of permeability between hitherto separated centers of awareness, so that each of the subselves or alters comes to know what happens at any given time not only in the external world, through perception, but also in the inner world of that spatio-temporal individual's other locus, or loci, of awareness. Successful integration is often described by appeal to the epistemological notion of coconsciousness. When there is *coconsciousness* between two selves *A* and *B*, on Braude's (1991, 77) analysis, *A* is "cosensory" and/or "intraconscious" with *B*. (*A* is *cosensory* with *B* when both *A* and *B* seem to be simultaneously aware of external events, such as sights and sounds; *A* is *intraconscious* with *B* when *A* claims knowledge of *B*'s mental states.) Braude's taxonomy allows us to recognize additional distinctions concerning action. *A* is *intraactive* with *B* when *A* can influence *B*'s experience or behavior, and *A* is *copresent* with *B* when *A* and *B* appear to share executive control of the body.

At the least, then, integration is understood as involving *A*'s becoming intraconscious and/or cosensory with *B*, and thus coconscious with *B*. But ambiguity remains. Is the outcome or product sought one self or a confederacy of several all-knowing, all-controlling selves? The notion of coconscious integration invites further interpretation, or at least terminological clarification. The integration of selves *A*, *B*, and *C* may be said to result in a new creation, *Y*, which is a composite of, but distinct from, the self comprising traits of *A*, *B*, and *C*. Some accounts of therapeutically effected successful integration seem to suggest this model.[7]

The mere notion of coconsciousness, however, implies something rather less: the coexistence of *A*, *B*, and *C*, unchanged except in respect of their epistemic relations to one another. This is the confederacy model, and some descriptions appear to identify the achievement of integration or fusion with such a state.[8]

Finally, there is a more radical conception of this process whereby some of *A*, *B*, and *C* are actively eliminated through integration.[9] Thus in Prince's case (1906), some of his patient's characters or selves were "killed," eliminated to secure the ascendancy of the "real" Christine Beauchamp. Writing in contemporary times, Irving Yalom (1989) portrays a "cannibalistic" process in which one self, Marge, was expanded and fattened by absorbing and adopting traits of another self, "me." In revealing how this work with multiples challenges the therapist's loyalties and raises questions of what he calls "therapeutic monogamy," Yalom describes how he determined where his loyalties lay and resolved to eliminate "me": "The moment demanded a decision, and I chose to stand by Marge. I would sacrifice her rival to her, pluck her feathers, pull her asunder, and, bit by bit, feed her to Marge" (1989, 226).

Integration is also understood in relation to stretches of time. It involves recasting past experience so that a sense of continuity through time is recognized—or superimposed. As Putnam describes it, the patient must come to view past experience as a continuous whole, rather than as "flashes and fragments of memory," and the therapist "must help the patient assimilate his/her past history as a continuous experience and memory while integrating the new continuous sense of self that now runs through the course of events" (1989, 318).

The means by which these goals or ends are effected themselves throw some light on the notions of self and identity presupposed in such descriptions. The goal of complete integration, whether or not understood in any of the ways outlined above, is explicitly raised and discussed in therapy, naturally. But the method of integration must be incremental and seemingly indirect. Coconsciousness is often sought by means of hypnotism. Partial fusions between selves most like each other are sometimes effected, after much preparation, by the use of ritual (Putnam 1989). Subselves must learn, as Putnam puts it, "a sense of self-identification" (1989, 308). They must learn a new sense of identity and, in some cases, it would seem, a sense of their new identity. This process is not portrayed as one of reintegration or recovery of a prior wholeness now lost, notice. So early was the trauma effecting the self's dissociation in these cases, it seems now widely believed, that little previous integration may have been achieved (Putnam 1989, Kluft 1982, Braun 1984). Moreover, it is shared memory, as well as qualitative similarity of personality, that marks the more integrated self. *B* must learn not only that *A*'s tastes and style are hers but also that *A*'s memories are her memories too.

Finally, something may be learned from the emphasis on the subjective sense of continuity and oneness necessary for such integration. Putnam speaks of developing and, after fusion has been effected, of "firmly rooting" and "consolidating" the patient's new sense of internal unity so as to achieve "a new and more integrated sense of personal identity" (1989, 316). Making use of Braude's (1991) distinction between indexical and autobiographical states we may say that an expansion is sought among autobiographical as well as indexical states for each self.

This emphasis on the patient's subjective response and understanding of her unity or continuity through time is not merely a decision to favor the introspective account, however. Abnormal psychology is a scientific discipline with claims to objectivity, and therapists working with multiplicity of this kind require public verification of the integration they seek. (Public verification is particularly necessary in this area, it has been pointed out, because patients may pretend or imagine fusion to please an eager therapist.) Thus psychologists have devised and use tests for integration that attempt to go beyond the subjective (Kluft 1984a). This emphasis on developing the sense of unity in the patient, then, must spring from the role that subjective sense plays in promoting the publicly verifiable oneness sought. Only when the patient feels herself to be a unity through time, we might put it, will the necessary unity of experience and continuity of personality and memory prevail, and also reveal themselves to others.

Self-Knowledge in Insight Therapies

Today we have lost the Platonic confidence that knowledge alone ensures right action. So greater self-knowledge in the patient or client is usually not or perhaps never judged to be a demonstration of therapeutic effectiveness. Self-knowledge may in principle function as an end in itself and be seen as an intrinsic good, as it is, for instance, by Charles Taylor (see page 203). But in the context of the goals of therapy, self-knowledge is more often judged to have instrumental value. Certainly this was true for the psychoanalysis from which most contemporary psychotherapies derive. Rather than as intrinsically valuable, Freud saw the new knowledge gained through psychoanalysis as instrumental in enhancing our ability to love and work. It is worth seeking because it is applicable to conduct.

Functional goals, then, are closely entwined with the notion of insight, as they are with integration, we saw. This requires answers to empirical and pragmatic questions. How much can knowing affect doing? What kind of self-knowledge is most helpful to further the functional goals we seek? Although I will not explore the complex correlations required for a thorough empirical treatment of this inquiry, we must acknowledge one proposed conceptual connection that gives confidence in the practical efficacy of self-knowledge and demonstrates another entwining of the broad goals under discussion. Autonomy, in the sense of acting unaided, is apparently a separate aim of much therapy (as such, it will be explored later in this chapter). Autonomy is linked with self-knowledge: the kind of self-knowledge or self-understanding that therapy allows us to achieve is believed to enhance or increase our autonomy or self-determination. It allows us both to act without restraint and to act from a unified and coherent motivational structure. This correlation permeates discussion and theory about insight therapy. Interpreting the ideas of Spinoza, Stuart Hampshire has argued that we are free to the highest degree when we are engaged in an intellectual inquiry whose subject is the order of our own thoughts "as an instance of something that may be understood *sub specie aeternitatis,* and not as it is affected by particular causes in the common order of nature" (Hampshire 1968, 60). Thus, "the more the sequence of a man's own ideas can be explained without reference to causes outside his own thinking, the more active and self-determining he is, regarded as a thinking being.... The more self-determining and active he is, and the more free, in this sense of 'free', the more he can be regarded as a real individual" (Hampshire 1968, 55).

Self-knowledge is related to the therapeutic goal of integration, and to the central liberal notion of the self's unity, as well. Insight gained is often represented as learning of hitherto unconscious states of mind, so the work of insight therapy is in important respects analogous to efforts to achieve fusion in the integration of multiples. The divided self reflects separated awarenesses and separate agent sources. What is desired is a state of translucency. A state of translucency ensures some form of unity.

An interesting conundrum arises here, however. The discovery of conflicts hitherto unknown to us may be said to replace one disunity, observed from without, with another, experienced from within. My initial state of believing *p* may be rendered more heterogenous and conflicting through the revelation of a hitherto unconscious belief implying not *p*. Short of some theory of cognitive dissonance that would have us naturally disposed to reduce conflicts and inconsistencies in our beliefs and desires upon recognizing them, self-knowledge brings something equivalent to coconsciousness without necessarily ensuring unanimity. The unity achieved through insight is not so perfect and complete as to admit of no conflict.

This point may be revealingly exhibited if we return again to clinical discussions of the therapeutic endeavors required with multiples. The "mopping up" operations involved after permanent fusion has been effected include helping the patient or client to deal with mixed feelings and ambivalence. Previously, dissociative barriers prevented such experience of division and disunity which, for less deeply fractured selves, is a subjective commonplace. The multiple must discover the gentler heterogeneity associated with being of two minds (Putnam 1989).

What understanding of the self is presupposed here? Distinct epistemological models of the process of gaining self-knowledge or insight emerge from descriptions of the therapeutic endeavor, each with a slightly differing answer to this question. The continuity of the self across time as determined from within, or subjectively, may be seen primarily as created or constructed by the intellectual effort of insight. On this view, the self is a product of the imagination as much as, or more than, it is derived from remembrance or recollection. (Interestingly, this view comports with certain contemporary philosophical theories about the self: in its telling, we forge the narrative that is our lives and makes our selves (Dennett 1988, 1989, 1991; Flanagan 1992).

Alternatively, we may stress the visual metaphor suggested by 'insight', so that an "inner sense" is presupposed.[10] Kant postulated an ability to scan the internal horizon, just as with our five perceptual senses we scan the outer one. Such a metaphor is realist in tone. It conveys that inner states, the objects of inner sense perception, correspond to the outer, spatiotemporal world, which comprises the objects of outer sense perception. The patient or client is sometimes portrayed as exercising her inner sense. Through therapy she is assisted in uncovering or identifying unconscious mental states, early memories and recollections, and other psychological dispositions in a process close to discovery.

The practice of psychoanalysis in particular has been associated with this second, "discovery" epistemology. In a recurrent metaphor employed by Freud, the task of analysis was "archeological." The graphic notion of the *return* of the repressed and, indeed, much else of Freud's metapsychology invite us to see the process of therapy as one of discovery, rediscovery, and recovery of what was once present to consciousness and later lost. Just as field archaeologists uncover the artifacts of past reality, so, on Freud's notion, psychoanalysts disclose historical facts about the patient's mind and experience.

While he employed the archeological metaphor, however, it was also Freud who introduced what most urgently invites the contrary understanding of insight: the notion of a screen memory, or fantasy. For Freud, the pathological symptom was not only a reflection of a wish or impulse, rather than an actual historical event; it was subject to further distortion through the same processes of displacement and condensation we find in dreams. By such processes it became unrecognizably transformed. Moreover, in the carefully wrought clinical tales Freud tells, he must be seen as appealing to a kind of "narrative" truth, Donald Spence and others have shown (Spence 1984, Lear 1990). In contrast to historical truth, which is time-bound and dedicated to the strict observance of correspondence rules between propositions and the world, narrative truth relies on coherence. Interpretations are persuasive not, or not merely, because of their likely truth but because they make sense and hang together. Conviction emerges, as Spence puts it, not because we have necessarily made contact with the past but "because the fit is good" (Spence 1984, 32). A master at taking pieces of the patient's associations, dreams, and memories and "weaving them into a coherent pattern that allows us to make important discoveries about the patient's life and to make sense out of previously random events" (Spence 1984, 21), Freud made us aware of the persuasive power of coherent narrative.

In a more extreme constructivist position, Hacking (1995) has argued for the indeterminacy of the past itself. Rather than portraying the past accurately or distortedly, he insists, we make it up in the act of "remembering." Our reconstructions "may not have been true in the past" (Hacking 1995, 249).

The reconstruction and transformation involved in psychoanalysis and other forms of psychotherapy are thus today acknowledged to be creative, selective, and interpretive—a complex synthesis of psychological reality and historical actuality. The relation of self-knowledge to historical reality (which events occurred), and even to earlier psychological reality (how things seemed at that time), is at best complex and tenuous.

Which of these contrasting discovery and construction epistemologies better reflects what takes place during therapy does not depend only on the conception of therapy adopted, however. Some therapy is avowedly "abreactive." In calling for the uncovering of repressed traumatic memories, it must necessarily resemble more closely the discovery model. But abreactive therapy, thus understood, is applied only to particular patient groups. When describing their early work with hysteria, Freud and Breuer (1955) observed that some patients suffer primarily from "reminiscences," for which discovery therapies are apt. Not all patients suffer from hysteria, to which abreactive therapies are suited.

A group of patients whose apparent memories of trauma seemed at first most urgently to require abreaction in the discovery sense was multiples, whose condition we have explored earlier in this chapter. Dissociative-identity disorder, or as it was then known, multiple-personality disorder, was seen as a form of chronic post-traumatic stress disorder, based on exogenous childhood trauma (Kluft 1983, 1984a, 1984b, 1986). Part of the work of integration is clearly "archeological": producing coconsciousness, we saw, involves discovering actual but hidden experiences and memories. Yet even here there has been a recent shift in understanding the abreaction used in the treatment of sufferers of dissociative disorders: emphasis has been directed toward the narrative truth, rather than the historical truth, to be found in patients' accounts of their early trauma. Moreover, there is recognition that the distortion and construction of nonfactual "memories" is likely to be greater among this group of patients, who are highly hypnotizable and vulnerable to distortion effects (Ganaway 1989).

These observations suggest at least that the conceptual distinction between the archeological discovery and fantasy-based construction epistemologies is blurred in real-life therapeutic settings. Here elements of each model blend and merge: no interpretation, memory, or reported experience is an unproblematic reflection of historical fact. (The recent extrapolation from the preceding observations to today's memory wars, while of political and legal significance, has added little to our understanding of the tension between these two different epistemologies.)

Helping the Client Help Herself: The Value of Self-Determination

The freedom of the self-determining individual and the self-determined life is judged as a central ingredient for liberal societies, a sine qua non of democratic systems. And perhaps more than any other, the goal of enhanced self-determination, or as it is sometimes termed, autonomy, is constant across different therapeutic approaches and techniques and different patient and client categories and needs. In a recent discussion of the values of psychotherapy, Holmes and Lindley quote with approval from a guide to would-be therapy subjects: "The only value that can be emphasized in the selection and conduct of a therapy is the pursuit of free, autonomous choice. Neurosis enslaves" (1989, 52).

Self-determination sometimes is regarded as an end in itself, a good that requires no justification. It is also judged as the end toward which other instrumental goods, such as insight, are directed. As a general capacity, it is valued as a means to more specific goods and a precondition of other qualities we cherish. Thus if enhanced self-determination involves acquiring a consistent and coherent set of intentions and values, these are seen to aid in the realization of more pragmatic and particular goals of day-to-day living and in the promotion of individual well-being. Finally, self-determination is treated as a precondition of something else we particularly value: responsibility. If the individual's action is self-determined, that individual may rightly be held responsible for it.[11]

What is included in the expression 'self-determination'? Certainly we are familiar with what is not self-determined: behavior not freely chosen. Such behavior may stem from forces within the person that are unknown to the self of conscious awareness or motivationally at odds with that self's goals (as in compulsive action). Or they may derive from outside the self. Neurosis enslaves, but so too does slavery. When not self-determined, behavior is sometimes determined by others, literally and immediately, as in enslavement, and also psychologically and mediately, through manipulation, coercion, or brainwashing, for example. It seems plausible to extend this notion of constraints and acknowledge that any hindrance preventing the realization of her goals and desires, including economic and social constraints, renders a person less than fully self-determining or self-determined. Customarily, however, psychotherapy has concerned itself with eliminating constraints that are psychological and self-originating. As one contemporary discussion explains it, those who choose psychotherapy as a solution are frustrated not by their circumstances but by themselves (Holmes and Lindley 1989).

Thus far my portrayal of self-determination has been compatible with the view that it is what distinguishes free and voluntary action from what is unfree or involuntary. And so self-determination is often understood when it is sought in therapy. Here self-determination is an attribute of voluntary actions. Compulsive, self-destructive, haphazard, impulsive actions and actions that are the products of defensive fantasy and of delusion lack the quality of self-determination in being less than free. The task of much therapeutic intervention is to improve the patient's or client's behavior act after act by reducing or eliminating the elements that stand in the way of each act being free, or voluntary, in some minimal respect.

But as a goal of therapy, self-determination is also construed more fully. Autonomy, in the context of psychotherapy, implies "taking control of one's life" (Holmes and Lindley 1989, 52). And concealed

within that phrase lies a more complex ideal. Self-determination becomes a quality of *lives*, or stretches of lives, and not merely of individual actions. Action that are self-determined will be woven together
with other actions, linked and interconnected through their reflection
of long-term dispositions and traits, values and goals, principles and
policies.

Hierarchical desire theories are again helpful here (Frankfurt
1971; Wolf 1980, 1987, 1990). Humans alone experience second-
order desires, desires about which desires they want for themselves,
Frankfurt has argued. And these second order desires are involved
when we seek self-determination: a coherent set of wishes and intentions about who we are, or want to become, and what shape we
would like to see our lives take; what we want to want. Freedom of
the will, as Frankfurt understands it, occurs when the hierarchy of our
desires permits us to act on our second-order desires.[12]

Also useful here is terminology introduced by Diana Meyers
(1989), who distinguishes *episodic* from *programmatic* or *life-plan* autonomy. When it encompasses more than the quality of voluntariness
minimally construed (Meyer's episodic autonomy) and approaches
programmatic or life-plan autonomy, self-determination resembles the
more political notion of self-government. Indeed, contexts where we
speak of self-determination or self-government for a nation or group
yield useful analogies for our analysis here. National self-determination sometimes conveys the idea of obedience to rules or laws that
persist over time and shape the life of a political entity, a people, say.
Colonial or foreign domination forms one contrast with the self-
governing, self-determined state, tyranny forms another, and anarchy
yet another. A people are self-governing in one respect when they
have shaken off the yoke of a tyrant's power; they are self-governing
in a fuller way, however, only when they subject themselves to some
kind of self-government, with all that this conveys: laws and regu-
lations, procedures and institutions. A state of anarchy may be said to
be a state of freedom. But no group enjoys the full freedom of self-
government or self-determination without rules and rule-governed
order. By analogy, we may say, to ascribe self-determination or self-
government to an individual's action is to imply that more than mere
voluntariness or freedom attaches to that action.

This fuller meaning of self-determination corresponding to Meyers's "programmatic autonomy" is central to its role in mental health. Buchanan and Brock, for example, in their work on substituted judgment in psychiatric settings (1989), emphasize how our human capacity for reflective self-evaluation, for considering and deciding on what kind of lives we want to lead and what kind of persons we want to become, invites the conclusion that it is part of our telos as humans (it is, as they say, good for humans) to make significant decisions about their lives themselves. Since they marshal normative arguments of this kind in support of the value of self-determination, Buchanan and Brock clearly view an action as self-determined in relation to its place in a life or a stretch of a life that has this quality.

How must we understand the self when self-determination or autonomy are proposed as the goals of therapy? The category of voluntariness (or episodic autonomy) brings fewer presuppositions about the self and its enduring values and second-order desires. An action may be voluntary while contravening some self-imposed policy. When I willfully disregard my earlier resolve to finish some undesirable task, my action may reveal lack of tenacity or even moral fiber, but not of voluntary capacity. Acting on a whim or impulse, acting, as we say, for "no reason" (in choosing a flavor, for example), we nonetheless act voluntarily (although it may be true, as Frankfurt [1971] insists, that the creature incapable of *any* but these "wanton" acts would be less than a person). A modicum of continuity between self stages seems required even for this voluntary action. We would not distinguish acting on a whim or acting impulsively from acting for reasons unless there were some basis for the contrast. And acting for reasons presupposes that there are enduring agent patterns and traits, motivations not merely of the moment but effective through longer stretches of time. The continuity requirements for whimful or impulsive action, in contrast, are fewer, and less.[13]

The self that is self-determining is the author of second-order desires about what it wants for itself. Developing this hierarchical view, Susan Wolf (1980, 1987, 1990) has entitled the self-determining self in compliance with whose second-order desires and values that we use to revise, correct, and improve ourselves the "real self." Presupposed here are certain identifiable traits, dispositions, and agent patterns that are part of, or ascribable to, the self. By their nature as dispositional states, these must be invariant through time. A constantly changing psychological flux would not provide sufficient stability for the foresight and planning required by self-determination. The person who enjoys or achieves some degree of self-determination possesses a self with considerable continuity, whether viewed from the public perspective or from the subjective perspective.

Does self-determination also require that the unified and relatively continuous self be introspectively recognized to extend through time and be felt to do so? Does a concept of self as enduring underlie this notion? It seems so. To be self-determining, one must be able to recognize, and to be aware or capable of becoming aware, that one's decisions and actions spring from a coherent cluster of values and beliefs. Moreover, it is to recognize these values and beliefs attributable to oneself as somewhat settled, constant, and unchanging through time. Self-determining policies, principles, and rules are temporally extended: they span a number of occasions and require a degree of consistency across time.

To sum up, then, the degree of continuity between past and present self stages required for claims of sameness or invariance increases with one's realization of, and thus are presupposed in one's adherence to, the ideal of self-determination. They decrease as we shift to the ascription of mere voluntariness or episodic autonomy. But this is a relative judgment: some degree of continuity is presupposed even in the slimmest description of voluntary action, and while more continuity or invariance seems to be demanded for self-determination, understood in the full sense sketched here, than for voluntariness, minimally understood, yet the degree of continuity or invariance required for self-determination is not so great as to preclude shifts through time on the part of the self-determined and self-determining individual.

Finally, what normative understanding of self is implicit in self-determination? Nancy Chodorow (1986) has coined the term 'relational individualism' to characterize a tenet of object-relations psychology that resonates through much contemporary thought: the self of relational individualism is embedded in the world of social relations.[14]

This concept has application whether we speak of the concept of self or of the person's self concept, understood subjectively. My identity, in the richer sense this term acquires when I distinguish myself as unique, may be deeply socially embedded, so that when my relationships alter, I no longer judge myself the same person. Changes in the lives of others centrally affect who I am and who I become. An individual's own sense of self will be variously relational between one person and another person (and perhaps even between earlier and later selves or self stages).

Much in past writing about the self-determination and autonomy sought through therapy has championed the "autonomous" individual rejected in today's emphasis on relational individualism. And the notion of autonomy still carries some of the nonrelational connotations of acting and deciding in isolation. But the isolation of the traditional autonomous self of the liberal tradition and of—it is now acknowledged—rather exclusively male experience and definition has been challenged in two ways. For their development, selves are not so isolated and independent as this portrait of autonomy suggests, it has been argued (Gilligan 1982, 1986; Gilligan, Lyons, and Hanmer 1990; Gilligan, Ward, and Taylor 1988; Chodorow 1986, 1989; Benhabib 1987). If in maturity they become so isolated, moreover, they ought not to: their isolation and independence represents a weakness or insufficiency. The autonomous and isolated self of liberal tradition decides and acts alone to determine the life of an individual defined and understood in social isolation. In better accord with both moral and mental-health norms is the self of relational individualism, which may decide and act in community to determine the life of an individual defined and understood relationally.

This is not to say that the more relational self will not undergo and/or understand personal change through time in a distinctive way. A socially embedded self experiences and understands herself and her identity relationally. Changes in the social world within which she is embedded will affect her self identity, and her publicly observable responses and behavior will reflect these changes. Through a new friendship or the death of a parent, a different "self" may emerge. Perhaps the more separate individual of traditional liberalism and of traditional male self-description would be less vulnerable to personal transformation through the rearrangement of his social constellation. But part of the message of the relationalist revisions I have been discussing is that he is more affected than his distorted self-identity would show.

Relational individualism, then, is at least compatible with continuity and an identity-conserving survival threshold. But it may be more. In entering, and constituting myself through, relationships, I extend my self boundaries in several dimensions. With the added knowledge, experience, and feeling that social relations bring, I expand, on some metaphorical measure. But I also adopt a series of new temporal relations, subjectively speaking. Knowledge of my friends or child's past memories adds to the complexity of my memory. My child's future extends and in some ways becomes mine. Obscure and complex as these self extensions are, they suggest that the relational individual may have a need for, and be constituted of, at least as much continuity and temporal stretch as the isolated self of traditional individualism.

Rather than being neutral, psychotherapeutic practice is a deeply normative endeavor, committed to, and vested in, the values of individualism. Not only those whose clinical practice concerns the extremes of self fracture examined in this book but all who participate in psychotherapeutic endeavors have a stake in the answer to the question asked next: how much continuity is required for the normative concepts and categories we value?

Continuity Sufficient for Individualism

What if, tempted by the extreme cases of multiplicity found in abnormal psychology and spurred by the applicability of the language of successive selves to such cases, we are drawn to an identity-multiplying metaphysics? Is much at stake? What of the therapeutic goals of unity, self-knowledge, and self-determination, reflecting the individualism to which our liberal society and values have been so wedded? What of our moral concepts and responses? Must we abandon talk of virtues and character?

In assessing the attractions of the dependency theses concerning the normative tug of individualism, several distinct questions need to be separated. To begin with, I will ask whether our valued moral concepts and categories require the strict numerical identity and unifying subject of Cartesian and Kantian metaphysics. The answer, we will see, is that they apparently do not. For flexibility in neo-Humean theories of the self permit us to adopt a perfectly singularity-conserving survival threshold that would in no way alter traditional identity presumptions. In this chapter, two further inquiries are pursued. First, would we lose our moral concepts and categories if we adopted a language and metaphysics that allowed us to speak of multiplicity and succession only in rare and extreme cases? Our customary responses will put to rest the concern expressed in this question. Our concepts and categories do prove inapplicable and incoherent when we confront the extremes of multiplicity like those exhibited in dissociative-identity disorder, yet because these anomalous cases represent such a rare extreme, our concepts and categories are not threatened, diminished, or unseated by them. A second question then follows: would we lose our moral concepts and categories if we adopted a language and metaphysics permitting us to speak of a degree of multiplicity and succession in most or all ordinary lives as well? I will argue that some modest degree of multiplicity and succession may indeed be compatible with almost all of our valued concepts and categories, so long as such succession remains orderly, predictable, and shared.

There are misapprehensions and overstatement in arguments about the normative tug of individualism. Once resolved, they leave us free to embrace a notion of psychological continuity sufficient for many, at least, of the concepts and categories we value, such as agency, moral categories, trust, the notion of character and of the virtues, integrity, self-understanding, unity, and self-determination or autonomy. These assorted goods, we saw, are purported to depend on the unitary self of the "one to a customer" rule. And it is true and important that these assorted goods call for at least a moderate degree of self-continuity. But the invariance, and thus continuity, of self that such goods allegedly require has been exaggerated. Moreover, within a threshold hospitable to a language and metaphysics of successive selves for the extreme mental disorders in which we are interested, the normal selves encountered in everyday life will almost always remain unities. For normal selves are relatively invariant. The exception is instances of personality or character change due to religious or ideological conversion. But such cases combine with the successive selves of abnormal psychology to form a small class.

Perhaps our prized concepts and categories would be jeopardized were we to adopt a threshold that allowed us to see most ordinary lives as fractured into a series of selves. But the more "conservative" (identity-conserving) threshold required by our commitment to the language and metaphysics of successive selves for the special cases of multiplicity noted here seems to represent little threat to our norms.

Each of the group of dependency theses introduced in chapter 13 asserts that there is a valuable category or concept that requires the self's identity through time. These theses are associated with attempts to maintain the very strongest notion of strict personal identity for the self, the identity associated with a Cartesian soul or Kantian transcendental subject. In this respect, however, they distort the important insight they would recognize. So long as an identity-conserving threshold ensures the traditional identity assumption of the "one to a customer" rule, an empirical self loosely held together by one or several psychological continuities—memory and consciousness, psychological states, personality traits—will equally suffice to ensure the goods we cherish. So too, we will discover, will a threshold permitting some modest succession of selves inhabiting the same spatiotemporal body during its lifetime.

Continuity Sufficient for Agency

The supposition that a lifetime span is required to sustain agency as an intelligible concept and category would seem to rest on the idea that because some is better than none, much more than some is better than some. But this is mistaken. The features of human agency linking earlier and later moments of a life, thought and action, plan and execution, expectation and outcome, need not span a human lifetime to be meaningful. We make and execute plans for an hour away or a day or five years, and to do so seems to require the same concept of agency, and all it implies, as the one we employ when we plan for a lifetime.

The significant distinction here is between the invariance of traits, and thus continuity, that is sufficient for preserving of categories and concepts like that of agency, and that which is insufficient. And while there can be found a degree of self fracture or discontinuity insufficient for the application of these concepts and categories, sufficient invariance or continuity may involve a good deal less than the lifetime span associated with the notion of perfect or numerical identity.

One aspect of valuing agency is valuing a lifetime of devotion to a single goal, idea, or cause, it is true. This point has been emphasized by MacIntyre, who quotes with approval Kierkegaard's remark that purity of heart is to will one thing. On this notion of singleness of purpose throughout a whole life, MacIntryre comments that it "can have no application unless that of a whole life does" (MacIntyre 1981, 189).

Admitting the possibility of successive selves does not preclude the possibility that in some instances a single self may inhabit the same body for that body's lifetime. But 'willing one thing' must also be understood as willing one thing for a stretch of time within a human lifetime. The related concept of wholeheartedness will serve to clarify my point. Frankfurt has argued that when coherence and harmony mark our second-order desires—desires about what we want to want—we reach a condition of wholeheartedness (Frankfurt 1987). The plan, once mapped, will be wholeheartedly sought, i.e., without the introduction of conflicting or alternative desires and goals. Yet not all plans and goals to which we give wholehearted allegiance are life plans, without variance in direction or purpose until death. Short- and medium-term plans and goals too may be embraced and sought wholeheartedly. The lives and stories of some of our revered exemplars reveal a Kierkegaardian lifelong singleness of purpose (in their devotion to God, perhaps) or a falling short while striving for such an ideal. Yet other lives, in contrast, are radically and willfully fractured, by ideological conversion and circumstantial possibilities. They reveal interruptions of continuity and contrasting goals and projects severally embraced and sought wholeheartedly.

The Kierkegaardian ideal has been interestingly challenged by Mary Catherine Bateson, who associates it with monotheism and male experience:

But what if we recognize the capacity for distraction, the divided will, as representing a higher wisdom? Perhaps Kierkegaard was wrong when he said that "purity is to will one thing." Perhaps the issue is not a fixed knowledge of the good, the single focus that millennia of monotheism have made us idealize, but rather a kind of attention that is open, not focused on a single point. Instead of concentration on a transcendent ideal, sustained attention to diversity and interdependence may offer a different clarity of vision, one that is sensitive to ecological complexity, to the multitude rather than the singular. (Bateson 1990, 166)

At the least, Bateson's remarks require us to reconsider singleness of purpose as a goal and ideal and to recognize that it might have imposed its own kind of blinder effect, to our cost.

Continuity Sufficient for Our Moral Categories

The theme developed here in relation to agency may be extended to each of the dependent goods enumerated earlier. Moral categories associated with responsibility, like the ascription of blame and the practice of promise keeping, presuppose for their application some temporal span in the subject's life.[1] Were personal identities so fluid that they changed minute by minute or day by day, we would be able to make no sense of persons keeping promises or deserving blame. The cases of dissociative-identity disorder examined earlier well illustrate this. That self 1 is not responsible for all the intentional and voluntary deeds perpetuated by her own body (although in pragmatic contexts, such as the legal one, she may need to be held responsible) is in part because the succession of selves here shifts so rapidly as to deter us from applying our customary concepts.[2] And our usual expectations and presumptions about blame, reproach, and praise become inapplicable when we are confronted with multiples. Exacting a promise from a multiple also strains to breaking point the notion of promising. How can self 1 promise what self 2 may not consent to uphold? Self 1's "promise" must be so hedged with qualifications ('I promise that if I can, I will meet you') as to be meaningless.

These concepts are rendered unintelligible or at least radically problematic, then, when we attempt to apply them to the flux and discontinuity of dissociative disorder. Were there widely found such dizzying multiplicity and succession as the multiples exhibit, it would indeed doom the responsibility concepts of blame, praise, and promise keeping as we know them. Nevertheless, the case must not be overstated. In between the extreme multiplicity illustrated here and the invariance of traditional identity presuppositions a modest degree of succession may prove to be compatible with responsibility concepts such as promise keeping. I may make and keep a promise for a day or a year, as well as for a lifetime, after all ('I cannot promise you what will happen after this job ends, but while it lasts, I will support you'). Moreover, if we concede that some responsibility-related attributions, such as blame, praise, and culpability, require a relatively unified self, it perhaps need not be one with a perfect identity that endures through a lifetime. As long as responsibility itself is understood to admit of degree, such responses may be compatible with the latitude provided by a modest degree of succession, even in every normal life.

Would we alter or even risk losing our responsibility concepts by conceding that diminished responsibility, lessened blame, and reduced praise should accompany increased change between earlier and later selves or self stages? This issue is more difficult. For severe crimes, traditional deontological conceptions of responsibility permit neither the passage of time alone nor personality or character change through time to lessen the blame accorded to individuals. On the other hand, statutes of limitations (which govern lesser crimes) have been seen to adhere to time- and change-relative notions of responsibility.

Real-life examples where the passage of time and/or radical psychological transformation seem to invite the language of successive selves are rare in the sphere of normal psychology. One may be that of Katherine Anne Power, imprisoned in Boston in 1993 for murder and robbery after twenty years of evading authorities by changing her identity and successfully constructing a new life on the other side of the country. Her youthful revolutionary zeal enabled Power to commit crimes as a college student that would be unimaginable for the seemingly gentle and conventional middle-aged woman who recently submitted herself for punishment twenty years later. As the contrary and ambivalent reactions to her sentence illustrate, people's moral intuitions founder and diverge on the question of whether culpability and blame should transfer undiminished from one self or self phase to another in such cases (Radden 1995). But because it is customary to allow such intuitive responses to guide our metaphysics of personal identity, this uncertainty leaves us without a methodology to determine whether and how much our customary responsibility concepts and categories are threatened by a metaphysics of successive selves.

Continuity Sufficient for Moral Concepts and Emotions

Of the several time-spanning and seemingly self-directed moral concepts and emotions sometimes introduced to argue against a metaphysics permitting successive selves, remorse, contrition, and guilt present the most stubborn cases. Others offer little difficulty. For example, although they are time-spanning and self-directed, pride and gratitude are customarily extended toward others with whom the individual is closely identified. To feel pride or gratitude over the feats and fortunes of another self with whom one shares a body thus seems a natural extension of those concepts. Similarly, shame and at least some forms of regret seem to have latitude in their ordinary application sufficient for us to extend them to embrace attributes of the several selves we might house within our body. We feel shame and regret over deeds we did not do. More closely tied as they are to individualism, however, remorse, guilt, and contrition reflect the same sort of difficulties that, we saw above, arise with responsibility and the concepts with which it is allied. If we accept a metaphysics of successive selves, must we relinquish or change our notions of guilt, contrition, and remorse? At least to the extent of acknowledging them to be relative to time and change (as we saw responsibility must be deemed to be), this is so, it would seem.

Continuity Sufficient for Trust

The development of judicious trust, Lorraine Code (1991) has shown, presupposes the unifying frame of character: we are entitled to trust in and because of the oneness between earlier and later self stages, captured in the notion of another's character. Again, the extreme multiplicity associated with mental disorder prevents such oneness. The subject of rapid and unpredictable mood swings between phases of mania and despair challenges our ability to extend (judicious) trust; as a composite person, the mercurial multiple is not trustworthy, for all that each of the separate selves she comprises may be, while they reign.

   Because her sympathy lies with postmodern rejections of the unified modern self, Code finds disquieting this recognition that self unity is required for trust and casts it in the form of a paradox. We want to assert "constancy of traits and attributes—of 'character'" while at the same time repudiating "the politically vexed implications of unified, humanistic subjectivity" (Code 1991, 183). But Code's disquietude may be unnecessary. Characters change, on occasion transformatively: the constancy of others' traits and attributes necessary for the intelligibility of trust, or character, call for something less than lifelong invariance. Through a lifetime a person may become, and then later cease to be, "worthy," as we say, of trust. Moreover, the one trusting may recognize this relative and conditional aspect, even as she places her trust in the other ('I trust your judgement now because you have no stake in the matter, but were you to buy shares in the company, . . .'). That her character is trustworthy through one phase of her life only, say her youth, means that if a person's lifetime is divided in phases of some duration, each must be long enough for such dispositions to develop. Hourly or daily fluctuations would not permit us to ascribe character traits to another, whether the trait of trustworthiness or any other. But a transition through phases lasting years or decades would. Again, then, it seems that continuity or sameness sufficient for trust may not need to span a physical lifetime.

Continuity Sufficient for Self-Understanding

The same qualifications apply to claims about self-understanding, both as a deeply held value of the Western intellectual tradition and as a goal sought by those undertaking forms of psychotherapy. Unless it reflects a tautology, the assertion that self-knowledge requires continuity with the "temporal depth and narrative" of a life span (Taylor, 1989) exaggerates in its implication that no self-knowledge is possible without such continuity. We may want the future to "redeem" the past, as Taylor puts it, to make it "part of a life story which has sense or purpose, to take it up as a meaningful unity" (Taylor 1989, 51). But ascription of 'self-knowledge' and 'self-understanding' usually apply to insights falling short of such an exhaustive understanding.

And perhaps necessarily so: as it is expressed, Taylor's is not a realistic or reachable goal. Such extensive self-knowledge may better be understood as an ideal, an end, that is by its nature unreachable. Naturally, then, more self-knowledge will be better, and a lifetime's worth will be best. But we do not reserve the term 'self-understanding' for what Taylor's argument seems to imply, nor is it clear why we should. True, self-understanding and self-knowledge will require some temporal span and a coherence that calls for memory sequences stretching beyond momentary, discrete experience. If the narrative is central, as Taylor and many contemporary theorists believe, then such temporal span and memory sequences are especially requisite. Stories require temporal duration, by their nature and for their construction. Invariance sufficient for the limited and partial self-knowledge within our human capability, however, is less than the oneness of a lifetime.

Continuity Sufficient for Virtues

Like theorists who have exaggerated the degree of continuity required for the substantive goods and values of autonomy and the moral categories and emotions of self-assessment and self-knowledge, Alasdair MacIntyre also overstates a dependency thesis in his discussion of virtue based moral systems. Influenced as he is by Kierkegaard, MacIntyre fails to recognize a misleading polarity in that thinker's distinction between the ethical and aesthetic ways of life. The Kierkegaardian aesthetic life, as MacIntyre puts it, is one "in which a human life is dissolved into a series of separate present moments, in which the unity of a human life disappears from view," while in the ethical life, "the commitments and responsibilities to the future springing from past episodes in which obligations were conceived and debts assumed unite the present to past and to future in such a way as to make of a human life a unity" (MacIntyre 1981, 225).

But we need not choose between such stark alternatives. When regarded as less than a whole lifetime, a life does not dissolve into separate present moments, nor is it robbed of all moral attributes. Commitments, responsibilities, and obligations pertain for parts of lives, as well as for lifetimes. And while we venerate the constancy of a lifetime, we also honor constancy of twenty years or even twenty months. Moreover, we honor change, resolve, considered changes of mind and course; we honor second thoughts.

MacIntyre's general claim remains true: Without some degree of oneness in individual selves, the notion of character and dispositionally analyzed states like the virtues of integrity and constancy would be untenable as moral ideals. They could have no application; literally, they would make no sense. But this is compatible with the position that some degree of continuity is sufficient for such application. Just as trustworthiness may mark a character through a limited stage only, so may constancy or integrity.

Because it concerns unity itself, the virtue of integrity, we have seen, has a special place in this discussion. But not only may integrity be compatible with personal change and some discontinuity; it is arguable that integrity resides in a set of traits that embrace and even encourage revision, flexibility, and openness to change, Victoria Davion (1991) has shown. If we understand moral integrity not in terms of unchanging and unconditional commitments, Davion insists, but instead as being committed to one's development, then integrity involves "being careful and paying attention to one's growth process" (Davion 1991, 184).

This emphasis on paying a certain sort of attention to one's life, invokes again the concept of second-order desires. Once a certain minimum degree of continuity is presupposed, a second-order desire is consistent with continuity and invariance, and it is equally compatible with radical change, as Davion demonstrates. This is not a self of hourly or daily transformations. The aspect of the self that monitors its other changes stays relatively constant, after all. But much else may be transformed during the ideological conversions that Davion envisages.

Continuity Sufficient for Self-Determination and Autonomy

Davion's concept of moral integrity, with its emphasis on the second-order desires we have about our selves and the lives we want to lead, suggests self-determination or autonomy. For as we saw in an earlier chapter, it is often just such forming, entertaining, and attending to second-order desires that marks the state of self-determination sought through therapeutic engagement. And while more continuity is required for self-determination than for voluntariness or episodic autonomy minimally understood, we learned, the degree of continuity required for self-determination need not be great.

Much therapeutic endeavor is directed toward the goal of improving, and thus altering, sometimes thoroughly, the client's behavior and dispositions in accordance with newly minted, self-imposed, and self-regarding rules, principles, and policies. Moreover, continuity or sameness through time is not a simple guide to self-determination: the invariant behavior and dispositions of the enslaved victim of neurotic patterns is not self-determined. The possibility of adopting and adhering to second-order desires about who we want to be and what we want to want—forged, perhaps, through therapeutic effort—lies at the heart of our conviction that self-determination is valuable. Therapy grounds itself on the recognition that people can thus come to take control of their lives, to shape and change their characters and destinies.

Life Changes in More Normal Lives

The successive selves and cases of multiplicity that are the particular focus of this book are relatively rare. Even if we add to cases from abnormal psychology instances of personality and character change resulting from other sources, like brain damage and disease, mind-affecting drugs, and religious and ideological conversion, we are left with too small a group of cases to threaten the viability of the concepts, values, and categories purportedly in jeopardy from the several "dependency" arguments examined here. But the misapprehensions and overstatement in those arguments seem to suggest a bolder claim. Even a threshold that permitted us to see most or all lives, normal and abnormal alike, as a fairly modest succession of selves may be compatible with many of our valued concepts and categories. While it must not allow a life to fracture into a succession of Korsgaard's "merely present selves" (1989) sufficient continuity may be achieved through a threshold less stringently identity-conserving than some have supposed.

By their nature, human lives are made up of changing phases or stretches. Once we dismiss the hypothesis that these phases are held constant or contained by a Cartesian unifying principle of some kind and accept instead an empiricist theory of psychological continuity, we discover much that suggests a gradually changing succession of "selves"—not daily or hourly shifts but several transformations in a lifetime—which may offer sufficient continuity for the dependent goods we prize.

With their theories of self, Hume and neo-Humeans like Parfit permit us to recast and look differently on a fact of utmost human importance: there are construed to be relatively stable, gradually changing stretches of lives, lasting months, years, or decades, which together make up the temporal patchwork of a physical lifetime. These are discontinuous but usually overlapping. They may be understood to correspond to the stages distinguished by developmental psychologists (and common sense): infancy, childhood, youth, middle age, old age (Kegan 1982). They may be mapped onto occupational patterns, such as schooling, working life, before and after a change of job, retirement, or onto emotional and maturational patterns, such as marriage, parenting, and dying. Some of these patterns are biological and "natural." Some are cultural, but shared. Others, in contrast, are deeply idiosyncratic and personal, following moral and spiritual fault lines (before and after ideological conversion; sinning, then reborn and redeemed) or psychiatric ones (stability, illness, recovery, recurrence).

Some of these idiosyncratic changes, we have seen, are dramatic and sudden, particularly those associated with mental illness and with ideological conversion.

Whether understood as a series of stages taking place within an invariant self or as separate and distinguishable selves, those of these transformations that are shared and undramatic reflect neither the flux and impermanence of Korsgaard's "merely present selves" nor the steady and enduring oneness of a lifetime exemplified by the Cartesian subject of experiences. We accept and rely on this modest and moderate degree of succession and continuity. It is an unsurprising and commonplace way in which we construe the sequence of our physical lifetimes. And quite possibly the degree of continuity fitting these several shared and predictable divisions, I would suggest, most closely approximates the continuity sufficient for the goods we value.[3]

IV

Divided Minds

The Divided Minds of Mental Disorder

In the two chapters that follow, we turn from discontinuities of selves through time, reflecting successive selves, to disunities inviting a description of divided minds. A daunting array of clinical descriptions suggests minds more divided than what we know from the kinds of heterogeneity experienced and observed in everyday life, however. We may limit ourselves, excluding data from commissurotomy and from the extensive amnesias of brain damage and disease, which seem to fracture and divide the person as much at a given time as through time. Yet there remain a diverse cluster of disorders and symptoms: the division and disunity evidenced in descriptions of the coconsciousness of dissociative-identity disorder, hypnoid states, and other dissociative conditions and the felt division and disownership experienced subjectively in states of depersonalization and derealization, possession, "copresence" in dissociative-identity disorder, and the ego-alien, "made" experiences (such as thought insertion) associated with other severe mental disorders.

Evidence of divided minds comes from two sources, this collection shows. There are behavioral attributes, which may be observed by others, and there are subjectively experienced divisions. Notable among the former is the evidence of "coconsciousness" in dissociative-identity disorder—shared knowledge apparently acquired first-hand by nonreigning selves through forms of "eavesdropping," or "listening in," on the experience of the reigning self. Seemingly less common is the purported interference from other selves reflected in the occasional "waverings" of the reigning self-interruptions and anomalies in the smooth flow of control linking the reigning self's cognitive states and desires to their execution. Such evidence and its interpretation will be the initial focus of this chapter. Later I will review the reported evidence of subjectively experienced states, particularly the feeling of copresence. Evidence of divided minds from each source is opaque, fleeting, and equivocal. Neither such introspective reports of felt disunity or possession nor publicly observable division will eventually prove sufficient to refute certain philosophical claims and commonsense presumptions about the self's unity. They deserve close examination nonetheless, because they are opaque—open to, and even inviting, conflicting interpretation.

Unlike my previous discussion of successive selves, the following analysis of divided minds involves findings that are without pressing moral and pragmatic consequences. Nevertheless, these findings are important and far-reaching from a theoretical standpoint. How we choose to understand the behavioral evidence suggesting disunity and to describe these experiences of duality will influence our concepts of mind, self, awareness, and subjectivity.

Divided Minds and Questions of Evidence

Some of this evidence has attracted the attention of philosophers in recent years (Kolak and Martin 1991). And it has been the subject of ambitious claims—about multiple minds, selves, and persons, about forms of disunity and division—more extravagent than anything entertained here. To delimit the discussion, I must formulate the particular claim in support of which I will review these several forms of evidence.

The dispositional nature of selves makes relatively uncontroversial any answer to the question of whether selves are to be regarded as simultaneous rather than sequential, it was shown earlier. Granted the satisfaction of certain criteria built into the notion of self used in this discussion, several selves sharing the same body may be said either to coexist or to succeed one another. The considerations affecting our decision to put it one way rather than another are not philosophically weighty. In contrast, the decision to speak of simultaneous rather than successive centers of *awareness* will be more problematic. Awareness is not usually treated as a dispositional concept. Thus the claim that more than one separate center of awareness inhabits the same body at the same time is a philosophically significant one with serious conceptual implications. It will affect how we must understand selves and minds. It has bearing on the notions of awareness and subjectivity. And it is the more significant philosophical claim toward which our evaluation of the evidence from abnormal psychology will be directed.

Does the evidence suggest that the divided states of awareness in dissociative identity disorder are simultaneous or successive? These alternative interpretations may be illustrated through a passage from the account of a multiple named Sybil (Schreiber 1973) which, although fictionalized, contains close and careful description. This account includes exchanges between the therapist (psychoanalyst Dr. Cornelia Wilbur) and several of the separate selves inhabiting the body publicly identified as Sybil Dorsett. One of these selves, Victoria Antoinette Scharleau, is portrayed as enjoying the unique epistemic advantage of knowing everything that goes on.

Sybil has just been given a silver pendant. Sybil is reigning in this scene, and the author speculates on her thoughts and inner monologue. But, Schreiber goes on, "Victoria Antoinette Scharleau, who knew everything, watched Marion Ludlow give Sybil the silver pendant" (Schreiber 1973, 86).

The two verbs 'knew' and 'watched' in this passage are interestingly chosen. Schreiber says Victoria had watched the gift giving. Yet she draws license to do so only from the earlier claim: that Victoria *knew* of the gift. 'Watched' implies some form of direct personal awareness. If Victoria watched while Sybil received the pendant, then Victoria's presence seems to have been simultaneous with Sybil's. There was coconsciousness. If, after the event, Victoria merely knew that it had occurred, then this is not obviously so.

The question of whether Victoria can rightly be described as having watched the exchange, is the one asked here: whether there can be simultaneous divided states of awareness, or coconsciousness.[1] First we will consider the behavioral evidence and then the subjective evidence.

Behavioral Evidence for Coconsciousness

Separate awareness in dissociative–identity disorder

Evidence of coconsciousness that may be identified by an outside observer of multiples is of two kinds. First, there are observable waverings in the reigning self's progress, which seem to indicate interference from a cognizant but nonreigning self. Second, there is an indication at a later time that the nonreigning self (here, Victoria) is in possession of information acquired by the reigning self (here, Sybil) at an earlier time, i.e., the fact that Victoria "knew."

Let us deal with waverings first. A brief example from real life (provided by a clinician) will illustrate: a multiple is grocery shopping, filling her cart with the staples of an adult diet. What occurs next appears to be inconsistency: although she lives alone, she reaches for several brightly colored packets of animal-shaped children's cereal. The hypothesis proposed to account for this wavering is that the impulse was not hers but rather was a challenge to her reign interjected by another self, a child "alter." To the outside observer, this apparently aberrant and alien impulsive intervention reflects a wavering in the steady course of the reigning adult self's agency.

We saw earlier in this book that observed across stretches of time, the erratic behavior of multiples strongly invites us—if it does not actually require us—to attribute more than one source of agency to the composite person. In contrast, viewed at any given time, the corresponding waverings of multiples constitute considerably less compelling evidence in support of the presence of simultaneous divided centers of awareness. Indeed, the very rarity of these waverings is itself puzzling. If the multiple comprises all these contenders for control, why is there not more of a visible struggle for ascendancy, we want to ask? Why do other selves meekly accede to the power of the reigning self so often?

When such a struggle is purported to take place, what do we observe publicly? An eccentric taste in cereal or a self-indulgent impulse. Nothing more. From within, the adult self in our example may sense the alien impulse and respond to it without a sense of ownership. But to the outsider, this instance of wavering is not compelling as evidence for divided minds.

What of evidence of shared knowledge acquired by nonreigning selves? If a nonreigning self (Victoria) knew p at t_1, must we conclude that awareness was simultaneous? Several possible interpretations avoid such an inference. The simplest of these is that while Victoria acquires sensory information at t_1, this information was acquired without her being aware (or being able to become aware) of this acquisition at t_1. Another interpretation is that at t_2 Sybil informed Victoria that p.

If we rely on a nonintrospective method, by which there is no subjectively established awareness of p, there seem to be no better grounds for ascribing awareness at t_1 to the nonreigning self (Victoria) than for attributing sense-produced knowledge that p after t_1. We know from the case of normal subliminal perception that not all the sensory information we acquire is, or could be, acknowledged in subjective awareness—or, as we say, consciously. Certainly, we sometimes extend the word 'awareness', just as we extend 'perception', so that it encompasses sensory input of this subliminal kind. Indeed, perhaps this looseness in the notion of awareness explains the attribution of two separate awarenesses to the alleged divided mind of dissociative-identity disorder. But rather than attributing simultaneous separate awarenesses to the multiple's two selves, it seems simpler, and at least equally plausible, to suppose that the distinctive beliefs were derived in the way normal persons acquire beliefs based on unnoticed sensory input.

Analogous reasoning is invited when we reflect on two other phenomena suggesting divided minds: the postoperative behavior of commissurotomy patients and the "hidden observer" phenomenon associated with the experimental study of hypnoid states. The two behavioral sources of alleged evidence for divided minds in multiples, observable waverings and shared knowledge, have proved to offer us little. And behavioral evidence about commissurotomy and hidden observers is similarly unconvincing, as I will demonstrate.

Alleged separated awareness in hypnotic states and commissurotomy

Anesthesia, deafness, and various additional and particular sensory effects may be induced during hypnotic trance. The entranced subject does not seem to feel extreme and normally painful heat, for example, or to hear words spoken to her. Yet these effects are later revealed to be known by what, in discussions of hypnosis, has come to be designated as the "hidden observer," an entity that exhibits subsequent knowledge of the hypnotically inhibited states (of painful heat or sound) and is to be identified neither with the entranced subject nor with the self of normal awareness, which remains ignorant

of the entire episode. One study describes how, even with hypnotically induced deafness, a subject's hidden observer was able to give
informed answers afterward to questions about what was heard during
the period of hypnotic deafness, answers that neither the hypnotized subject nor the posttrance subject could provide (Hilgard 1973,
1984).

Again we may postulate two explanations for this phenomenon,
corresponding to the two hypotheses distinguished earlier (divided
states of awareness are simultaneous or successive). There may be
simultaneous separated centers of awareness, only one of which suffers hypnotically induced deafness during the trance. A second and
simpler interpretation is that sensory information is received, without
awareness, at the time of the trance. This information is stored in
some part of the brain accessible neither to the hypnotically deaf
subject nor to the posttrance subject and later provides the hidden
observer with knowledge not available to either the hypnotized subject or the posttrance subject.

The alleged evidence for divided minds in commissurotomy
patients is more complicated, but is analogous. Consider the following key/ring example, which illustrates the behavioral peculiarities
associated with the surgical separation of the two commissures.[2]
When the words 'key' and 'ring' are briefly flashed on the two sides
of a divided screen, the left eye of the postoperative commissurotomy
patient communicates only 'key' to the right brain. So later, when
asked to use his left hand to pick out what he saw from an array of
items concealed from sight, the patient retrieves the key but leaves the
ring. And used together, left and right hands act independently, the
right hand picking up but rejecting a key in favor of a ring, the left
hand selecting a key. These actions of the hands seem to permit us,
indeed, perhaps force us, to ascribe awareness of the key to the right
hemisphere and ignorance of the key to the left hemisphere. But if
we rely on a nonsubjective, nonphenomenological method, in which
there is no introspectively established awareness of p, there seem to be
no grounds for ascribing to the right hemisphere 'awareness' of p at
t_1, rather than merely attributing to that hemisphere sense-produced
knowledge that p after t_1.

In a thorough discussion of the question of divided minds and
split-brain patients, Marks (1980) has exposed errors of reasoning

likely to have led philosophers and neuropsychologists to extravagant claims about commissurotomy, claims that postulate simultaneous divided awarenesses and even separate selves. And these errors suggest that successive, rather than simultaneous, awareness is the preferred interpretation here.[3] Those who attribute divided minds have been ineluctably drawn to the wrong picture of the information exchange between the brain's two hemispheres, construing it on the model of two people talking. Whatever the proper account is, Marks concludes, this picture of it cannot be accurate, for "the exchange of information via the commissures does not differ in principle from other neural exchanges of information within the hemispheres" (1980, 45). We do not need to suppose that awareness or intentionality accompany the neural exchanges of information between the two hemispheres, any more than we do for any exchange of information among our bodily systems. Similarly, we do not need to suppose that when the left eye sends a message to the right hemisphere, which results in a new and accurate belief in that hemisphere as evidenced by selective hand motions, the sensory input involved is an act of *seeing*, as we usually understand this notion, i.e., as an experience of the kind that we are aware, or could become aware by an effort of attention.

Thus reminded of how neural exchanges of information occur in the brain, which is very unlike two people talking, we may rightly be reluctant to attribute simultaneous separate centers of awareness to the commissurotomy patient. But the force of this argument shifts when we return to the cases with which we began. There is no subjective and introspective evidence of simultaneous separate centers of awareness from commissurotomy patients, as there is from multiples. Moreover, some of the purported exchange between separate selves in dissociative-identity disorder appears much more like two people (or selves) talking than do the exchanges between the hemispheres, at least as descriptions of subjective phenomena like copresence attest. Before deciding whether Marks's analysis is as useful in explaining the implausibility of a hypothesis of simultaneous separate awarenesses for dissociative-identity disorder as for commissurotomy, we must evaluate the subjective evidence for the hypothesis of simultaneous divided awarenesses. No useful subjective evidence from commissurotomy or hypnotic states allows us to hypothesize about divided

minds. Dissociative disorder and seemingly allied states do allow us
to do so. It will prove that even what feels like two people talking
is not plausibly understood this way at all. But when we have introspective reports asserting that this is how it feels, we need to pay
careful attention.

Subjective Evidence for Divided Minds

Perhaps Sybil experienced Victoria's presence through the phenomenon, similar to some possession states, described as copresence. Just as
the multiple whose selves have been effectively integrated through
therapeutic intervention complains of a feeling of loneliness, so clinical descriptions sometimes attribute an "accompanied" feeling to a
reigning self when another self is present.

The evidence of divided minds in multiples is importantly like,
if not introspectively identical with, other subjectively experienced
disunity experience, such as disownership, possession, depersonalization, and derealization. Whether they are qualitatively distinguishable may indeed be an unprovable proposition.[4] It is not apparent
that these kinds of experience differ from forms of copresence in
subjective quality, or feel, and they will be reviewed alongside these
other states. As symptoms of larger symptom clusters, or syndromes,
these experiences differ. Understood not as syndromes but as isolated
experiences, however, it is difficult—and may add conceptual confusion—to distinguish them. Once we have freed ourselves of nosological and syndromic categories in order to compare these apparently
similar experiences of disunity, we find, in depersonalization, derealization, possession, out-of-body hallucinations, and ego–alien experiences, more vivid and richly developed descriptions than are yielded
in dissociative-identity disorder.

Because they are such a common human response to stress, because they take diverse forms, or at least descriptions, and finally,
because they are often brief or even fleeting reactions, rather than
states of longer duration, this group of dissociative experiences does
not readily submit to generalization.

Thought insertion
Seeming failures and errors of self-attribution and cases of "disowning" some experience are vividly described in accounts of mental

disorder. The group of symptoms discussed here are characteristically cognitive and affective. They involve the subjective belief that some experiences originate outside the person's own mind or will. They are also accompanied by feelings of alienation. These experiences, sometimes known as ego-alien experiences, may best be summed up in the term 'disownership'.

In a less extreme and lasting form, related and at least surprisingly similar experiences to these disownership experiences are found in temporary states of depersonalization, in out-of-body experiences, and in some possession states, as we will see presently. But disownership also occurs in more severe, nondissociative disorders. Associated with schizophrenia is thought insertion, the occurrence of thoughts judged by the patient to be another's. The experience is as of their having been placed in the patient's mind from some outside source. Complaining of this condition, one woman is reported to have, "I look out of the window and I think the garden looks nice and the grass looks cool, but the thoughts of Eamonn Andrews come into my mind. There are no other thoughts there, only his.... He treats my mind like a screen and flashes his thoughts on it like you flash a picture" (Davidson and Neale 1986, 339).

Not only thoughts but also feelings, impulses, and actions are described with this language of alienation or disownership. States and actions not acknowledged to be the patient's own are known as "made" responses. Such made feelings were reported by another patient in the following way: "I cry, tears roll down my cheeks and I look unhappy, but inside I have a cold anger because they are using me in this way, and it is not me who is unhappy, but they are projecting unhappiness on my brain. They project upon me laughter, for no reason, and you have no idea how terrible it is to laugh and look happy and know it is not you, but their emotions" (Davidson and Neale 1986, 340).

Made volitional acts, or "dissociated will," are described similarly. The patient feels that her actions result from a consciousness and will other than her own. Not merely does she experience an irresistible and undesirable impulse whose origin feels to be external, however. In addition, the impulses in, and movements carried out by, her body feel to be another's. Rather than as active in bringing them about, she experiences her body as the other's passive instrument.

These descriptions suggest divisions of the mind at a given time rather different from, and in excess of, those unremarkable heterogeneities of self like ambivalence, or as we say colloquially, being of two minds. Disowned experiences challenge a very fundamental tenet of subjective experience, the notion that all and only my experiences—thoughts, feelings, impulses to act, and seemingly voluntary actions—are mine.

We saw earlier that Braude's (1991) taxonomy of self-ascription was helpful in identifying the several different epistemic attitudes adopted by the separate selves of a multiple vis-à-vis one another's experiences. A state is *indexical* when a person believes it to be his or her own, *autobiographical* when a person experiences it *as* his or her own. The ambiguities involved in some disowned experiences seem to go beyond these categories, however. The patients described do not experience their made responses as theirs. Rather, they experience them as alien. And in one way they do not believe them to be theirs. Yet in another respect these descriptions reveal that the subject both knows the responses to be hers (and "owns" them) and experiences them as hers. The first patient quoted complains of Eamonn Andrew's thoughts invading her mind, i.e., she *experiences* them; the second speaks of unhappiness, a *felt* state, in her brain. So although they are both nonindexical and nonautobiographical, disowned experiences are not *simply* nonindexical and nonautobiographical.

Depersonalization, derealization, possession states, and out-of-body experience

Usually classified as dissociative states are forms of depersonalization where the individual experiences a temporary sense of division or estrangement within the self, commonly in the form of an inner dialogue between observing and participating selves.

Depersonalization disorder, or neurosis, is a persistent or recurrent feeling of detachment from one's mental processes or body. It is often accompanied by derealization, where an alteration of the perception of one's surroundings throws the seeming reality of the outside world into question. Writing of his own episode of severe depression and suicidal obsession, the author William Styron (1990, 64) describes his sense of being accompanied by a second self, a wraithlike observer who, not sharing the dementia of his double, is able to watch with dispassionate curiosity as his companion struggles against the oncoming disaster or decides to embrace it. William Styron's "darkness visible" descended, unexpectedly, in his middle age. No precipitating external cause or origin suggested itself in his life and circumstances, no particular new-found reason for despair. But in the following passage to which James draws our attention in his discussion of the divided self, another literary artist, Alphonse Daudet, describes a comparable splitting as a part of normal grieving:

"Homo duplex, homo duplex!" writes Alphonse Daudet. "The first time that I perceived that I was two was at the death of my brother Henri, when my father cried out so dramatically, 'He is dead, he is dead!' While my first self wept, my second self thought, 'How truly given was that cry, how fine it would be at the theatre.' I was then fourteen years old." (James 1902, 144)

Daudet's description illustrates a significant feature of depersonalization. It is as much a phenomenon of normal people in abnormal situations as of abnormal people in normal situations. It is a common, and thus perhaps adaptive, response to stress. Although the exact relationship between traumatic events and dissociative conditions remains unresolved, strong correlations are evident. Research indicates that during and after traumatic events, approximately half of all adults experience a sense of detachment from their physical and psychological self or from the social and material world (American Psychiatric Association 1995, 489). A continuum appears to allow us to connect nonclinical adaptive forms of dissociation, such as the grief-induced depersonalization described by Daudet, with severe, chronic, and pervasive clinical dissociative experiences, such as the copresence found in multiples. But the fact that depersonalization is in these respects a normal response, at least in its more fleeting forms, adds to the difficulty of reaching generalizations when it is proffered as evidence for some philosophical thesis concerning the disunity of the mind.

When they are understood as psychological phenomena rather than as religious or magical phenomena, possession states too appear to reflect an extreme of subjectively felt division or disunity. Subject to little controlled examination, these states must be introduced as evidence with caution, but one psychiatric study at least allows us to distinguish two main forms: lucid, or obsessional, and somnambulistic, or hysterical (Oesterreich 1966). In its less extreme, lucid form, possession is an introspectable experience. The one possessed remains self-aware throughout and remembers the experience afterward, but feels invaded and engaged in a struggle for control. In contrast, with the somnambulistic form the one possessed retains no awareness or memory of the possessive state after returning to normal: this subject may experience no disunity. The kind of possession experience that might provide introspectable, subjective evidence of a divided mind, clearly, is lucid. But the distinction between the two forms is not one that allows us to distinguish among actual possession experiences, for shifts from lucid to somnambulistic states occur. Such shifts are revealed in the following description. The patient was a middle-aged Japanese woman whose physician reported her purported possession by "the fox," a state that, she complained, recurred several times a day.

At first there appeared slight twitchings of the mouth and arm on the left side. As these became stronger she violently struck with her fist on her left side, which was already swollen and red with similar blows, and said to me: "Ah, sir, here he is stirring again in my breast." Then a strange and incisive voice issued from her mouth: "Yes, it is true, I am there. Did you think, stupid goose, that you could stop me?" Thereupon the woman addressed herself to us: "Oh dear, gentlemen, forgive me, I cannot help it!"

Continuing to strike her breast and contract the left side of her face . . . , the woman threatened him and abjured him to be quiet, but after a short time he interrupted her and it was he alone who thought and spoke. The woman was now passive like an automaton, obviously no longer understanding what was said to her. It was the fox which answered maliciously instead. At the end of ten minutes the fox spoke in a more confused manner, the woman gradually came to herself and assumed back her normal state. She remembered the first part of the fit and begged us with tears to forgive her for the outrageous conduct of the fox. (Jaynes 1982, 356–357)

It remains uncertain how possession states, such as this one, are related to mental disorder and to what extent they, like certain other dissociative states, reflect normal responses to abnormal situations that are subjectively stressful and/or religious (Oesterreich 1966). While not fully understood, the lucid possession of which its subject remains conscious is nonetheless the source of vivid introspective experiences of disunity, as this account illustrates.

Subjectively experienced disunity of the most intense kind is described in out-of-body experiences, which are understood in psychiatric nosology as a stress-induced form of dissociation. Here the person vividly experiences a separation between the mind or sense of awareness and the body. Often associated with "near death" episodes, these experiences are portrayed in the following account of sensations accompanying a nearly fatal car accident: "I kind of lost my sense of time, and I lost my physical reality as far as my body is concerned—I lost my body. My being or my self or my spirit, or whatever you would like to label it—I could sort of feel it rise out of me . . . , and it wasn't anything that hurt, it was just a sort of lifting and being above me" (Moody 1976, 50–51).

Depersonalization, derealization, possession, and out-of-body experiences have each been understood as forms of dissociative states. This category is itself vague, however, and suggests more rigor than is commonly found in discussions of these and other purportedly related phenomena, such as the dissociative symptoms that are only, or at least more easily, observed behaviorally: hypnoid states, somnambulism, somnambulistic possession, aspects of coconsciousness in multiples, and the effects of dissociative amnesia, for example. Moreover, subjectively experienced dissociative symptoms also share much with other responses, such as some medium and other trance states, as well as, for example, Cotard syndrome and *le délire de negation*, whose primary symptom is a complete denial of the existence of the self (Enoch, Trethowan, and Barker 1967).

Thinking in terms of syndromes and reliance on subjective report combine to sow confusion here and, it seems likely, also to multiply taxonomic entities unnecessarily. Regarded as mere symptoms and detached from their context within a larger syndrome, little appears to distinguish some of these subjective states and experiences from one another. Choice of language and classification create misleading and arbitrary barriers. Thus, in a more obvious example, the felt presence of another source of will is "copresence" within dissociative-identity disorder, but it is "possession" in religious and ceremonial contexts or in the mind of a patient familiar with the language and concepts of fundamentalist religion.

Some of the confusions wrought by the different discourses of religion and psychiatry have long been acknowledged. (The faithful's "religious visions" may be the clinician's "hallucinations.") Less obvious, perhaps, have been the risks of duplication resulting from nosology and the syndromic thinking it engenders. Copresence may be "possession," but it is perhaps also "made volitional acts" in nondissociative disorder.

What, then, can we conclude from the nonbehavioral indications of divided minds? As instances of simultaneous separate awarenesses, these subjective experiences and states constitute evidence that is far from univocal. What seems clear is that here are minds more divided than normal and heterogeneities of self far exceeding those associated with everyday life experience. Feelings of disownership, depersonalization, and possession reflect a sense of disunity in excess of that found in the commonplace state of ambivalence that we call being of two minds. But if divided minds means simultaneous separate centers of awareness, then the evidence seems to direct us toward contradictory conclusions. On the one hand, we want to insist, the mere fact that these are subjective experiences ensures their unity. When they *are* subjective experience, and not behavioral observation, they are in the final analysis a report from one, albeit fractured, center of awareness, as they could only be, issuing from the lips of one person and spoken in the language of the first person, singular. And this must preclude their constituting any kind of evidence in support of separate centers of awareness. On the other hand, these odd disownings and detachments between "this experience" and the quality of "mineness" seem to impel us to look more closely at what we may take for granted about self-ascription in the normal case. These abnormal cases perhaps illustrate that the *process* by which we attribute our experiences to ourselves must be recognized to be just that, a process, requiring in every case an inferential step from 'this experience' to 'my experience'.

In a tradition dating to the eighteenth century, philosophers have concerned themselves about issues of ownership and self-attribution, albeit their experience has been limited, until very recently, to normal experience. It will be useful, then, to turn to philosophical theory at this point and to let it inform our interpretation of the ambiguous subjective evidence for divided minds.

The Grammar of Disownership

The philosophical tradition following Hume has yielded insights helpful in understanding a language fitting for the radically discontinuous selves of severe mental disturbance. But this tradition is also germane to the apparently divided minds revealed in abnormal psychology. There are philosophical theories of self-ascription, or ownership, that offer guidance as we try to describe, place, and explain experiences suggesting division and disunity greater than that found in everyday life. The purpose of this chapter is to review these theoretical claims and to use them in clarifying our understanding of such extreme and puzzling introspective phenomena as the ruptures of self revealed through descriptions of copresence in multiples and the dualities of other disorders broadly classified as dissociative (possession states, depersonalization, derealization and out-of-body experiences), as well as the strange subjective reports of the "thought insertion" or "made" experiences suffered by some mental patients.

Philosophers have customarily approached the question of ownership or self-ascription with reference to the normal case, in which ownership is assumed, and also to the subjective perspective. On one formulation, the philosophical question has been, 'How do I know that my experiences are mine?' It is understood here that I do know. It is a question not about identification or reidentification—whether my experiences might be mine—but about epistemological features of my knowledge of that incontrovertible fact. Beginning with this approach, we must recognize that the abnormal case and a more detached perspective may add to or alter the questions to be asked and the answers found.

Are these minds divided in any strong sense? We saw that behavioral evidence of coconsciousness will not provide unequivocal

support for the hypothesis of simultaneous separate centers of awareness. And the following analysis of the subjective experience of mental
division in the light of philosophical accounts of self-ascription yields
the same conclusion. As evidence of simultaneous separate centers of
awareness, such experience is insufficient, because of the inviolable
unity presupposed by the subjectivity that allows patients to report
and describe symptoms of disownership.

Philosophical Accounts of Ownership

Philosophical accounts of ownership say what they have to say about
disowned experiences even before real case material is introduced.
(We will presently see whether case material can or must alter these
expectations and the theories on which they are based.) Until recent
interest in abnormal psychology, disowned experiences have been
treated as hypothetical cases, or logical possibilities, at best.

Different accounts share the tenet that ownership of experience
is grammatically guaranteed. Our usual understandings of concepts
like experience and self, it seems widely agreed, prevent my speaking
of having experiences that are not mine. Making the point that all his
experiences are his, Sydney Shoemaker asserts that an experiencing is
predicated of a subject: the states of a self are as attached to that self as
are a material thing's attributes to that material thing—a book's shape
to that book, for example. We can no more speak of an experience
without its subject than of the shape of the book without the book
(upon which it is adjectival) (Shoemaker 1986).[1] Stressing that only
my experiences are mine, Owen Flanagan remarks that I alone "am
hooked up to myself in the right way to directly experience my own
mental states" (Flanagan 1992, 159).

Accounts of why this is so and whether it is significant differ. In
traditional Kantianism, for example, a transcendental unifying principle unavailable to subjective experience ensures ownership. A nonempirical posit explains and necessitates the grammatical fact. In the
barer empirical tradition, within which both James and contemporary thinkers like Parfit must be placed and which eschews transcendental entities, the inviolable unity-of-ownership grammar is also
maintained. Here too, however, there are divergent accounts of the
meaning and significance of that grammar. Some theorists emphasize

the psychological necessity of ownership: as a contingent fact about humans, shaped, perhaps, by evolutionary imperative, we naturally ascribe all and only our experiences to ourselves, it is asserted. On the other hand, if we accept that information-processing systems are natural kinds, as some thinkers do, then the unity of ownership may be less noteworthy. The notion of persons as information-processing systems invites us to expect that, unremarkably and like other such systems (e.g., computers), persons will have access to their own experience.

Despite such differences, each of these analyses rejects the possibility of radical disownership, or acknowledges it as no more than a hypothetical, a heuristic for explaining theory. Their points of agreement require our attention initially. If ownership is ensured, as these theories suggest, instances of disowned experience, hypothetical or real, must submit to the same analysis. The mental patient's complaint that she is possessed or that she is experiencing another person's thoughts would have to be dismissed as a misleading or mistaken description. The allegedly disowned experiences of possession or thought insertion encountered in abnormal psychology must be understood to reduce to some form of delusion.

This emphasis on the grammatical necessity of ownership may be illustrated by considering how we employ possessive pronouns in other contexts. Some of the things we call our own we are able to give away, sell, or otherwise make no longer ours. (By an action I may give you my book: now it is yours, not mine.) Others we can merely disown. I may disown a relative, a cousin, let us say. This means I feel estranged from her, I refuse to acknowledge her existence or relationship to me, I cut her out of my will. But it does not, and cannot, mean that I effect some magical transformation by which, any way but figuratively, she ceases to be my cousin. The term 'disown' aptly describes the cases we have been discussing here precisely because it conveys this constraint. If the grammar of self and experience dictates ownership, unity, and self-ascription, then our subjective states, like our cousins, may be disowned at most.

This philosophical point of view and approach appears to find some correspondence, and thus corroboration, in the way paranormal phenomena are portrayed. We do not need to accept the evidence for telepathy to acknowledge how it ought to be described were compelling instances found. The hypothetical telepathic awareness by which person X is said to enjoy access to the contents of the mind of another person (person Y) can only be understood as the recurrence in X's mind of an exactly similar token of Y's thought. X experiences Y's thoughts, only in the sense that X experiences thoughts qualitatively the same as Y's (Braude 1986). They are X's own thoughts, not Y's, and in this sense X is entitled to use the possessive grammar of ownership with regard to them: 'They are mine.'

Related to these observations is a feature noted by philosophers of mind emphasizing the privileged access or privacy we enjoy in relation to our mental states. In the phenomenal or mental realm, distinctions that undergird the activity of doubt, like that between 'seems' and 'is', have no purchase. To doubt too is to think, as Descartes pointed out (Descartes 1964, 70). But without the possibility of doubt, we have no way to question whether an apparently owned experience might be disowned. If they are experiences, then they must be owned. Despite the alien and detached quality they may exhibit as experiences, these states are objects of awareness. As such— however alien they may be described as feeling or seeming, however removed, remote, and separated—they are the subject's own experiences, and none other's.

This analysis encourages us to examine the language in which any clinical experiences of disownership are reported. 'Some of *my* mental contents feel not to be mine' (my emphasis). '*My* actions do not emanate from my will (but from an alien possessor's).' Those possessives seem to be an admission that while something is wrong, unusual, or alien about these experiences and actions, they are nevertheless the person's own, and self-ascription is not in question. A less confusing account introducing 'as if' language would entirely capture all that such avowals can coherently mean. Thus, 'It feels as if this feeling (I experience) were not mine', or 'It feels if my actions do not emanate from my will'.

An explanation for some of these strange locutions is not hard to find. Our speech is filled with ambiguities of identity language, we saw earlier in this book. Such ambiguity is certainly sufficient to have distorted the meaning or intent of these introspective reports and descriptions of unusually fractured experience. In insisting that she is thinking another's thoughts, a patient may mean merely that the content of her thought echoes the other's, i.e., her thought is qualitatively similar to, though not numerically identical with, his. Since context alone allows us to distinguish when a phrase like 'the same thought' is used in each way, the confusion comes by default: there exists no unambiguous linguistic form for the patient to employ.

Cases of real disowned experience in abnormal psychology may give us reason to adjust or question these sorts of analyses and the entrenched philosophical tradition about ownership that they make up, for such analyses were developed to accommodate the normal case, not abnormal ones. Before we consider such abnormal cases, let us trace the origins of these philosophical analyses in the identity theories associated with the Humean and post-Humean tradition.

Hume, James, and the Self's Unity

If there is no introspectively identified unchanging subject of experiences, as Hume's critique suggests, then the unifying function purportedly ensured by this subject is lost. That function, on Hume's reductionist account of the self, devolved onto the imagination. If I could not confuse my bundle of experiences with yours or question whether some experiences were mine, then it must be because the imagination ensured the unity of consciousness at any given time.

To understand why we treat the self as a unity at a given time and why the philosophical tradition concurs over the grammar of ownership, we would do better to follow not Hume's notion of the unifying role played by the imagination, but rather a theme that—although it is actually identifiable in Kant's critique of Hume—is most clearly expressed and developed in James's account of the unity of consciousness. James's views, in turn, may be traced through Wittgenstein to contemporary analyses of ownership, such as were outlined previously. Self-attribution, on these analyses, is ensured by the grammar of references to experiences and to the self (Wittgenstein 1963, secs. 246, 288, 408).

The distinction between unity and continuity, around which the present essay is shaped, has not always been emphasized in the history of philosophy (see Introduction, note 3). Only with James, writing at the end of the nineteenth century, do we find a useful marriage between a methodology recognized by Hume and the insights of Kant's, to which Hume was blind.

Like Kant, James saw the need for an account of how experiences come bundled one to a person at a given time. But his analysis falls within the methodological tradition developed out of Hume's empiricism, for like Hume, he shunned an explanation of the unity of consciousness that appeals to transcendental entities. Because of his methodological assumptions, moreover, James was able to recognize the need for an account of the unity of experience distinct from that by which the self's continuity through time is to be understood.

The Cartesian subject, or self, encompasses a unifying principle which links items in the imagination at a given time and, remaining unaltered through time, ensures perfect identity throughout the individual's lifetime. Since the same principle serves to unify the self at a given time and through stretches of time, little emphasis was placed on these distinguishable kinds of oneness.

While challenging these notions of self-identity, Hume too failed fully to acknowledge the distinction between the unity of the self at a given time and the continuity unifying experiences and traits across stretches of time. For him, the distinction was illusory or insignificant. This was because he believed that each separate perception we might apparently experience simultaneously is actually sequential. The sound of the dripping tap and the dog's bark, the thought of lunch and the sight of the bowl of peonies on the table, each actually succeed each other, in his view, albeit with "inconceivable rapidity," which will make imperceptible their being sequential rather than simultaneous (Hume 1888, 253). All separable impressions share the same feature. Both those that appear to do so and those that do not occur sequentially. Not surprisingly, then, Hume offered but one principle to explain their seeming oneness: the unifying role of the imagination. But if, *pace* Hume, we distinguish rather than conflating simultaneous and sequential experiences, we may find the unifying role of the imagination insufficient, or at least different, in each case. And something like this seems to be so.

Hume's assertion that through imagination experience at any given time is unified in a bundle at best reveals little about how this unifying process is effected, and the explanation he proffers appears to be incomplete. After all, as Hume's contemporary Kant and later James have both pointed out, relations of contiguity, causation, and resemblance may conjoin a set of ideas present in two separate (i.e., spatiotemporarily distinct) persons. Only when the ideas come together in one mind will we concede that they belong to the same bundle. James is perhaps the clearest and firmest on this point, and he makes it in a number of different and graphic ways. Take a sentence of a dozen words, he says, and take twelve men and tell to each one word. "Then stand the men in a row or jam them in a bunch, and let each think of his word as intently as he will; nowhere will there be a consciousness of the whole sentence" (James 1890, 199). The thoughts, which we actually know to exist, "do not fly about loose," as he puts it elsewhere (1890, 201). Rather, they seem each to belong to one thinker and not to another. And finally,

In this room—this lecture-room, say—there are a multitude of thoughts, yours and mine, some of which cohere mutually, and some not. They are as little each-for-itself and reciprocally independent as they are all-belonging-together. They are neither: no one of them is separate, but each belongs with certain others and none beside. My thought belongs with *my* other thoughts, and your thought with *your* other thoughts. Whether anywhere in the room there be a *mere* thought, which is nobody's thought, we have no means of ascertaining, for we have no experience of its like. The only states of consciousness that we naturally deal with are found in personal consciousnesses, minds, selves, concrete particular I's and you's. (James 1892, 20)

That thoughts do come owned in every case and that we can distinguish my bundle from another's James accepts because of the "mutual coherence" among our thoughts, which we know through experience. The "mineness" of experience is a phenomenological fact of the matter that is almost irreducible. It is not quite irreducible: my current experiences have a warmth, intimacy, and immediacy by which I know them to be me and mine. "So sure as this present is me, is mine, ... so sure is anything else that comes with the same warmth and intimacy and immediacy, me and mine" (James 1890, 204).

For James, there can be no knowledge, introspective or otherwise, of any transcendental unifying center or subject of experience. And certainly for James, pursuing the empirical and introspectionist discipline of psychology, there can be no place for further discussion of such an entity, and none is required. We have introspective grounds for our claims as to the self's unity at a given time. There is no need to postulate a unifier, no need, as he put it, to posit "a sanctuary within the citadel" (James 1890, 303).

If, as James supposes, we are not able to refer to experiences without ownership of them being understood, this is a central feature of all experience, a key phenomenological fact about our lives. Moreover, while grammatically ensured, it may not rest, as many grammatical particulars do, on arbitrary convention. There may be good reasons for this form of self-ascription. Without it, some contemporary philosophers have proposed and James believed, we humans would be disadvantaged in evolutionary design (James 1890, Dennett 1991, Flanagan 1992, Shoemaker 1986). The ownership of experiences and the quality of mineness may be neither mere convention nor a metaphysical or transcendental principle but rather some kind of psychological necessity (Hirsch 1982).[2] The likely reason for such design is fairly obvious. As Dennett points out, no sooner does something get into the business of self-preservation than boundaries become important. For if you are setting out to preserve yourself, you don't want to squander effort trying to preserve the whole world; "you draw the line" (Dennett 1991, 174).

Another feature of self-attribution now deserves attention. Since Kant, ownership has often been cast not as a form of propositional knowledge (I know that in every given instance this experience is my experience) but as a capacity (I can recognize which experiences are mine). Self-ascription is something that I am able to do. If we want to understand this Kantian insight in modern psychological language, we may recognize this as the capacity to distinguish self from nonself, or to employ the spatial metaphor in which the self is sometimes described, the capacity to distinguish self boundaries. Self-attribution is the *capacity* to "draw the line."

To summarize, then, Hume accurately sees that at any particular time experiences come bundled one to a person. A process of imagination, in his view, ensures that I am always able to recognize my bundle as mine. To supplement Hume's account, we may appeal to James's analysis of the unity of consciousness. Of the elusive transcendental ego, which those following in the Kantian tradition saw as the ultimate, albeit unknowable, unifier, we need say nothing; like James, we may acknowledge this transcendental entity or principle to be a datum that, in psychology, must be off limits. But its alleged effects (if such they are) in ensuring the self's unity at a given time we can recognize to be a grammatical, logical, or perhaps psychological fact of the matter. Bundles of experience come owned, one to a person or self; this is part of how experience and self are understood.

The Meaning of Disowned Experience

What must we say, then, about the disowned experiences of abnormal psychology? Is such experience necessarily owned, its subject the unfailing possessor of the capacity of self-ascription? And if so, is this a psychological or a logical necessity? Finally, if there are psychological reasons for ownership grammar rather than logical ones, as some theorists have proposed, might it not be that in abnormal cases, such as disowned experience, there is a breakdown of the usual psychological connections? Although in normal psyches "this experience" is inextricably linked to "my experience," perhaps under conditions of stress or mental illness these ties give way.

We must first notice that, fractured and divided as they are, the disowned and detached experiences with which we are concerned do not constitute a challenge to the self's capacity to distinguish self from nonself, to separate my experiences from those that are not mine. The patients described earlier do not have any doubt that it is their own mind on which are imposed others' thoughts, feelings, and impulses, their own body that is made the instrument of others' actions. Nor, in the case of copresence or possession, does the reigning subject doubt the boundary between herself and the other self "accompanying" or "invading" her. To the contrary, it is the sharpness of the boundary between the reigning self and her ghostly accomplice that constitutes this symptom and, indeed, accounts for the qualitative distinctness of this experience. These symptoms do not provide evidence that the boundary between self and nonself is eroded or absent.[3]

Something more can be learned from this discovery that disowned and detached experiences do not reflect an incapacity to distinguish self from nonself, and it is of the utmost methodological significance. The experiences that are our particular concern do not reveal a breakdown or incapacity of self-attribution. But neither will any symptoms that, as observers, we might begin to understand. Disorders more extreme than those we have been considering may truly rob a person of the ability of self-ascription. Attempts to understand autism have postulated something to this effect, as have descriptions of those suffering the extreme disintegration or fragmentation associated with brain damage and disease and with forms of schizophrenic disorder. But what is significant in these suggestions is that they are mere postulations, tentative interpretations of behavior observed by others. They do not come from subjective or introspective reports. This is because such reports, for intelligibility, require a unified subjectivity. They presuppose the capacity to distinguish self boundaries and to recognize that, however alienated and detached from them she may feel, their subject knows that her experiences are hers.

Philosophical claims about ownership are thus not refuted by the particular delusions of disownership isolated here. In revealing where the usual cohesion of experience is fractured, these delusions can nonetheless teach us something about self-ascription, something that the normal oneness of experience conceals.

This view is suggested in recent writing by George Graham and Lynn Stephens (Graham and Stephens 1994a; Stephens and Graham 1994a, 1994b), and their analysis is particularly apposite here in hinting at some distinctions concerning memory developed earlier in this book. These authors assert that normal self-ascription—applying the label 'my experience' to this experience—is analyzable into two elements, or what in my earlier discussion (chapter 6) I called cognitive components. One concerns ownership ('Experience M occurred to me'), the second agency ('Experience M is my mental action'). The disowned experiences of mental disturbance reflect a separation of these two elements overlooked in the indissoluble oneness of normal ownership, which we find reflected in normal grammatical possessive forms.

These authors are concerned with cases of disowned experiences in nondissociative disorders, such as that of the patient who claims that she has the thoughts of another (their term is 'introspective alienation'). Thus a person suffering from introspective alienation with respect to mental episode M acknowledges that he is the subject in whom M occurs, but he feels that somebody else is the agent of M (Graham and Stephens 1994a, 95). Graham and Stephens derive this distinction from another philosopher, Frankfurt. Frankfurt has tried to distinguish and define a sort of mental state, associated with normal experience, that goes undistinguished in the usual grammar and language of ownership: unbidden thoughts. Frankfurt (1976) has postulated that such thoughts, which seem to occur to us without our will or wish, are not thoughts that we think at all but rather are thoughts that we find occurring in us.

If we accept Graham and Stephens's use of the distinction between thoughts we think and thoughts that merely occur in us, then self-ascription and the grammar of ownership are ambiguous. 'This is my experience' accommodates 'This is not my experience'. Thus while expressing mistaken beliefs, these authors insist, the subject of disowned experiences does not utter claims that are incoherent or unintelligible.

The sense in which she attributes the thought to herself is not the same as the sense in which she attributes it to the other and denies that it is hers. So her attributions may be taken literally and they are mutually consistent. One answers the question 'Who is the subject in whom M occurs?' the other answers the question 'Who is the agent who produces M (wherever M occurs)?' (Graham and Stephens 1994a, 100).

The force of this analysis, as these authors recognize, depends on two additional elements: it requires a useful explanation of when and why the subject disowns some experiences in this way, and it calls for an account of why our notions of the common and normal experience of unbidden thoughts, which seem to invite the same analysis, has failed to accommodate them until Frankfurt's analysis. Although neither is of immediate concern for us here, Graham and Stephens offer both. A self-referential, narrative explanation of my mental states and behavior is sometimes available through my understanding or "theory" of myself. (This is a set of enduring intentional states sufficient to yield such an explanation.) If my theory of myself ascribes to me the relevant intentional states or if a mental state or bit of behavior is random and is not the apparent creation of some other intentional source, I unproblematically and fully regard this episode as mine. In this case, agency and ownership elements are both present. If a mental state or bit of behavior is inexplicable in terms of these intentional states, then it is judged as something that happens to me but is not mine. Unbidden thoughts, although they happen to me, are not the seeming product of another source of agency, for they lack the coherence, intelligence, and direction that invites us to postulate a separate source of agency.

Until philosophers directed their attention away from normal psychology and toward abnormal states and experiences, it may be added, they failed to recognize the complexities in the seemingly simple judgments of ownership and in the individualistic grammar of self-ascription.

This account of the complexities underlying "mineness" seems to permit a reconciliation between the apparently conflicting explanations of the inviolable unity of self-consciousness put forward by different theorists. My ownership of those of my states of which I am subjectively aware at a given time is ensured by the grammar of experience. But just as, we saw, 'I remember doing x' broke into two cognitive components, one concerning ownership and the other agency, so 'my experience' contains two parts. My experience is mine when it emanates from a unified subjectivity. This is logically guaranteed. It is not mine when disownership renders it "another's" mental action instead of mine. This is a psychological matter.

The evidence of disownership in abnormal psychology may seem to refute those who postulate that self-ascription is an uninteresting logical necessity, derivable from acknowledgment of humans as a species of information-processing system. But this analysis suggests otherwise. The judgment 'This experience is mine' involves a logically ensured element but also a psychological element that relates to agency. The answer to the question of whether the grammatical necessity of ownership is logical or psychological appears to be that it is both.

So my inviolable ownership of my experiences is compatible with my believing them—falsely but not incoherently—to be another self's experience. It is also compatible with my believing them to be alien and/or experiencing them as alien and/or believing them to emanate from an alien source. (It is compatible with their being nonindexical and/or nonautobiographical, in Braude's [1991] terms.) But whatever extremes of inner heterogeneity these several forms of disowned or divided experience reveal and whatever disunities of self they suggest, they are not sufficient to elude the conclusion that the self of a given moment remains one while it is many. There is no absolute and categorical sense in which even these subjectively fractured selves are mere heterogeneities.

Conclusion

This inquiry was stimulated by questions about what attitudes we should adopt toward radical personality change as it is reflected in descriptions from abnormal psychology. But the process of searching for an answer to such questions and seeking a suitable methodology for this search has taken us far beyond these initial concerns.

First, several different, cross-cutting distinctions emerged from an exploration of the empirical phenomena. We saw evidence both of the self's disunity at a time and of its discontinuity through time, breaks and radical alterations of the self from one day, or year, to the next. Other evidence suggested more: the presence of multiplicity, where several selves inhabit one body successively and even simultaneously.

A divided mind, we saw, must be distinguished from one that is utterly fragmented, without center, sequence, or memory. Neuropsychology provides dramatic descriptions of this extreme *fragmentation* of the self, where disunities are so radical and pervasive that our response is to question whether the sufferers described have selves at all. Rather than no self, cases of *multiplicity* reveal several more or less complete selves. Because descriptions of extreme dissociative disorder invite us to speak of multiple selves simultaneously inhabiting the same body, they have perhaps captured the disproportionate attention of philosophers. But other clinical descriptions from abnormal psychology and neuropsychology were shown to offer as much of a challenge as dissociative disorder to some of our usual ideas and expectations about the singularity and unchanging nature of the self.

Phenomena from everyday life and experience were introduced, including reactions undergone by otherwise normal people in abnormal contexts, such as the brief dissociative states so common to human distress. While apparently introspectively indistiguishable from them, these states were placed in contrast to rare cases from psychiatry, such as those of dissociative-identity disorder, which are apparently the products of a causal story particular to the individual sufferer's brain or psyche. And this distinction proved significant when we considered philosophical attempts to draw generalizations about the mind and self from these differing sources.

We encountered conditions of disunity and discontinuity resulting from known physical causes and those whose causes remain a mystery. In the context of medical psychiatry, where an expectation of future discovery of organic origins for all conditions makes what used to be known as functional disorders presumptively organic, this distinction goes unstressed. But it too proved important, both for generalization from the experience of statistically abnormal subgroups and when ethical issues were raised about the moral authority of advance care directives issued by those who will be victims mental disorder.

Only initially were abnormal conditions of memory loss; dissociation and disownership; cognitive, perceptual, and affective disharmony; and personality change introduced in the light of stardard psychiatric nosology, where symptoms are clustered in syndromes and understood according to their natural history or causation. Not so understood, we saw, these descriptions link unlikely occasions in strange patterns: the ideologically converted with the brain damaged or diseased, the bereaved with the psychotic, the hypnotized and possessed with the chemically altered. Diagnostic categories in psychiatry reflect many factors, including pragmatic and ideological concerns and historical accident. By isolating the symptom descriptions, we are able to see more clearly the import of the empirical data for conceptual and normative claims about the self.

As some of these contrasts suggest, the self's disunity may be understood in two ways: introspectively and from the more detached perspective of the public stance. And with these differences in perspective, it was shown, come critical moral distinctions and consequences central to our understanding of the self.

While nuanced and qualified, some answers have emerged to the cluster of questions about moral attitudes, and in particular about multiplicity and personal responsibility, with which we began. We found a plausible response to the question of why and how disordered memory of the kind attributable to successive selves might serve to protect one self from responsibility for the deeds of another self with which it shares a body. The sense of self that is appropriately forensic, in Locke's sense, requires subjectively experienced continuities and agent memory of actions. Given certain other conditions, we discovered that both disorders of memory or awareness found in multiples and those that often divide earlier and later selves resulting from other, nondissociative disorders, such as schizophrenic and affective conditions, should prevent us from according full responsibility between separate selves. Called for are ascriptions of *divided responsibility* ('Self 1 was responsible for the misdeed, but self 2 was not', for example), and the *adoption of differential reactive attitudes* toward the separate selves involved (sympathy toward one self, together with reproach toward another, for example).

Responsibility ascription is importantly dependent on context, however. Some therapeutic and everyday contexts permit, and even require, the ascription of divided responsibility and the adoption of differential reactive attitudes. But the dispositive purposes of the legal context and the interests dictated by certain inpatient settings work differently. Responsibility must be ascribed to multiples as unitary persons where these purposes and interests prevail.

Moving from forensic responsibility over past deeds to attitudes of responsibility toward the future, I distinguished a discourse of care within which, I argued, one self may have special obligations concerning another with which it shares a body. I explored the moral question of the more particular case of advance care directives for successive selves. Is paternalistic intervention justified, whether this intervention is on the part of other spatiotemporally distinct persons or other selves? Only in the case of advance directives concerning future self-destructive behavior, I argued, does one self retain moral authority over another.

Nuanced and qualified though they are, these outcomes may be applied to practical and policy-related concerns. Yet this analysis has gone beyond the several puzzles about change and responsibility invited by an acknowledgement of multiplicity in abnormal psychology, in pointing out the complexity of these puzzles and their relation to deeper, more abstract questions about the self and its identity.

A second set of conclusions concern the proposed language of successive selves. Should we adopt a language of successive selves to describe the extremes of multiplicity found in abnormal psychology? The informal language of successive selves was shown to invite a series of questions. Are there practical reasons to use it? Are there theoretical reasons to eschew it or to see it as merely figurative? Are there normative reasons to avoid its use, related to our moral and cultural commitments to individualism? Answers to each of these questions emerged from our inquiry into the web of empirical findings, theory, and values surrounding self identity.

Are there practical advantages to adopt such a language? The answer, we saw, is yes. When it is refined and clarified, such a language, whether figuratively or more literally interpreted, proves an important aid to understanding and working with some forms of mental disorder. Its applicability is context- and purpose-relative, true, but it is valuable nonetheless.

The answer is no, we saw, to the question of whether we should see the language of successive selves as a merely figurative one, because to confer more serious status on it would be to violate metaphysical or theoretical dictates. A metaphysics of successive selves is incompatible with the traditional theory of self associated with the Cartesian and Kantian tradition. But the Humean analysis, traceable through William James to the theory of neoempiricists like Grice and Parfit, is entirely hospitable to such a language, nonfiguratively understood.

Moreover, we also arrived at a negative answer to the question of whether there nevertheless remain moral and normative reasons to avoid adopting such a language and metaphysics. While great normative costs attach to a metaphysics of successive selves when it employs a threshold that readily multiplies identities, we are free to adopt a fairly identity-conserving threshold. In so doing, we need not fear for the individualistic values and concepts we hold dear.

Many of the findings of this essay were more solely methodological than those named thus far. How should we approach questions about personal change, multiplicity, and moral responsibility that were the impetus for this essay? Here we reach conclusions to guide other and future inquiries, and these outcomes are the most far-reaching.

One group of these findings reflects the peculiar difficulties attached to this exercise as an interdisciplinary study. The moral, philosophical, and theoretical explorations of metaphysics and the philosophy of mind here share a subject matter with abnormal psychology. Yet abnormal psychology, and particularly the clinical disciplines of psychiatry and psychotherapy associated with it, are empirical in approach, particular in disposition, and value-neutral, at least in intent. Philosophy, in contrast, is by its nature nonempirical and general, always seeking after conclusions that go beyond the particularities of any given experience, context, or case and deeply concerned with the place and nature of moral norms and values. These two approaches should have much to offer to one another. But because of these differing dispositions, the impediments to success at this interdisciplinary boundary are considerable.

Here I have explored and emphasized two of these impediments in particular. First, we saw that clinical and nosological concerns, which place symptoms in syndromic symptom clusters and resort to causal definition, serve to separate what may be states that are introspectively and conceptually indistinguishable (one example: dissociative disorder, possession, and the made experiences of severe psychotic states). Again, these factors of syndromic and causal definition yield a discourse so insulated from the descriptions of everyday experience and from philosophical, literary, and even psychodynamic writing that radical uncertainty prevails over, for example, the phenomenon of self-deception and its relationship to the dissociative states that are within the narrow purview of clinical understanding.

Second, it was shown how psychiatry's presumption of organicity, which leaves unstressed the contrast between conditions whose causal origins are fully understood and those in which they are not, stands in the way of two distinct kinds of conclusions important to our overall inquiry here: those we would draw about responsibility and culpability in relation to the mentally disturbed wrongdoer and those we might reach through generalization to all minds or selves from rare and unusual cases.

The contrasting discourses and interests of the several disciplines that intersect here are not alone in raising methodological issues,

moreover. Also implicated in our uncertainty over how to find satisfactory answers were methodological traps that beset us within philosophy. Most notable of these are two: the dilemma associated with
choosing between real and imagined cases and the delicate interplay
between moral intuition and metaphysical postulation.

The simplest strictures of scientific method seemingly necessitate
the use of thought experiment and imaginary, "science fiction" cases
for some inquiries into philosophical questions about personal identity. Yet the imaginary cases we construct are at the same time not
realistic enough for the purposes to which we would put them.

The risk of unacceptable and unproductive circularity is ever
present when conclusions about moral responsibility are grounded
in general claims of metaphysics while at the same time questions of
metaphysics are answered—as it seems they must be—by appeal to
moral intuitions about particular cases. To avoid such circularity, we
saw, an exacting method of "reflective equilibrium," circling but not
circular, must be developed and employed.

While writing this book at home on a sabbatical leave, I made a
succession of visits to a man who fixes chairs, every week or so
bringing him another small repair job. At the very start of our association, he declared himself and his work, gesturing toward the dis-
assembled parts of a rocker neatly arranged on his workbench (two
carved wooden slides, two arms, flat back, and seat): "If it comes
apart, I take it apart!" Then he scrapes it clean, he explained, and
reglues it, and "Then it's cured!"

Analysis. Synthesis. Cure. Would that I could have achieved so
much in this book, but I have not. There are few unqualified public-
policy recommendations and no specific proposals for ethical codes.
Very little regluing. No cure. But if it comes apart, I have taken it
apart, revealing the complexity of the parts and the interdependencies
involved: empirical, theoretical, and normative.

Notes

Introduction

1. See Rosenbaum (1980).

2. Nineteenth-century speculation about multiple selves also raised some of these legal concerns, it is true (see Hacking 1995, 49).

3. Should we—can we—separate the self's unity and continuity this way? At least two considerations have invited philosophers to connect and even conflate questions about the unity or division of minds at a given time with those about the continuity or discontinuity of selves through time. First, if we are persuaded by Kant's (1781, 1787) transcendental arguments in the Deduction, we may well believe, with him, that the self's unity at a given time depends, at some deep level, on the experience of its continuity through time, that the possibility of any experience entails that we know any "now" as placed in relation to some, and indeed several, "then"s. There has also been a more recent attempt to sketch conceptual links between unity and continuity: that of Shoemaker (1984). Mental states, Shoemaker argues, are unified at a given time in virtue of what they jointly cause or are capable of causing, and what they cause will be something later in time with which they are continuous through stretches of time. These are compelling arguments. But the self's unity and continuity may be metaphysically interdependent, as I believe they are, for all their empirical distinguishability.

Second, the distinction between unity and continuity flies in the face of an influential tradition where the self's unity at a time and its continuity through time have been represented as products of the same unifying force. Personal identity—the numerical sameness of the self or person from one time to another—is provided, on this view, by the transcendental subject of experiences. Some posit, variously taken as a substance (Descartes) and a transcendental principle (Kant), remains unvarying through the everchanging rush of experiences and inner states that the conscious person is the subject of. This subject of experiences acts to unify the self in two ways. Because it, and it alone, is the subject of *my* experiences, it has been appealed to in explaining the so-called "unity of consciousness"—the self's unity at a given time. In addition, because the transcendental subject is invariant through time, it has been used to explain the identity of the person through time—here the self's continuity. The person is a unity in these two ways because of the unifying effect of the transcendental subject.

These Cartesian and Kantian theories, I surmise, go far to explain why discussions of divided minds and disunity have not been distinguished from those about discontinuous and even successive selves, and why questions about these apparently distinct notions have often been treated together and even conflated in theoretical writing. Because of the force and persistence of versions of the Cartesian and Kantian tradition, we are inclined to use the phrase 'the unity of the self' to apply indifferently to both of the distinguishable unities implied in the distinction between divided minds and successive selves.

4. Compare this definition with the definitions of a self offered by Segal and White. For Segal, a self is "a highly integrated structure of the personality that typically exists only partially formed within a person" (1991, viii–ix). For White, "The self . . . is a subject of intentional states, such as beliefs and desires, as well as qualitative states, such as pains. . . . Selves . . . are persons as they are represented to themselves from the first-person point of view" (1991, 1). This is also at least close to Hacking's "soul": "that strange mix of aspects of a person that may be, at sometime, imagined as inner" (1995, 6). For a fuller explication of the connotations of 'self' and associated terms such as 'person', 'character', and 'individual', see Rorty 1976.

Chapter 1   Heterogeneities of Self in Everyday Life

1. For a sensitive discussion of the dangers lurking when a rigid subjective/objective dichotomy is embraced, see Code 1991.

2. The distinction between unity and continuity is one that well accords with subjective experience. We seem to understand the "now," or as it has sometimes been termed, the "specious present," involved in distinguishing the self's unity at a time, as many philosophers have pointed out (e.g., James [1890], Daniels [1979], Mackie [1976], Wilkes [1988], Korsgaard [1989], Braude [1991]). Moreover, so long as we trust appearances as they are given in subjective experience, we are able to establish a rough definition of the specious present. *Experiences E_1 and E_2 are united at a time, or in a specious present, just when they are believed, on the basis of memory or introspection, to be simultaneous* (this is an adaptation from Grice 1941).

3. An interesting set of arguments that challenge the notion that conversions can be rapid are offered by Swinburne (1984).

Chapter 2   A Language of Successive Selves

1. This may be only a very loose invariance. Should their qualitative changes through time be gradual—imperceptible or incremental—it is arguable that our attribution of sameness may not be in acknowledgment of their continuity as particulars (the sense noted in (a)). Instead, it may be because, as Reid (1785) insisted, qualitative sameness of the kind intended in (b) admits of degree, and in

an ever-changing world, it will be linguistically convenient to overlook lesser, or less abrupt, qualitative alterations in things. When we are speaking of divisible wholes, entities whose meaning elevates them to something over and above the sum of their parts, such as nations or, to use one of Reid's examples, regiments, this point is irrefutable. Attributions of sameness to spatiotemporal particulars like refrigerators and curtains, on the other hand, are more opaque: they may be a reflection of the understanding implied in (a).

2. The causes of these alterations in persons differ significantly, of course. My psychological states transform me, from within, into a feminist; my states also determine, from without, that the curtains will be dyed green.

3. It may be said to be something worse: inaccurate. In the strict parlance of analytical philosophy, this "secondary" sense of sameness corresponds to exact similarity, it is true. Nevertheless, the loose language of everyday discourse utilizes 'sameness' and its cognates in the manner indicated here (see Mackie 1976, chap. 6). In theoretical writing, however, ambiguities surround not only 'identity' but the apparently less formal 'sameness'. I am adopting the position that 'identity' differs from 'sameness' in not admitting of degree; this position equates sameness with exact similarity. In contrast, some theorists would acknowledge "relative" or "qualitative" identity, which, unlike strict or numerical identity, admits of degree (see, e.g., Brennan 1988, chap. 1). Moreover, others would preserve 'sameness', equating it with strict or numerical identity so as to preclude an equation between sameness and exact similarity (Reid [1785], Mackie [1976, chap. 6]). Reid, for instance, permits 'same' to cover exact and even inexact qualitative similarity when we speak of bodily things, but he insists that when we speak of persons, we must use the "strict and philosophical" sense of sameness, i.e., numerical identity. (See also Chisholm 1969.)

The role of continuity introduces additional variations: some theorists ascribe 'identity' but not 'sameness' to an entity to which changes have occurred in its nonrelational properties while it proceeded through a continuous spatiotemporal path (see Price 1977).

4. Elster (1987) perhaps too readily assumes that it does in his otherwise valuable attempt to rank on a scale of literalness the various theories and phenomena proposed by philosophers and social scientists to support the ascription of multiple selves. The most literal accounts, on this scale, propose different "hardware" in the brain to account for its seemingly different functional subselves, and the least literal is Freud's theoretical tripartite division into ego, superego, and id. In the less literal accounts, as Elster puts it, the selves are more like aspects than agents; in the most literal, they are relatively durable, stable, autonomous systems that have distinct functions in the the life of the mind. It would be a crude mistake, of which one hopes Elster is not guilty, to identify the self with the hardware. (Contemporary theorists who take issue with the patriarchal and modernist "plunge into self objectification" [Keller 1986, 194] apparently attribute the same sort of overly literal apprehension to those they criticize.) Yet unless one identifies the self with the hardware, the question raised in the text seems to arise. Because selves are closer to angels than to curtains, the criteria for literal and figurative applications will be problematic and theory-dependent.

5. Not all theorists have adopted the view that identity judgments rest on analyzable criteria. It has been claimed, for example, that personal identity judgments are noncriterial and nonanalyzable (see Butler 1736). A recent variant on this view is to be found in the writing of Chisholm (1969).

6. It is not regarded as sufficient by Bernard Williams (1973), for example.

7. This is the distinction between "strong" and "weak" continuity, introduced by Hirsch (1982, chap. 1) and helpfully explicated by Brennan (1988, chap. 1).

Chapter 3   Multiplicity through Dissociation

1. The term 'dissociation' is used in several different ways within abnormal psychology. It may mean (1) a disconnection between states of consciousness or different mental systems, (2) an experiential feeling of disconnection, or (3) a defense mechanism to ward off pain. The first of these uses is intended in this discussion.

2. Another poignant expression of the loss of self comes from a patient suffering the advances of Alzheimer's disease: "I am hungry for the life that is being taken away from me. I am a human being. I still exist.... What I ask for is that what is left of my life shall have some meaning.... Help me to be strong and free until my self no longer exists.... Every few months I sense that another part of me is missing. My life ..., my self ..., are falling apart. I can only think half thoughts now. Someday I may wake up and not think at all ..., not know who I am. Most people expect to die some day, but whoever expected to lose their self first?" (quoted in Cohen and Eisdorfer 1986, 21).

3. These cases interestingly resemble the hypothetical result of "brain zap" discussed by some theorists (Perry 1976a, 1976b).

4. The fragmentation accompanying such conditions has been vividly documented by Laing (1960), for example.

5. This point has been recognized by de Sousa: If we are drawn to the homunculi picture, he remarks, "we must ... conceive of them as relatively stable intentional systems." This concerns him, for "to accommodate the variety of our strategies, priorities, attitudes, and projects, the boundaries of the homunculi would have to be constantly changing." (1976, 224).

Yet because and to the extent that the full separate selves identified by our criteria reflect stable agent and personality patterns and dispositions, they deserve this title. De Sousa's criterion was not at fault. Rather, the fault lies with thinking that certain kinds of phenomena suggest homunculi.

6. This assertion forms a criterion for unified consciousness or a specious present, as we saw earlier (chapter 1, note 2): two simultaneous conscious experiences E_1 and E_2 belong to the same unified consciousness just when they are believed (on the basis of memory or introspection) to be simultaneous (Grice 1941).

7. By encompassing more than mere amnesia or forgetting, the notion of disordered awareness and memory allows us to acknowledge the range of memory disturbances that some theorists judge to be importantly related. Spiegel and

Cardeña (1991) have linked amnesia or forgetting with those forms of memory disturbance that involve unbidden memories, flashbacks, and "intrusive recollection." Although seeming to be contraries, these very different disturbances of memory are each consequences of trauma, they argue. Thus they are syndromically and causally related.

8. Compare the multiplicity criteria identified here with the important philosophical account of multiplicity provided by Stephen Braude. Braude (1991, 77) has argued that among related phenomena (depersonalization, hypnoid states) multiples alone comprise separate selves, which are distinct "apperceptive centers," i.e., the autobiographical and indexical status of each are largely nonautobiographical and nonindexical for the other. Thus subself 1 regards a high proportion of subself 2's states in a detached way (as "hers" not "mine"). Braude's terminological distinctions are useful, we will find, in classifying the epistemology of selves vis-à-vis one another's experiences.

9. See White 1991.

10. Amélie Rorty has argued that while akrasia (and self-deception) may in certain ways challenge the traditional notion of the self as a unified source of agency, they also presuppose that very notion. For a self that *cares* to avoid akrasia and self-deception, she observes, is already a unified agent, rather than a "loose confederation of habits" (Rorty 1986, 136). Rorty's remarks illustrate and confirm the point made here: the relationships both among propositional attitudes and between propositional attitudes and action (mental and physical) are open to several interpretations when we are looking at how they reveal agency. Indeed, we *are not clear* how to derive conclusions as to single or multiple sources of agency from cases of whole human beings. But as I have pointed out, we are also not clear about something else that Rorty's comments seem to imply: that some overall agent unity must preclude all talk of coexisting subselves with distinguishable and conflicting sets of goals and purposes.

11. See also Cardeña et al. 1995.

12. The point has been recognized by Coons (1980, 1984), and *DSM*-IV (American Psychiatric Association 1995) has seen the restoration of amnesia— expunged in *DSM*-III-R (APA 1987)—as a feature of dissociative-identity disorder. This confusion over the role of amnesia is the product of the different perspectives from which to view this condition: the limited view revealed through the presenting symptoms available to the diagnostician or the purportedly detached and objective view provided by the all-seeing eye.

13. Another interest of philosophers has been the ascription of incompatible predicates to multiples, which an acknowledgment of the seeming multiplicity attributable to dissociative conditions seems to impel. How do we describe the patient, one of whose subselves knows some proposition *p* while another does not? Regarded as a whole, does that patient know *p*? (See Wilkes 1988.)

14. Compared with ordinary unitary selves, the separate selves of multiples typically suffer a paucity of traits, Braude (1991, 215) insists. Nonetheless, most descriptions of such selves indicate a number of traits sufficient for identification and reidentification, although see note 15 below.

15. The paucity of identifying traits found in some "selves" may preclude their ranking as full selves.

16. For a full discussion of the several skeptical doubts about the putative phenomenon of multiple personality or dissociative-identity disorder, see especially Hacking 1986, 1995, and the concept Hacking introduces of "dynamic nominalism."

For various reasons, some similar to those elaborated here, several philosophers have judged descriptions of this disorder to exhibit multiple selves; some have gone further and ascribed multiple persons, minds, and consciousnesses in addition. One, Bernard Williams, has firmly declined to extend the term 'person' to these cases, however, and while his reasoning may not apply as easily to 'self', with its rather different nuances, it is nevertheless worth rehearsing here. Individuation of Miss Beauchamp's various personalities by reference to character, attainments, and memories was possible, Williams argues, only because it took place in the context of the continuity of a certain body. Thus "what we have succeeded in doing on these principles is individuating particular personalities of Miss B, who is bodily identified" (Williams 1973, 17).

Williams's argument rests on two assumptions that may be questioned: (a) that identity or unity precludes multiplicity and (b) that all individuation is interpersonal. Take (a). If Miss Beauchamp is one person, she cannot also be several persons, Williams argues. His insistence that personal identity requires bodily continuity obliges him to describe Miss Beauchamp as one person, since there is but one body. No such obligation need constrain others, however, unless they, with Williams, are committed to a bodily criterion of personal identity. Presumably, others are free both to speak of Miss Beauchamp's various personalities as separate selves or persons and to speak of multiplicity as coexisting within or alongside the unity of personal identity. With regard to (b), we have seen that interpersonal and intrapersonal individuation are to be distinguished. For the therapist's purposes of helping a multiple identify and reunite separate selves, deeper efforts of identification and reidentification may be unnecessary and irrelevant.

17. An interesting exception is to be found in the writing of the psychoanalyst Roy Schafer. He describes the defenses thus: "One does not know that one knows something, wishes something, considers something emotionally, or is doing or has done some other action; one keeps oneself from discovering what one does not know, etc., thus deceiving oneself once; and one keeps oneself from discovering *that* and *how* one is deceiving oneself in this way ('unconscious defence'), thus deceiving oneself a second time or in a second respect" (Schafer 1976, 234).

18. White (1991, 141) distinguishes "one-shot" cases of self-deception from "full-blown" self-deception, in recognition of something close to this point. However, White's otherwise clear and useful discussion of self-deception does not sufficiently emphasize the difference between the results of mild and those of entrenched self-deception. By subsuming all cases of genuine (not merely one-shot) self-deception under the same homuncular model, he fails to explore the variations in, and range of, separate-self development that distinguish extreme from less extreme instances. This failure has costs for White's concerns over our

responsibility for self-deception. At its extreme in dissociative-identity disorder, one is probably not responsible for self-deception, whereas in everday and fleeting self-deception, it seems plausible to suggest that one is.

Chapter 4   Succession and Recurrence outside Dissociative Disorder

1. For a discussion related to this, see Tony Hope's (1994) remarks on mania and identity.

2. Actions here include acts of mind, like perceiving and deciding. This definition is from Rorty 1986, 119. See also Mele 1987.

3. For example, few judge compulsive or impulsive action as culpable in the way that everyday weakness of will is generally taken to be—a fact that may create difficulties for Frankfurt's (1971) hierarchical account, it has been noted (see White 1991).

4. Like Schelling, Jon Elster has explored akrasia through the idea of advance directives and other strategies adopted to prevent subsequent, less rational choices. By initiating such strategies in advance, Elster (1984) emphasizes, one may improve one's prospects by eliminating certain options from the feasible set. In the most obvious case, we protect ourselves against weakness by avoiding the "near occasion" of sin. (If I cannot resist macadamia nuts, I leave them off the grocery list.) But in addition, it seems possible, Elster points out, that I anticipate my preventive strategies and "try to make myself invulnerable against the strategies that I might later use to get my way." If we were to engage in such strategies, he concedes, it may be necessary to speak of one self's manipulating another: "If two or more parts of the person are really engaging in mutual strategic manipulation, there would seem to be good grounds for referring to several selves" (Elster 1984, 10).

While these maneuvres are not in any way logically impossible, Elster observes, they do not appear to occur frequently enough to constitute the grounds we need to change our traditional idea of the self as one. Elster is surely right to note the infrequency of these elaborate maneuvres, but he is mistaken to suppose that acknowledging them as instances of separate selves would unseat our traditional identity presuppositions. According to the notions of multiplicity developed in this essay, he is also mistaken in judging them to be plausible candidates for separate selves.

5. See Fingarette 1969, and also Pears 1984, Radden 1984, Mele 1987, White 1991, and essays in Martin 1985 and in McLaughlin and Rorty 1988.

Chapter 5   From Abnormal Psychology to Metaphysics: A Methodological Preamble

1. For additional examples of science fantasy, see White 1991.

2. The literature reveals considerable intuitive disagreement over Parfit's own case of the Nobel laureate (Parfit 1984), for example.

3. See MacIntosh 1969.

4. An example of such an exercise in futility can be found when we ask a specific question about an issue in psychiatric ethics with policy-related answers: should mentally disturbed defendants be drugged to stand trial? In a detailed discussion of the intricacies of this question, I have argued elsewhere (Radden 1989) that because of the uncertainty of our intuitions in this case, the threshold concept of accountability involved, and the difficulty in choosing between the several metaphysical accounts of identity on which this concept seems to rest, we had better turn from metaphysics and from cases and appeal instead to pragmatic considerations for the policy answers we seek.

5. For a fuller discussion, see Radden 1985, chaps. 2 and 3. The broader context here concerns the concept of mental disease or illness, for which see Boorse 1975, Engelhardt 1975, Fulford 1989, Reznek 1991, and essays in Graham and Stephens 1994b and Sadler, Wiggins, and Schwartz 1994.

6. The physiological facts and experimental findings centering around commissurotomy have been rehearsed too frequently to require much introduction. The brain, we know, comprises two hemispheres, each of which controls and receives sensory input from its contralateral side and which perform separate functions. Joining the two hemispheres at the left and right cerebral cortex are bundles of nerve fibers, the cerebral commisure, or commisures. Commissurotomy, which involves partial or complete severance of the cerebral commissure, has been practiced on animals and on human epilepsy sufferers. While a medical success in reducing patients' epilepsy and apparently leaving them unimpaired and unchanged in their everyday functioning, behavioral tests postoperatively given to these human subjects reveal fractures of awareness and disunities between the severed hemispheres, which suggest that some kind of bifurcation has been the result.

7. Notice that (1) is vague on the matter of whether these contrived circumstances include all the commissurotomy patient's postoperative experience or only the experimental setting.

8. Braude (1991, chap. 5) has developed a similar argument. Not all agree, however. This position that a second mind is brought into existence by the surgery sits uneasily with our conception of what a mind is, as Nagel has remarked ("So unusual an event as a mind's popping in and out of existence would have to be explained by something more than its explanatory convenience" [1971, 408]). But how "unusual" such an event is depends on what sort of thing we think a mind is, it must be emphasized, and this is precisely what has become uncertain. At just this point we need an open mind and, as Marks (1980, 12) rightly notes, a *theory* about what minds are.

Chapter 6   Memory, Responsibility, and Contrition

1. It is not only the extension of Locke's principle to less straightforward clinical cases of successive selves that brings concerns over how such a principle is to be applied and understood. Even in application to the normal person in everyday

settings these ideas are complex and opaque. They require qualification and explication, yet even with such clarification, they remain difficult to formulate.

One difficulty is that despite the methodological individualism usually associated with responsibility for deeds, we sometimes speak as if one may be responsible for another's actions. If memory were necessary for responsibility, we might wonder about the person accorded such responsibility whose memory can encompass the experience not of doing the deed but merely at best of requesting (delegating, ordering, demanding) it. This seeming challenge to Locke's principle may be shown to rest on a confusing ellipsis, however. We are held responsible for our act (requesting), and those acts of others' in which it results here count as some of our act's foreseeable consequences. We cannot remember the acts of others that ensue, of course. But if we forget our act (of requesting), the forgetting itself is culpable. (We should not have forgotten.) We might similarly wonder about the corporations found guilty of wrongdoing: they cannot remember. Corporations comprise persons who decide, act, and request, however. It is these persons' memory—when culpable forgetting is not present—is required required for responsibility ascription (see French 1972, Thompson 1987).

Another apparent challenge to Locke's claim understood as a general principle lies in legal traditions concerning amnesia. Amnesia alone has not served as an excuse in criminal law, for reasons that, while they are critical to the purposes and context of the criminal law, may be set aside in the less pragmatic context of this discussion: problems associated with differentiating genuine from fraudulent or simulated amnesia and with the frequency with which amnesia is a concomitant to the commission of violent crime in otherwise normal wrongdoers. The first of these problems allows us to emphasize a distinction important for our discussion between moral considerations and epistemological considerations. Without a means to distinguish fraudulent from genuine amnesia—a severe epistemological impediment—the purposes and context of criminal law may be incompatible with policy that would allow amnesia to excuse. But divorced from such pragmatic considerations, purely moral reasoning permits us adopt the principle that amnesia ought to be treated as an excuse. Even without a means of distinguishing genuine amnesia in actual cases, we may determine Locke's principle to be true. (Locke acknowledged this distinction in his own discussion when he recognized the seeming contradiction to his principle in the man whose drunken commission of a crime enabled him to forget it. The law does not accept as excuses the amnesia wrought by drunkenness or sleepwalking, Locke insists, because it can have no proof that these claims are not fraudulent. But on the day of judgement God will hold us responsible only for remembered deeds. (II.xxvii.22, n.). Again, important though it may be to criminal law, the fact that amnesia is a frequent concomitant to violent crime need not affect our less circumscribed moral reasoning. The many nonlegal wrongs we encounter in everyday life, which such reasoning encompasses, are not similarly accompanied by amnesia.

2. The first and best known statement of this objection is by Butler (1736).

3. Although the conclusions and focus here differ from Strawson's, they are in no way incompatible. Strawson's discussion influenced what follows both in the category of ("reactive") moral attitudes and in the style of argument that accords them centrality.

4. Understood as culpability, guilt is, as we saw, constrained by individualism. But guilt and guilt feelings must be carefully distinguished. We do not ascribe guilt to others ('She is guilty') merely on the basis of the feelings they may experience and express. Separate grounds warrant the ascription of guilt and the ascription of guilt feelings. The grounds warranting ascriptions of guilt at least include an individualistic tenet. 'He is guilty' conveys that the self same person who is the subject of the ascription (he) did the deed. For a further discussion of these points, see Radden 1995.

5. This conviction was emphasized in the discussion "MPD and Personal Responsibility" at the Annual Meeting of the American Psychological Association, Toronto, August 1993.

6. This point was emphasized by clinicians at the meeting cited in note 5, above.

7. Responsibility also depends on a degree of voluntary control and of rational functioning likely absent in such cases. Moreover, some would treat the presumed organicity of Mr. M.'s manic excesses as exculpating.

The presumption of organicity, widely adopted when there are functional psychiatric disorders such as that suffered by Mr. M., complicates our conclusion here. The conviction that Mr. M. is not responsible for the harm he inflicted upon his family during the fish-tank episode may rest with the intuition that diseases excuse and that he suffered a disease, albeit one whose origin remains unknown. However, we must set aside this and other possible grounds to excuse Mr. M.'s behavior for the purposes of this discussion. In determining whether the peculiarities likely to characterize his subsequent memory of this episode should absolve Mr. M. of responsibility *according to Locke's principle*, the presumption of organicity must play no part.

This will not be easy, and at such times we most strongly see the advantage of science-fiction cases, such as Carol Rovane's (1993) forgetful person. This is someone who only remembers for 24-hour stretches and must resort to "identification criteria." Only by looking up a written record and remembering that she has a short memory can this hypothetical forgetter assert ownership ('It was I who did it').

There is no presumption of organicity to distract us here. Yet the case suffers as a means of determining whether responsibility spans over these memory losses. Unlike Rovane, I remain uncertain in my intuitions over this case, and feel that it is underdescribed. Why is this woman so incapacitated, I want to ask? And exactly how much memory has she left? What are the other unrealistic features of the world in this story?

Chapter 7 Purposes and Discourses of Responsibility Ascription

1. This claim is derived from conversation with clinicians, particularly those undertaking therapy with victims of sexual abuse, victims in whom shame is a cruel and damaging emotional legacy of their earlier experience.

2. This must be expected; that it occurs in fact was emphasized by Dr. Mitchell Eisen, speaking on "Multiple Personality Disorder and Personal Responsibility," American Psychological Association Annual Meeting, Toronto, August 1993.

3. For discussion of attempts to use the insanity defense with dissociative disorders, see Cleary 1983, 1985; Perr 1991; and Saks 1992, 1995.

4. Normal unity itself is less than complete: normally united persons are complexly heterogeneous, we know. They are what Flanagan (1994) has called "multiplex."

5. My information derives from discussion at a conference at the Institute of Pennsylvania Hospital in February 1992 on managing multiples as inpatients, where speakers included Richard P. Kluft, the director of an inpatient unit for patients suffering dissociative disorder.

Chapter 8   Multiplicity and Legal Culpability

1. Significant variations occur among actual cases. There are even cases where the ineffectual self is witness to the wrongdoing of the reigning self but lacks control. For a useful discussion of these differences, see French and Shechmeister 1983, and Perr 1991.

2. Kopelman (1987) has stressed how many amnesic subjects either have reported the crime themselves or have made no attempt to conceal it.

3. See Bradford and Smith 1979.

4. For an account of the Milligan case, see Keyes 1982. For a discussion of why and how attempts to use the insanity defense with dissociative disorders have succeeded and failed, see Cleary 1983, Perr 1991, and Saks 1992, 1995.

5. McNaghten's rule states that to establish a defense on the ground of insanity, it must be clearly proved that at the time of committing the act, the party accused was laboring under such a defect of reason, from disease or defect of the mind, as not to know the nature and quality of the act he was doing, or if he did know, then as not to know that he was doing what was wrong (*Regina v. McNaghten* 1843).

   The Bonnie rule states that a person charged with a criminal offense should be found not guilty by reason of insanity if it is shown that as a result of mental disease or mental retardation, he was unable to appreciate the wrongfulness of his conduct at the time of the offense (Bonnie 1983).

   The ALI test is found in section 4.01 of the *Model Penal Code:* a person is not responsible for criminal conduct if at the time of such conduct as a result of mental disease or defect he lacks substantial capacity either to appreciate the criminality (wrongfulness) of his conduct or to conform his conduct to the requirements of law (ALI 1955).

6. That unconsciousness may not result from being of unsound mind is established in *People v. Kitt* 1978, *People v. Lisnow* 1978, and *People v. Caldwell* 1980. For a discussion of the legal doctrine that unconsciousness excuses, see Hart 1968. In U.S. law the defense of unconsciousness is set forth in the Penal Code, section 26: all persons are capable of committing crimes except those

belonging to certain classes, one of which is persons who committed the act charged without being conscious of doing it (*People v. Kitt* 1978).

7. Changes to the Californian Penal Code that took effect in 1982 prevented evidence of mental disease, defect, or disorder from being admissible to negate the capacity to form any mental state (see section 28). For a recent analysis of the Californian experiment with diminished capacity, see Bursztajn, Scherr, and Brodsky 1994, 613.

8. The therapy offered must be the right kind of therapy, appropriate to the condition. See Putnam 1989 and Hall 1989.

Chapter 9   Paternalistic Intervention

1. These justifications may show intervention to be merely permissible or to be obligatory, as Fulford (1989, 189–190) has emphasized.

2. Susan Wolf's development of hierarchical theories of desire is particularly associated with the application of a "real self" theory to questions of responsibility and mental disorder (see Wolf 1980, 1987, 1990). These questions are discussed in chapter 14.

3. In subsequent writing (1983) Macklin has acknowledged—without offering a solution for—something close to this problem. She proposes a drawback to defining autonomy in terms of authenticity in the following terms: "In this sense of the term, the person with a lifelong history of mental illness may nonetheless turn out to have autonomy, so long as attitudes and values remain consistent, or 'in character' " (Macklin 1983, 49).

4. In addition to these various theoretical presuppositions, arguments about the restoration of authenticity presuppose that therapeutic means are effective in restoring an earlier, more authentic self. On these empirical issues little can be said here. But we do know that some forms of therapeutic intervention, such as that provided by psychotropic drugs, have marked and even extreme effects on personality and may be expected with some reliability to return patients to a self at least more like his or her original one than the disturbed self. (Moreover, these means can often be relied on to restore some measure of autonomy, in Macklin's sense of self-directed action.) A thoughtful recent discussion about the restoration of authenticity is found in Hope 1994, 140.

5. For documentation of this trend, see Gutheil and Appelbaum 1985.

6. For the phrase ' "thank you" theory' and for illumination on this and related topics, I am indebted to Alan Wertheimer.

Chapter 10   Responsibilities over Oneself in the Future or One's Future Selves

1. The term is Dresser's (1984).

2. I am not satisfied, however, with the criteria of personhood that these authors adopt (namely, the abilities to be conscious of oneself as existing through time,

to appreciate reasons for acting, and to engage in purposive sequences of action) (see Radden 1992). They are open to interpretation, but even on a fairly generous reading, these criteria would prove overly stringent in excluding many people from the status of personhood at least temporarily during phases of mental disturbance. For a similar dissatisfaction with Buchanan and Brock's (1989) analysis, see recent discussion by Hope (1994).

Chapter 11   A Metaphysics of Successive Selves

1. Hume's attacks on metaphysical reasoning were directed not at the scope of the conclusions sought so much as at the method of reasoning employed in the "dogmatic" metaphysics of his time. The term 'metaphysics' bears several distinguishable meanings, some very narrow, as in 'dogmatic metaphysics', and some looser and broader. Whenever we delve into abstract theoretical and philosophical ideas, we approach metaphysics understood in this broader way. Thus all the exploration conducted in this book may be described as metaphysical if we follow James, who defined 'metaphysics' as only an unusually obstinate attempt to think clearly and consistently (1890, 461). My analysis is directed toward selves at some remove from the particular settings of embodiment, action, and interaction within which we encounter them in everyday life or clinical experience. This detachment and generality, together with the depth and detail required for such an analysis, capture one sense in which this whole endeavor is metaphysical.

2. Although, as Parfit has pointed out, strikingly similar conceptions of identity influence Indian philosophy, this last claim may be too immodest: other cultures and other ontologies with different metaphysical and normative presuppositions may yield identity theories different from any imagined by Anglo-American philosophy. On these issues of relativism, see also White 1991, chap. 5.

3. Hume, in his *Treatise* (1888, 169), asserts that identity is merely a quality that we attribute to our separate and distinct perceptions of things "because of the union of their ideas in the imagination when we reflect upon them." The qualities that unite ideas in the imagination are, for Hume, the relations of resemblance, causation, and contiguity (by which he means proximity, or closeness). He concludes, "Identity depends on the relations of ideas," and "these relations produce identity, by means of that easy transition they occasion. But as the relations, and the easiness of the transition diminish by insensible degrees, we have no just standard by which we can decide any dispute concerning the item when they acquire or lose a title to the name of identity. All the disputes concerning the identity of connected objects are merely verbal, except so far as the relation of parts gives rise to some fiction or imaginary principle of union, as we have already observed" (Hume 1965, 262).

4. A related concept is that of emergence in the writing of George Herbert Mead (1932).

5. This is at least true unless we include as part of memory the "implicit memory" identified by psychologists that enables a person to know without knowing that she knows.

6. The term 'survival' is associated with Parfit's earlier description (1970, 1971); later he uses 'psychological continuity and connectedness' (1984).

7. But survival is what is important in the relation between self stages, Parfit insists.

8. Leibniz's law is that if x is identical with y, then anything that is true of x is also true of y. For a useful discussion of this aspect of identity, see Brennan 1988.

9. Again the question turns on whether we accept "implicit memory" as memory.

10. See especially Parfit 1984, pp. 206, 213, 240.

11. Parfit's theory does not commit itself on this point.

Chapter 12   The Normative Tug of Individualism

1. See MacIntyre (1981, 114). On the other hand, Owen Flanagan (1991, 292) has reminded us that some cultures are considerably less enamored than ours of the global-trait terms in which we cast the language of virtues, preferring instead descriptions qualified by context.

2. So MacIntyre (1981, 35) believes, at least.

3. For a fuller discussion on integrity, see Taylor 1985, 108–141.

4. In his discussion of the virtue-based moral life of eighteenth-century English society, reflected in Jane Austen's novels, MacIntyre (1981, 189) has singled out constancy and integrity. They are virtues for Jane Austen, and MacIntyre treats them as special virtues, or as aspects of a single special virtue. His discussion is ambiguous on this matter, and with some reason. A want of integrity may, and often does, reveal itself with distressing regularity. But the steady moral reliability of true constancy would then not be found. And while integrity may appear to wax and wane through time, true integrity, we want to say, ensures stability. Possession of these virtues, MacIntyre remarks, is prerequisite for the possession of other virtues. MacIntyre appears to make the case I have been putting here (though conflating constancy and integrity) when he remarks, "There is at least one virtue recognized by the tradition which cannot be specified at all except with reference to the wholeness of human life [MacIntyre here means the span of a human lifetime]—the virtue of integrity or constancy" (MacIntyre 1981, 189).

5. A related thesis has been developed with respect to guilt by Sharon Bishop (1987), to which Barbara Houston (1992) has offered a measured response.

Chapter 13   Therapeutic Goals for a Liberal Culture

1. Other goals sought in therapy imply or presuppose complex theories of the self. There is, for example, building or enhancing the self-esteem of the client suffering affective disorders like depression. There is restoring or rebuilding an

inadequate self in personality disorders identified by self psychologists like Kohut (1971, 1977). An explicitly normative and ideological goal sought in the context of feminist therapy is to endorse and validate the relational self. The three goals chosen for analysis here—self unity, self-knowledge, and self-determination—have greater significance than these if only because they are the most widely shared goals.

2. My support for this claim comes from Tom Gutheil, M.D. (personal communication).

3. For a recent clear-eyed and honorably explicit discussion of this important dimension to psychiatric ethics, see Holmes and Lindley 1989, chap. 2.

4. The goal of integration is not unanimously accepted or adopted; dissention has been expressed by patients, by therapists, and by other theorists. Putnam (1989) and also Coons (1980, 1984) question whether compete integration is a realistic therapeutic goal for work with this disorder (see also Kluft 1984a, 1984b; Hale 1983; and essays in Braun 1986). The feminist theorist Naomi Scheman (1993, 103) rejects the solution of integrating all selves into one and making all but one go away in favor of "creating the possibility of respectful conversation among them."

5. See, for example, the therapist's epilogue by R. Phillips: "After I became aware of the MPD I fully expected that the goal of psychotherapy would be to find the central person and to integrate the others into the person of that one. However, I discovered that the 'core' was dead, and that the process of healing would most likely result in a number of persons who spoke through the 'shell' of a woman. The task became co-operation of many, rather than integration into one" (Chase 1987, 411–412).

6. Fusion has been achieved, according to one clinician when one finds "(i) at least three months of continuing memory, (ii) absence of overt behavioral signs of multiplicity, (iii) subjective sense of unity, (iv) absence of alter personalities under hypnosis, (v) modification of transference phenomena, and (vi) clinical evidence that the unified patient's self-representation included acknowledgement of attitudes and awareness which were previously segregated in separate personalities" (Kluft 1984a, 12).

7. In the case study of Evylyn reported by Osgood, Luria, Jeans, and Smith (1976), a new self is forged with the emergence of Evylyn and eventual disappearance of Gina and Mary.

8. See note 5, above.

9. Interestingly, Putnam seems to find of these models equally acceptable when he quotes another clinician, Caul, with approval: "After treatment you want a functional unity, be it a corporation, a partnership or a one-owner business" (Putnam 1989, 301).

10. The term is Kant's, introduced in the first *Critique* (Kant 1781, 1787, 77).

11. The force of this conviction has sometimes justified intervention against the patient's wishes, for example, requiring the use of psychotropic medicine to chemically produce a state of fitness to stand trial.

12. Frankfurt also understands moral responsibility in these terms, although serious theoretical problems have been identified in this aspect of his account (see Thalberg 1978; Watson 1975, 1977; White 1991).

13. To appreciate this point, it is important to emphasize that acting on a whim or for no reason is distinct from any of the psychological constraints, even self-caused ones, introduced earlier.

14. Versions of this view are to be found in much feminist writing today, and it appears in the communitarian critiques of traditional Western notions of individualism, as well (see Chodorow 1989).

Chapter 14   Continuity Sufficient for Individualism

1. The world seems to offer us policies and practices that would in many instances soften the rigidity of this stance, though. Not only statutes of limitations but even bankruptcy—with its opportunity for a fresh start, all past debts and obligations expunged—seem to reflect a notion of culpability that is relative to time and/or change (the law is ambiguous, notice). I am grateful to Sandy Levinson for drawing my attention to bankruptcy.

2. It may also be due in part to the kind of intuitions that undergird the insanity defense.

3. For a related discussion on issues raised here, see Meyers 1994, 143. Focusing on some of the heterogeneities encountered in normal selves, Meyers asks whether such inner diversity is compatible with "moral identity" and concludes that it is.

Chapter 15   The Divided Minds of Mental Disorder

1. The only attempt at purely philosophical support for a simultaneity thesis comes from an example developed by Parfit. In the example of the physics exam (Parfit 1984, 247), I manage to disengage my two hemispheres to simultaneously try different solutions to a problem, reuniting the two hemispheres after the math is done. My later memory is of "just having worked at two calculations, in working at each of which I was not aware of working at the other." But the example is underdescribed. What am I aware of during this stretch of time? Parfit fails to give a description of that. Even with his retrospective "memory" description there are problems. It is true that we can remember undertaking two activities simultaneously, e.g., listening to the radio while washing dishes. But such a case is quite different: I am aware of doing both because these two activities are not competing for the same kind of attention, as listening to two radios at once, or doing two math problems at once, must be. And they are bound by attention in such a way that they can be simultaneous. But I cannot read two books simultaneously, let alone make two sets of calculations.

2. The key/ring illustration has been developed by Marks (1980, 7).

3. For a particularly clear discussion of these issues, see Gillett 1986b.

4. Clinicians positioned to compare subjective reports from these two patient groups bring to their comparisons expectations and frames based on broader clinical and nosological considerations that seem all too likely to shape their judgments.

Chapter 16   The Grammar of Disownership

1. The same point seems to be attributable to Evans, when he claims that first-person reference is "identification free" (1982, 179). And the epistemological correlates of such a position are captured in Chisholm's (1981, 79) notion of "self-presenting" properties, whose nature is available to their subject.

2. Yet some theorists, like the materialist Armstrong (1968), may be seen to disagree. He follows the truth of Hume's observation that the subject of experiences cannot be met with introspectively to the conclusion that my certainty that my experiences are mine must be derived criterially. In speaking of minds and in using the first person singular, he insists that "we go beyond what is introspectively observed" (Armstrong 1968, 227). Armstrong's claims here seem to presuppose an act-object distinction and also an "inner sense" model of the mind. But there are real difficulties with these presuppositions. It is unclear, for example, what sort of epistemic operation or inference could be said to yield self-attribution. What features of my present experience could mark it as mine, except a kind of feeling attaching to every experience that seems to say 'mine'? (This is quite distinct from experiencing the "I.") What can it mean to say that I experience my experiences as possessed (by me)? I do not experience the separable whole self in relation to my experiences. But I *do* experience the gestalt of owned experiences. The act-object relation is irreducible and internal, our experience tells us (as, particularly insistently, do contemporary phenomenologists).

2. Following the innateness hypothesis of psycholinguistics and influenced by Piagetian structuralism, the theorist Eli Hirsch speculates that "as a matter of empirical fact, any human being is innately disposed to speak a language in which the boundaries of the self are drawn in the normal way" (Hirsch 1982, 303).

3. Hallucinations look more promising here. For they are customarily understood as a breakdown in the capacity to distinguish between reality and fantasy, or between the publicly confirmed and veridical perceptual experience, on the one hand, and subjective, nonveridical perceptual experience, on the other. But this portrayal of hallucinations best describes visual, olfactory, and tactile hallucinatory experiences. Auditory hallucinations, because they often take the form of inner voices communicating meaningful messages, are the most easily analyzed as "nonself" when this expression connotes another agent or source of agency. Yet this generalization also requires qualification. Much in phenomenological reports of auditory hallucination in particular belies the textbook definition and assumptions implicit in the view that hallucination is an in-

capacity to distinguish the subjective from the publicly verified and verifiable. Perhaps the victim of olfactory hallucination loses the capacity to distinguish between smells in the world and smells that are merely "in" herself. But the victim of auditory hallucination often does not fail in quite this way. There is a detachedness about the hallucinated voices sufficient to "disown" them, but they are not confused with embodied voices deriving from outside (Bleuler 1934; Fulford 1989, 1994; Graham and Stephens 1994a; Stephens and Graham 1994a, 1994b).

References

Abrams, S. 1983. "The Multiple Personality: A Legal Defense." *American Journal of Clinical Hypnosis* 25 (no. 4): 225–231.

American Law Institute. 1955. *Model Penal Code*. Sec. 4.01. Philadelphia: American Law Institute.

American Psychiatric Association. 1987. *Diagnostic and Statistical Manual of Mental Disorders*, 3rd ed., rev. (*DSM*-III-R). Washington, D.C.: APA.

American Psychiatric Association. 1995. *Diagnostic and Statistical Manual of Mental Disorders*, 4th ed. (*DSM*-IV). Washington, D.C.: APA.

Armstrong, D. 1968. *A Materialist Theory of the Mind*. London: Routledge and Kegan Paul.

Augustine, Saint, Bishop of Hippo. 400. *The Confessions of St. Augustine*. Translated and edited by J. G. Pilkington, 1876. Cleveland: Fine Editions Press, 1950.

Baier, A. 1985a. *Postures of the Mind: Essays on Mind and Morals*. Minneapolis: University of Minnesota Press.

Baier, A. 1985b. "What Do Women Want in a Moral Theory?" *Noûs* 19 (no. 1): 53–63.

Baier, A. 1986. "Trust and Antitrust." *Ethics* 96 (no. 2): 231–260.

Baier, A. 1991. "Whom Can Women Trust?" In *Feminist Ethics*, edited by C. Card. Lawrence: University Press of Kansas.

Baron, M. 1988. "Remorse and Agent Regret." In *Ethical Theory: Character and Virtue*, edited by P. French, T. Uehling, and H. Wettstein, Midwest Studies in Philosophy, no. 13. Indiana: University of Notre Dame Press.

Bateson, Catherine Mary. 1990. *Composing a Life*. New York: Plume Book.

Beahrs, J. 1983. "Co-consciousness: A Common Denominator in Hypnosis, Multiple Personality, and Normalcy." *American Journal of Clinical Hypnosis* 26 (no. 2): 100–113.

Benhabib, S. 1987. "The Generalized and the Concrete Other: The Kohlberg-Gilligan Controversy and Feminist Theory." In *Feminism as Critique: On the Politics of Gender*, edited by S. Benhabib and D. Cornell. Minneapolis: University of Minnesota Press.

Bishop, Sharon. 1987. "Connections and Guilt." *Hypatia* 2 (no. 1): 7–23.

Bleuler, E. 1934. *Textbook of Psychiatry*. Translated by A. A. Brill. New York: Macmillan.

Bonnie, R. J. 1983. "A Model Statute on the Insanity Defense." *Journal of the American Bar Association* 69 (Feb.): 194–197.

Boorse, C. 1975. "On the Distinction between Disease and Illness." *Philosophy and Public Affairs* 5 (Fall): 49–68.

Bradford, J., and Smith, S. M. 1979. "Amnesia and Homicide: The Padola Case and a Study of Thirty Cases." *Bulletin of the American Academy of Psychiatry and the Law* 7:219–231.

Braude, Stephen E. 1986. *The Limits of Influence: Psychokinesis and the Philosophy of Science*. London: Routledge and Kegan Paul.

Braude, Stephen E. 1991. *First Person Plural: Multiple Personality and the Philosophy of Mind*. London: Routledge.

Braude, Stephen E. In press. "Multiple Personality and Moral Responsibility." *Journal of Philosophy, Psychiatry, and Psychology*.

Braun, B. G. 1984. "Uses of Hypnosis with Multiple Personality." *Psychiatric Annals* 14 (no. 1): 34–40.

Braun, B. G., ed. 1986. *Treatment of Multiple Personality Disorder*. Washington, D.C.: American Psychiatric Press.

Brennan, A. 1988. *Conditions of Identity: A Study in Identity and Survival*. Oxford: Clarendon Press.

Buchanan, A. 1988. "Advance Directives and the Personal Identity Problem." *Philosophy and Public Affairs* 17 (Fall): 277–302.

Buchanan, A., and Brock, D. 1989. *Deciding for Others: The Ethics of Surrogate Decisionmaking*. Cambridge: Cambridge University Press.

Bursztajn, Harold, Harding, H., Gutheil, T. G., and Brodsky, A. 1991. "Beyond Cognition: The Role of Disordered Affective States in Impaired Competence to Consent to Treatment." *Bulletin of the American Academy of Psychiatry and the Law* 19 (no. 4): 383–388.

Bursztajn, Harold, Scherr, A., and Brodsky, A. 1994. "The Rebirth of Forensic Psychiatry in the Light of Recent Historical Trends in Criminal Responsibility." *Psychiatric Clinics of North America* 17 (no. 3): 611–635.

Butler, J. 1736. "Of Personal Identity." In his *Analogy of Religion*. Reprinted in *Personal Identity*, edited by John Perry. Berkeley: University of California Press, 1975.

Cardeña, Etzel, Lewis-Fernández, Robert, Bear, David, Pakianathan, Isabel, and Spiegel, David. 1995. "Dissociative Disorders." In *Diagnostic and Statistical Manual, IV: Sourcebook*, vol. 2. Washington, D.C.: American Psychiatric Press.

Chase, Truddi. 1987. *When Rabbit Howls*. New York: E. P. Dutton.

Chisholm, Roderick M. 1969. "The Loose and Popular and the Strict and Philosophical Senses of Identity." In *Perception and Personal Identity*, edited by Norman Care and Robert Grimm. Cleveland: Press of Case Western Reserve University.

Chisholm, Roderick M. 1981. *The First Person: An Essay on Reference and Intentionality*. Minneapolis: University of Minnesota Press.

Chodorow, N. 1986. "Toward a Relational Individualism: The Mediation of Self through Psychoanalysis." In *Reconstructing Individualism: Autonomy, Individuality, and the Self in Western Thought*, edited by T. C. Heller, M. Sosma, and D. E. Wellberg. Stanford: Stanford University Press.

Chodorow, N. 1989. *Feminism and Psychoanalytic Theory*. New Haven: Yale University Press.

Clark, Brian. 1980. *Whose Life Is It Anyway?* New York: Avon Books.

Cleary, M. 1983. "Dissociative States: Disproportionate Use as a Defense in Criminal Proceedings." *American Journal of Forensic Psychiatry* 4 (no. 4): 157–165.

Cleary, M. 1985. "Dissociative Reaction/Temporal Lobe Epilepsy: Psychiatric Excuses in Legal Proceedings." *American Journal of Forensic Psychiatry* 6 (no. 1): 30–37.

Code, L. 1991. *What Can She Know? Feminist Theory and the Construction of Knowledge*. Ithaca: Cornell University Press.

Cohen, D., and Eisdorfer, C. 1986. *The Loss of Self: A Family Resource for the Care of Alzheimer's Disease and Related Disorders*. New York: W. W. Norton and Co.

Coons, P. 1980. "Multiple Personality: Diagnostic Considerations." *Journal of Clinical Psychiatry* 41 (no. 10): 330–336.

Coons, P. 1984. "The Differential Diagnosis of Multiple Personality: A Comprehensive Review." *Psychiatric Clinics of North America* 7 (no. 1): 51–67.

Damasio, H., Grabowski, T., Frank, R., Galaburda, A. M., and Damasio, A. R. 1994. "The Return of Phineas Gage: Clues about the Brain from the Skull of a Famous Patient." *Science* 264 (20 May): 1102–1105.

Daniels, N. 1979. "Moral Theory and the Plasticity of Persons." *Monist* 62 (no. 3): 265–286.

Darwall, S. 1982. "Scheffler on Morality and Ideals of the Person." *Canadian Journal of Philosophy* 12 (no. 2): 247–255.

Davidson, Gerald, and Neale, John. 1986. *Abnormal Psychology: An Experimental Clinical Approach*. 4th ed. New York: John Wiley and Sons.

Davion, V. 1991. "Integrity and Radical Change." In *Feminist Ethics*, edited by Claudia Card. Lawrence: University Press of Kansas.

Dennett, D. C. 1969. *Content and Consciousness*. London: Routledge and Kegan Paul.

Dennett, D. C. 1988. "Why Everyone Is a Novelist." *Times Literary Supplement,* 16–22 Sept., p. 1016.

Dennett, D. C. 1989. "The Origins of Selves: Do I Choose Who I am?" *Cogito* 3 (no. 3): 163–173.

Dennett, D. C. 1991. *Consciousness Explained.* Boston: Little, Brown and Co.

Descartes, René. 1964. *Meditations on First Philosophy.* London: Nelson.

De Sousa, R. 1976. "Rational Homunculi." In *The Identities of Persons,* edited by Amélie Rorty. Berkeley: University of California Press.

Dresser, R. 1984. "Bound to Treatment: The Ulysses Contract." *Hastings Center Report* 14 (no. 3): 13–16.

Elster, Jon. 1984. *Ulysses and the Sirens: Studies in Rationality and Irrationality.* Cambridge: Cambridge University Press, in collaboration with Maison des Sciences de l'Homme, Paris.

Elster, Jon, ed. 1987. *The Multiple Self.* Cambridge: Cambridge University Press, in collaboration with Maison des Sciences de l'Homme, Paris.

Englehardt, H. T., Jr. 1975. "The Concept of Health and Disease." In *Evaluation and Explanation in the Biological Sciences,* edited by H. T. Engelhardt, Jr., and S. F. Spicker. Dordrecht, Holland: D. Reidel Publishing Co.

Enoch, M. D., Trethowan, W. H., and Barker, J. C. 1967. *Some Uncommon Psychiatric Syndromes.* Bristol: Wright.

Evans, G. 1982. *The Varieties of Reference.* Edited by John McDowell. Oxford: Oxford University Press.

Feinberg, J. 1986. *Harm to Self.* Vol. 3 of *The Moral Limits of the Criminal Law.* Oxford: Oxford University Press.

Fingarette, H. 1969. *Self-Deception.* London: Routledge and Kegan Paul.

Flanagan, O. 1991. *Varieties of Moral Personality: Ethics and Psychological Realism.* Cambridge: Harvard University Press.

Flanagan, O. 1992. *Consciousness Reconsidered.* Cambridge: MIT Press.

Flanagan, O. 1994. "Multiple Identity, Character Transformation, and Self-Reclamation." In *Philosophical Psychopathology,* edited by George Graham and G. Lynn Stephens. Cambridge: MIT Press.

Flanagan, O., and Rorty, A., eds. 1990. *Identity, Character, and Morality: Essays in Moral Psychology.* Cambridge: MIT Press.

Flax, J. 1990. *Thinking Fragments: Psychoanalysis, Feminism, and Postmodernism in the Contemporary West.* Berkeley: University of California Press.

Frankfurt, H. 1971. "Freedom of the Will and the Concept of a Person." *Journal of Philosophy* 68 (no. 1): 5–20.

Frankfurt, H. 1976. "Identification and Externality." In *The Identities of Persons,* edited by Amélie Rorty. Berkeley: University of California Press.

Frankfurt, H. 1987. "Identification and Wholeheartedness." In *Responsibility, Character, and the Emotions: New Essays in Moral Psychology*, edited by Ferdinand Schoeman. New York: Cambridge University Press.

Frankfurt, H. 1988. *The Importance of What We Care About: Philosophical Essays.* Cambridge: Cambridge University Press.

French, A., and Shechmeister, B. 1983. "The Multiple Personality Syndrome and Criminal Defense." *Bulletin of the American Academy of Psychiatry and the Law* 11 (no. 1): 17–25.

French, P., ed. 1972. *Individual and Collective Responsibility: Massacre at My Lai.* Cambridge, Mass: Schenkman Publishing Co.

Freud, Sigmund. 1911. "Psycho-analytic Notes upon an Autobiographical Account of a Case of Paranoia (Dementia Paranoides)." In his *Collected Papers*, vol. 3. London: Hogarth Press and the Institute of Psycho-analysis, 1957.

Freud, Sigmund, and Breuer, J. 1955. *Studies on Hysteria.* London: Hogarth Press and the Institute of Psycho-analysis.

Fulford, K. W. M. 1989. *Moral Theory and Medical Practice.* Cambridge: Cambridge University Press.

Fulford, K. W. M. 1994. "Value, Illness, and Failure of Action: Framework for a Philosophical Psychopathology of Delusions." In *Philosophical Psychopathology*, edited by George Graham and G. Lynn Stephens. Cambridge: MIT Press.

Ganaway, G. 1989. "Historical versus Narrative Truth: Clarifying the Role of Exogenous Trauma in the Etiology of MPD and Its Variants." *Dissociation* 2 (no. 4): 205–220.

Gazzaniga, M. S. 1970. *The Bisected Brain.* New York: Appleton-Century-Crofts.

Gazzaniga, M. S., and LeDoux, J. E. 1978. *The Integrated Mind.* New York: Plenum Press.

Gillett, Grant. 1986a. "Brain Bisection and Personal Identity." *Mind* 95 (no. 378): 224–229.

Gillett, Grant. 1986b. "Multiple Personality and the Concept of a Person." *New Ideas in Psychology* 4 (no. 2): 173–184.

Gillett, Grant. 1991. "Multiple Personality and Irrationality." *Philosophical Psychology* 4 (no. 1): 103–118.

Gilligan, Carol. 1982. *In a Different Voice: Psychological Theory and Women's Development.* Cambridge: Harvard University Press.

Gilligan, Carol. 1986. "Remapping the Moral Domain: New Images of the Self in Relationship." In *Reconstructing Individualism: Autonomy, Individuality, and the Self in Western Thought*, edited by T. C. Heller, M. Sosma, and D. E. Wellberg. Stanford: Stanford University Press.

Gilligan, Carol, Lyons, N. P., and Hanmer, T. J., eds. 1990. *Making Connections: The Relational Worlds of Adolescent Girls at Emma Williard School.* Cambridge: Harvard University Press.

Gilligan, Carol, Ward, J. V., and Taylor, J. M., eds. 1988. *Mapping the Moral Domain: A Contribution of Women's Thinking to Psychological Theory and Education*. Cambridge: Harvard University Graduate School of Education.

Glover, Jonathan. 1988. *I: The Philosophy and Psychology of Personal Identity*. London: Penguin.

Govier, Trudy. 1992. "Trust, Distrust, and Feminist Theory." *Hyaptia* 7 (no. 1): 16–33.

Govier, Trudy, 1993. "Self-Trust, Autonomy, and Self-Esteem." *Hypatia* 8 (no. 1): 99–120.

Graham, George, and Stephens, G. Lynn. 1994a. "Mind and Mine." In *Philosophical Psychopathology*, edited by George Graham and G. Lynn Stephens. Cambridge: MIT Press.

Graham, George, and Stephens, G. Lynn, eds. 1994b. *Philosophical Psychopathology*. Cambridge: MIT Press.

Gray, J. 1986. *Liberalism*. Minneapolis: University of Minnesota Press.

Grice, H. P. 1941. "Personal Identity." *Mind* 50. Reprinted in *Personal Identity*, edited by John Perry. Berkeley: University of California Press, 1975.

Gutheil, T., and Appelbaum, P. 1985. "The Substituted Judgement Approach: Its Difficulties and Paradoxes in Mental Health Settings." *Law, Medicine, and Health Care* 13 (no. 2): 61–64.

Hacking, I. 1986. "The Invention of Split Personalities." In *Human Nature and Natural Knowledge: Essays Presented to Marjorie Grene on the Occasion of Her Seventy-fifth Birthday*, edited by A. Donagan, A. N. Perovich, and M. V. Wedin, Boston Studies in the Philosophy of Science, no. 89, pp. 63–85. Dordrecht, Holland: D. Reidel Publishing Co.

Hacking, I. 1995. *Rewriting the Soul: Multiple Personality and the Sciences of Memory*. Princeton: Princeton University Press.

Hackler, C., Moseley, R., and Vawter, D., eds. 1989. *Advance Directives in Medicine*. New York: Praeger.

Haksar, V. 1979. *Equality, Liberty, and Perfectionism*. Oxford: Oxford University Press.

Hale, E. 1983. "Inside the Divided Mind." *New York Times Magazine*, 17 April, pp. 100–106.

Hall, P. 1989. "Multiple Personality Disorder and Homicide: Professional and Legal Issues." *Dissociation* 2 (no. 2): 110–115.

Hampshire, S. 1968. "Spinoza and the Idea of Freedom." In *Studies in the Philosophy of Thought and Action*, edited by P. F. Strawson. London: Oxford University Press.

Harlow, J. M. 1868. "Recovery from the Passage of an Iron Bar through the Head." *Publications of the Massachusetts Medical Society* 2:327–347.

Hart, H. L. A. 1968. *Punishment and Responsibility: Essays in the Philosophy of Law.* Oxford: Oxford University Press.

Held, V. 1990. "Feminist Transformations of Moral Theory." *Philosophy and Phenomenological Research* 50 (suppl.): 321–344.

Henriques, J., ed., 1984. *Changing the Subject: Psychology, Social Regulation, and Subjectivity.* New York: Methuen.

Hermann, D. 1986a. "Amnesia and the Criminal Law." *Idaho Law Review* 22:257–289.

Hermann, D. 1986b. "Criminal Defenses and Pleas in Mitigation Based on Amnesia." *Behavioral Sciences and the Law* 4 (no. 1): 5–26.

Hilgard, E. 1973. "A Neodissociation Interpretation of Pain Reduction in Hypnosis." *Psychological Review* 80 (no. 5): 403–419.

Hilgard, E. 1984. "The Hidden Observer and Multiple Personality." *International Journal of Clinical and Experimental Hypnosis* 32 (no. 2): 248–253.

Hirsch, Eli. 1982. *The Concept of Identity.* Oxford: Oxford University Press.

Hoagland, S. 1991. "Some Thoughts about 'Caring'." In *Feminist Ethics*, edited by C. Card. Lawrence: University Press of Kansas.

Hohfeld, W. 1923. *Fundamental Legal Conceptions as Applied in Judicial Reasoning, and Other Legal Essays.* Edited by W. W. Cook. New Haven: Yale University Press.

Holmes, J., and Lindley, R. 1989. *The Values of Psychotherapy.* Oxford: Oxford University Press.

Hope, Tony. 1994. "Personal Identity and Psychiatric Illness." In *Philosophy, Psychology, and Psychiatry*, edited by A. Phillips Griffiths. Cambridge: Cambridge University Press.

Houston, Barbara. 1992. "In Praise of Blame." *Hypatia* 7 (no. 4): 128–147.

Hume, D. 1888. *Treatise of Human Nature.* Edited by L. A. Selby-Bigge. Oxford: Clarendon Press, 1967. Reprint of 1888 edition.

Isenberg, A. 1980. "Natural Pride and Natural Shame." In *Explaining Emotions*, edited by Amélie Rorty. Berkeley: University of California Press.

James, Susan. 1984. *The Content of Social Explanation.* Cambridge: Cambridge University Press.

James, W. 1890. *The Principles of Psychology.* New York: H. Holt and Co.

James, W. 1892. *Psychology: The Briefer Course.* Edited by G. Allport. New York: Harper and Row, 1961.

James, W. 1902. *The Varieties of Religious Experience: A Study in Human Nature.* Page references are to the Collier Books edition, New York, 1961.

Jaynes, J. 1982. *The Origin of Consciousness in the Breakdown of the Bicameral Mind.* Boston: Houghton Mifflin.

Kant, Immanual. 1781, 1787. *Critique of Pure Reason*. 1st and 2nd eds. Page references are to the translation by Norman Kemp Smith, 1929, republished by Macmillan Co., London, and St. Martin's Press, New York, 1964.

Kegan, R. 1982. *The Evolving Self: Problem and Process in Human Development*. Cambridge: Harvard University Press.

Keller, C. 1986. *From a Broken Web: Separation, Sexism, and Self*. Boston: Beacon Press.

Keyes, Daniel. 1981. *The Minds of Billy Milligan*. New York: Random House.

King-Farlow, J. 1963. "Self-Deceivers and Sartrian Seducers." *Analysis* 23 (no. 5): 131–136.

Kluft, Richard P. 1982. "Varieties of Hypnotic Interventions in the Treatment of Multiple Personality." *American Journal of Clinical Hypnosis* 24 (no. 4): 230–240.

Kluft, Richard P. 1983. "Hypnotherapeutic Crisis Intervention in Multiple Personality." *American Journal of Clinical Hypnosis* 26 (no. 2): 73–83.

Kluft, Richard P. 1984a. "Aspects of the Treatment of Multiple Personality Disorder." *Psychiatric Annals* 14 (no. 1): 51–55.

Kluft, Richard P. 1984b. "Treatment of Multiple Personality Disorder: A Study of 33 Cases." *Psychiatric Clinics of North America* 7 (no. 1): 9–29.

Kluft, Richard P. 1986. "Personality Unification in Multiple Personality Disorder (MPD)." In *The Treatment of Multiple Personality Disorder*, edited by B. G. Braun. Washington, D.C.: American Psychiatric Press.

Kluft, Richard P. 1987. "Making the Diagnosis of Multiple Personality Disorder." In *Diagnostics and Psychopathology*, edited by F. F. Flach. New York: W. W. Norton and Co.

Kluft, Richard P., ed. 1990. *Incest-Related Syndromes of Adult Psychopathology*. Washington, D.C.: American Psychiatric Press.

Kohut, H. 1971. *The Analysis of the Self: A Systematic Approach to the Psychoanalytic Treatment of Narcissistic Personality Disorders*. New York: International Universities Press.

Kohut, H. 1977. *The Restoration of the Self*. New York: International Universities Press.

Kolak, Daniel, and Martin, Raymond, eds. 1991. *Self and Identity: Contemporary Philosophical Issues*. New York: Macmillan Publishing Co.

Kopelman, M. 1987. "Crime and Amnesia: A Review." *Behavioral Sciences and the Law* 5 (no. 3): 323–342.

Korsgaard, C. 1989. "Personal Identity and the Unity of Agency: A Kantian Response to Parfit." *Philosophy and Public Affairs* 18 (Spring): 101–132.

Kristeva, Julia. 1991. *Strangers to Ourselves*. Translated by Leon S. Roudiez. New York: Columbia University Press.

Laing, R. D. 1960. *The Divided Self: A Study of Sanity and Madness*. London: Tavistock Publications.

Lay, E. 1986. *Thinning from the Inside Out: The Proven, Personal Approach to Permanent Weight Loss*. New York: Bantom Books.

Lear, J. 1990. *Love and Its Place in Nature: A Philosophical Interpretation of Freudian Psychoanalysis*. New York: Farrar, Straus, and Giroux.

Livermore, J., Malmquist, C., and Meehl, P. 1968. "On the Justifications for Civil Commitment." *University of Pennsylvania Law Review* 117:75–96.

Locke, J. 1690. *An Essay Concerning Human Understanding*. Page references are to the Fontana Library edition, edited and abridged by A. D. Woozley and published by Wm. Collins, Sons and Co., London and Glasgow, 1964.

Lockett v. Ohio. 1978. 438 U.S. 586, 604; 98 S. Ct. 2954; 1978 U.S. LEXIS 133; 57 L. Ed 2d 973; 9 Ohio Op. 3d 26.

MacIntosh, J. J. 1969. "Memory and Personal Identity." In *The Business of Reason*, by J. J. MacIntosh and S. Coval. London: Routledge and Kegan Paul.

MacIntyre, Alasdair. 1981. *After Virtue: A Study in Moral Theory*. Notre Dame, Ind.: University of Notre Dame Press.

Mackie, John. 1976. *Problems from Locke*. Oxford: Clarendon Press.

Macklin, R. 1982. "Refusal of Psychiatric Treatment: Autonomy, Competence, and Paternalism." In *Psychiatry and Ethics: Insanity, Rational Autonomy, and Mental Health Care*, edited by R. Edwards. New York: Prometheus Books.

Macklin, R. 1983. "Treatment Refusals: Autonomy, Paternalism, and the 'Best Interests' of the Patient." In *Ethical Questions in Brain and Behavior: Problems and Opportunities*, edited by D. W. Pfaff. New York: Springer-Verlag.

Madell, G. 1981. *The Identity of the Self*. Edinburgh: Edinburgh University Press.

Margulies, Alfred. 1989. *The Empathic Imagination*. New York: W. W. Norton and Co.

Marks, C. 1980. *Commissurotomy, Consciousness, and Unity of Mind*. Cambridge: MIT Press.

Martin, M., ed. 1985. *Self-Deception and Self-Understanding: New Essays in Philosophy and Psychology*. Lawrence: University Press of Kansas.

McDougall, Joyce. 1985. *Theaters of the Mind: Illusion and Truth on the Psychoanalytic Stage*. New York: Basic Books.

McLaughlin, Brian, and Rorty, Amélie, eds. 1988. *Perspectives on Self-Deception*. Berkeley: University of California Press.

Mead, G. H. 1932. *The Philosophy of the Present*. Edited by A. E. Murphy. LaSalle, Ill.: Open Court Publishing Co.

Mele, A. 1987. *Irrationality: An Essay on Akrasia, Self-Deception, and Self-Control*. New York: Oxford University Press.

Meyers, Diana T. 1989. *Self, Society, and Personal Choice.* New York: Columbia University Press.

Meyers, Diana T. 1994. *Subjection and Subjectivity: Psychoanalytic Feminism and Moral Philosophy.* London: Routledge.

Mill, J. S. 1859. *On Liberty.* Page references are to the edition published by Bobbs-Merrill, Indianapolis, 1956.

Moody, R. A., Jr. 1976. *Life after Life: The Investigation of a Phenomenon—Survival of Bodily Death.* New York: Bantom Books.

Moore, M. 1984. *Law and Psychiatry: Rethinking the Relationship.* New York: Cambridge University Press.

Morris, H. 1968. "Persons and Punishment." *Monist* 52 (no. 4): 475–501.

Morris, H. 1987. "Nonmoral Guilt." In *Responsibility, Character, and the Emotions: New Essays in Moral Psychology,* edited by Ferdinand Schoeman. New York: Cambridge University Press.

Morris, H. 1988. "The Decline of Guilt." *Ethics* 99 (no. 1): 62–76.

Morrow v. State. 1982. 293 Md. 247; 443 A. 2d 108.

Nagel, T. 1971. "Brain Bisection and the Unity of Consciousness." *Synthese* 22:396–413.

Nicholson, L., ed. 1990. *Feminism/Postmodernism.* London: Routledge.

Nietzsche, F. 1966. *Werke in drei Banden.* Edited by K. Schlechta. Munich: Hanser.

Nietzsche, F. 1967. *Beyond Good and Evil: Prelude to a Philosophy of the Future.* 4th ed. London: Allen and Unwin.

Noddings, N. 1984. *Caring: A Feminine Approach to Ethics and Moral Education.* Berkeley: University of California Press.

Oesterreich, T. K. 1966. *Possession, Demoniacal and Other, among Primitive Races in Antiquity, the Middle Ages, and Modern Times.* New Hyde Park, N.Y.: University Books.

Osgood, C. E., Luria, Z., Jeans, R. F., and Smith, S. W. 1976. "The Three Faces of Evelyn: A Case Report." *Journal of Abnormal Psychology* 85 (no. 3): 247–286.

Parfit, Derek. 1971. "Personal Identity." *Philosophical Review* 80 (Jan.): 3–27.

Parfit, Derek. 1973. "Later Selves and Moral Principles." In *Philosophy and Personal Relations: An Anglo-French Study,* edited by A. Montefiore. London: Routledge and Kegan Paul.

Parfit, Derek. 1984. *Reasons and Persons.* Oxford: Oxford University Press.

Pears, D. 1984. *Motivated Irrationality.* Oxford: Clarendon Press.

People v. Booth. 1982. 414 Mich. 343; 324 N.W. 2d 741.

People v. Caldwell. 1980. 102 Cal. App. 3d 461; 162 Cal. Rptr. 397.

People v. Kitt. 1978. 83 Cal. App. 3d 834, 841; 148 Cal. Rptr. 447.

People v. Lisnow. 1978. 88 Cal. App. 3d Supp. 21; 151 Cal. Rptr. 621.

Perr, I. 1991. "Crime and Multiple Personality Disorder: A Case History and Discussion." *Bulletin of the American Academy of Psychiatry and the Law* 19 (no. 2): 203–214.

Perry, John. 1976a. "The Importance of Being Identical." In *The Identities of Persons,* edited by Amélie Rorty. Berkeley: University of California Press.

Perry, John. 1976b. Review of Bernard Williams, *Problems of the Self. Journal of Philosophy* 73 (no. 13): 416–428.

Price, M. 1977. "Identity through Time." *Journal of Philosophy* 74:201–217.

Prince, M. 1906. *The Dissociation of a Personality: A Biographical Study in Abnormal Psychology.* New York: Longmans, Green, and Co.

Puccetti, R. 1973a. "Brain Bisection and Personal Identity." *British Journal for the Philosophy of Science* 24:339–355.

Puccetti, R. 1973b. "Multiple Identity." *Personalist* 54 (no. 3): 203–215.

Puccetti, R. 1981. "The Case for Mental Duality: Evidence from Split-Brain Data and Other Considerations." *Behavioral and Brain Sciences* 4 (no. 1): 93–123.

Putnam, Frank W. 1989. *Diagnosis and Treatment of Multiple Personality Disorder.* New York: Guilford Press.

Quine, W. V. O. 1972. Review of M. K. Munitz, ed., *Identity and Individuation. Journal of Philosophy* 69 (no. 16): 488–497.

Quinton, A. 1962. "The Soul." *Journal of Philosophy* 59 (no. 15): 393–409.

Radden, Jennifer. 1984. "Defining Self-Deception." *Dialogue* 23:103–120.

Radden, Jennifer. 1985. *Madness and Reason.* London: Allen and Unwin.

Radden, Jennifer. 1989. "Chemical Sanity and Personal Identity." *Public Affairs Quarterly* 3 (no. 3): 64–79.

Radden, Jennifer. 1992. "Planning for Mental Disorder: Buchanan and Brock on Advance Directives in Psychiatry." *Journal of Social Theory and Practice* 18 (no. 2): 165–186.

Radden, Jennifer. 1994. "Second Thoughts: Revoking Decisions over One's Own Future." *Journal of Philosophical and Phenomenological Research* 54 (no. 4): 787–801.

Radden, Jennifer. 1995. "Shame and Blame: The Self through Time and Change." *Dialogue* 34:61–74.

Rawls, J. 1971. *A Theory of Justice.* Cambridge: Harvard University Press.

Reatig, N., ed. 1981. *Competency and Informed Consent.* Rockville, Md.: National Institute of Mental Health.

Regina v. McNaghten. 1843. 10 Clark and F. 200, 8 Eng. Rep. 718.

Reid, T. 1785. *Essays on the Intellectual Powers of Man*. Reprinted in *Personal Identity*, edited by John Perry. Berkeley: University of California Press, 1975.

Reznek, L. 1991. *The Philosophical Defense of Psychiatry*. London: Routledge.

Roesch, R., and Golding, S. 1986. "Amnesia and Competency to Stand Trial: A Review of Legal and Clinical Issues." *Behavioral Sciences and the Law* 4 (no. 1): 87–97.

Rorty, Amélie, ed. 1976. *The Identities of Persons*. Berkeley: University of California Press.

Rorty, Amélie. 1986. "Self-Deception, *Akrasia*, and Irrationality." In *The Multiple Self*, edited by Jon Elster. Cambridge: Cambridge University Press, in collaboration with Maison des Sciences de l'Homme, Paris.

Rorty, Amélie. 1988. *Mind in Action: Essays in the Philosophy of Mind*. Boston: Beacon Press.

Rosenbaum, M. 1980. "The Role of the Term 'Schizophrenia' in the Decline of Diagnosis of Multiple Personality." *Archives of General Psychiatry* 37 (no. 12): 1383–1385.

Ross, W. D. 1930. *The Right and the Good*. Oxford: Clarendon Press.

Roth, L., Meisel, A., and Lidz, C. W. 1977. "Tests of Competency to Consent to Treatment." *American Journal of Psychiatry* 134 (no. 3): 279–284.

Rovane, Carol. 1993. "Self-Reference: The Radicalization of Locke." *Journal of Philosophy* 90 (no. 2): 73–97.

Rubinsky, E., and Brandt, J. 1986. "Amnesia and Criminal Law: A Clinical Overview." *Behavioral Sciences and the Law* 4 (no. 1): 27–46.

Sacks, Oliver. 1970. *The Man Who Mistook His Wife for a Hat and Other Clinical Tales*. New York: Summit Books.

Sadler, J. Z., Wiggins, O., and Schwartz, M., eds. 1994. *Philosophical Perspectives on Psychiatric Diagnostic Classification*. Baltimore: Johns Hopkins University Press.

Saks, Elyn. 1992. "Multiple Personality Disorder and Criminal Responsibility." *U.C. Davis Law Review* 25 (no. 2): 384–461.

Saks, Elyn. 1995. "The Criminal Responsibility of People with Multiple Personality Disorder." *Psychiatric Quarterly* 66 (no. 2): 119–131.

Schafer, R. 1976. *A New Language for Psychoanalysis*. New Haven: Yale University Press.

Scheffler, S. 1982. "Ethics, Personal Identity, and Ideals of the Person." *Canadian Journal of Philosophy* 12:229–246.

Schelling, T. 1984. *Choice and Consequence*. Cambridge: Harvard University Press.

Schemen, N. 1993. *Engenderings: Constructions of Knowledge, Authority, and Privilege*. London: Routledge.

Schoeman, F., ed. 1987. *Responsibility, Character, and the Emotions: New Essays in Moral Psychology*. Cambridge: Cambridge University Press.

Schreiber, Flora Rheta. 1973. *Sybil*. Chicago: Henry Regnery Co.

Segal, Jerome M. 1991. *Agency and Alienation: A Theory of Human Presence.* Savage, Md.: Rowman and Littlefield.

Shoemaker, S. 1963. *Self-Knowledge and Self-Identity.* Ithaca, N.Y.: Cornell University Press.

Shoemaker, S. 1968. "Self-Reference and Self-Awareness." *Journal of Philosophy* 65:555–567.

Shoemaker, S. 1970. "Persons and Their Pasts." *American Philosophical Quarterly* 7:269–285.

Shoemaker, S. 1979. "Identity, Properties, and Causality." In *Studies in Metaphysics*, edited by Peter A. French, Theodore Edward Uehling, and Howard K. Wettstein, Midwest Studies in Philosophy, no. 4. Minneapolis: University of Minnesota Press.

Shoemaker, S. 1984. "Personal Identity: A Materialist's Account." In *Personal Identity*, by S. Shoemaker and R. Swinburne. Oxford: Basil Blackwell.

Shoemaker, S. 1986. "Introspection and the Self." In *Studies in the Philosophy of Mind*, edited by Peter A. French, Theodore Edward Uehling, and Howard K. Wettstein, Midwest Studies in Philosophy, no. 10. Minneapolis: University of Minnesota Press.

Singer, J., ed. 1990. *Repression and Dissociation: Implications for Personality Theory, Psychopathology, and Health.* Chicago: University of Chicago Press.

Slote, M. 1983. *Goods and Virtues.* Oxford: Clarendon Press.

Spanos, N. P. 1983. "The Hidden Observer as an Experimental Creation." *Journal of Personality and Social Psychology* 44 (no. 1): 170–176.

Spanos, N. P. 1986. "Hypnosis, Nonvolitional Responding, and Multiple Personality: A Social-Psychological Perspective." *Progress in Experimental Personality Research* 14:1–62.

Spanos, N. P., Weekes, J. R., and Bertrand, L. D. 1985. "Mulitple Personality: A Social-Psychological Perspective." *Journal of Abnormal Psychology* 94 (no. 3): 362–376.

Spanos, N. P., Weekes, J. R., Menary, E., and Bertrand, L. D. 1986. "Hypnotic Interview and Age Regression Procedures in the Elicitation of Multiple Personality Symptoms: A Simulation Study." *Psychiatry* 49 (no. 4): 298–311.

Spence, D. P. 1984. *Narrative Truth and Historical Truth: Meaning and Interpretation in Psychoanalysis.* New York: W. W. Norton and Co.

Sperry, R. W. 1966. "Brain Bisection and Consciousness." In *Brain and Conscious Experience*, edited by J. Eccles. New York: Springer-Verlag.

Spiegel, D., and Cardeña, Etzel. 1991. "Disintegrated Experience: The Dissociative Disorders Revisited." *Journal of Abnormal Psychology* 100 (no. 3): 366–378. Special issue: *Diagnoses, Divensions, and DSM-IV: The Science of Classification.*

Spiegel, H., and Spiegel, D. 1978. *Trance and Treatment: Clinical Uses of Hypnosis.* New York: Basic Books.

State v. Grimsley. 1982. 3 Ohio App. 3d 265; 444 N.E. 2d 1071; 3 Ohio B. Rep. 308; 27 A.L.R. 4th 1060.

State v. Rodrigues. 1984. 67 Haw. 70; 679 P. 2d 615.

Stephens, G. Lynn, and Graham, George. 1994a. "Self-Consciousness, Mental Agency, and the Clinical Psychopathology of Thought-Insertion." *Philosophy, Psychiatry, and Psychology* 1 (no. 1): 1–10.

Stephens, G. Lynn, and Graham, George. 1994b. "Voices and Selves." In *Philosophical Perspectives on Psychiatric Diagnostic Classification*, edited by J. Z. Sadler, O. Wiggins, and M. Schwartz. Baltimore: Johns Hopkins University Press.

Sternberg, R. J., and Kolligan, J., Jr., eds. 1990. *Competence Considered.* New Haven: Yale University Press.

Stevenson, Robert Louis. 1886. *Dr. Jekyll and Mr. Hyde, and Other Stories.* Page references are to the edition published by Grosset and Dunlap, New York, 1981.

Strawson, P. F. 1959. *Individuals: An Essay in Descriptive Metaphysics.* London: Methuen.

Strawson, P. F. 1968. "Freedom and Resentment." In *Studies in the Philosophy of Thought and Action*, edited by P. F. Strawson. Oxford: Oxford University Press.

Styron, W. 1990. *Darkness Visible: A Memoir of Madness.* New York: Random House.

Swinburne, R. 1984. "Personal Identity: The Dualist Theory." In *Personal Identity*, by S. Shoemaker and R. Swinburne. Oxford: Basil Blackwell.

Taylor, C. 1989. *Sources of the Self: The Making of the Modern Identity.* Cambridge: Harvard University Press.

Taylor, G. 1985. *Pride, Shame, and Guilt: Emotions of Self-Assessment.* Oxford: Clarendon Press.

Thalberg, I. 1978. "Hierarchical Analyses of Unfree Action." *Canadian Journal of Philosophy* 8:211–226.

Thaler, R. 1980. "Towards a Positive Theory of Consumer Behavior." *Journal of Economic Behavior and Organization* 1:39–60.

Thompson, D. 1987. *Political Ethics and Public Office.* Cambridge: Harvard University Press.

Tversky, A., and Kahneman, D. 1981. "The Framing of Decisions and the Psychology of Choice." *Science* 211 (no. 4481): 453–458.

VanDeVeer, Donald. 1986. *Paternalistic Intervention: The Moral Bounds on Benevolence.* Princeton: Princeton University Press.

Warren, M. 1988. "Marx and Methodological Individualism." *Philosophy of the Social Sciences* 18:447–476.

Watson, G. 1975. "Free Agency." *Journal of Philosophy* 72:205–220.

Watson, G. 1977. "Skepticism about Weakness of Will." *Philosophical Review* 86:316–339.

White, Stephen L. 1991. *The Unity of the Self.* Cambridge: MIT Press.

Wiggins, D. 1967. *Identity and Spatio-temporal Continuity.* Oxford: Blackwell.

Wilkes, Kathleen V. 1988. *Real People: Personal Identity without Thought Experiments.* Oxford: Clarendon Press.

Williams, Bernard. 1973. *Problems of the Self: Philosophical Papers, 1956–1972.* Cambridge: Cambridge University Press.

Wittgenstein, L. 1963. *Philosophical Investigations.* Oxford: Blackwell.

Wolf, Susan. 1980. "Asymmetrical Freedom." *Journal of Philosophy* 77:151–166.

Wolf, Susan. 1986. "Self-Interest and Interest in Selves." *Ethics* 96:704–720.

Wolf, Susan. 1987. "Sanity and the Metaphysics of Responsibility." In *Responsibility, Character, and the Emotions: New Essays in Moral Psychology*, edited by F. D. Schoeman. Cambridge: Cambridge University Press.

Wolf, Susan. 1990. *Freedom within Reason.* New York: Oxford University Press.

Wollheim, Richard. 1984. *The Thread of Life.* Cambridge: Harvard University Press.

Yalom, I. 1989. *Love's Executioner, and Other Tales of Psychotherapy.* New York: Basic Books.

Index

Accountability. *See* Responsibility
Advance directives, 143, 144–146,
    154, 159, 161–172, 174, 176–177,
    179, 268–269
Agent regret, 113, 115
Akrasia, or weakness of will, 20–23,
    59, 66–70, 72, 80
American Law Institute Model Penal
    Code rule, 132
stated, 283 (chap. 8, n. 5)
Amnesia
fraudulent, 130, 241, 253
meaning of term, 100
misleading connotations, 41
role of, in diagnosis of dissociative-
    identity disorder, 277 (n. 12)
when it should excuse, 281 (n. 1)
'Angels', as a figurative term, 30–31
Apparent memory (Swinburne), 97
Appelbaum, P., 155, 157, 164–165
Apperceptive centers (Braude),
    defined, 277 (n. 8)
Attention, 17
Augustine, Saint, 69, 198
Authenticity, restoration of, 143–144,
    150–152, 154, 210
Autonomy. *See* Self-determination

Baier, A., 170, 202–204
Beauchamp, Christine, case of, 212,
    214. *See also* Prince, M.
Williams's arguments concerning,
    278 (n. 16)
"Best interests" model of substituted
    judgment, 155–156

Bicycle-riding ability, 193–194
Bonnie rule, 132–133
stated, 283 (chap. 8, n. 5)
Borderline personality disorder, 60
Boy to general, case of changing from,
    187
Brain damage and disease, 6, 38, 63,
    148, 165
Braude, S., 46, 48–49, 96, 122, 136,
    213, 215, 250, 258
taxonomy of, 48–49, 96, 213, 215,
    250, 266
Brock, D., 148–149, 156, 161, 164,
    166–167, 171, 223
Buchanan, A., 148–149, 156, 161,
    164, 166–167, 171, 223

California Penal Code, 137
Cartesianism. *See* Descartes and
    Cartesianism
Cases, real and imagined. *See*
    Examples, real and imagined
Changes of mind, 166–169, 235
as "second thinking" (Baier), 170–171
Character, 203–206, 233, 235, 243
Coconsciousness, 47, 48, 49, 53, 213–
    214, 217, 219, 255
Code, L., 202, 233
Commissurotomy, or split brain
    operations, 67, 78, 80, 85, 88–89,
    241, 245–247
defined, 280 (n. 6)
Competence, 144–148, 154, 157–
    158, 159, 162, 173, 177
to stand trial, 126, 130

Continuants (Shoemaker), 190
Continuity condition, 40–41, 43, 53,
57, 59, 66, 71
Contrition and remorse, 200, 206,
232
Conversion, 19–20, 29, 59, 66–67,
103, 152, 173, 176, 193, 198, 228,
230, 237–238, 268
Copresence, 39, 241–242, 247, 251,
253, 263
Culpable forgetting, 89, 98, 100, 103–
104

Dangerous to society, 144, 173
Davion, V., 235
Degenerative brain disease. *See* Brain
damage and disease
Dennett, D., 25, 54, 88–89, 218, 262
Dependency theses, 198, 205, 227–
228, 237
Depersonalization and derealisation
experience, 59, 80, 241, 248, 250–
255
Descartes and Cartesianism, 7, 184,
192, 198, 227–228, 238, 258, 260,
270
Diachronic (and synchronic), 11–12
Differential reactive attitudes. *See*
Divided responsibility, or
differential reactive attitudes
Diminished capacity, 129–130, 133,
137, 139
Discontinuity, defined, 11
Disordered awareness and memory,
40, 41, 43, 47, 49, 57, 64–66, 68,
92
defined, 41
Disowned or ego-alien experiences,
65, 248–249, 263
defined, 248–249
Dispositive purposes of the law, 109,
117–118, 120–121, 133, 139, 269
Dissociated will, 50
Dissociation, defined, 276 (n. 1)
Dissociative-identity disorder, 37, 44,
46–48, 50, 52–56, 59, 62, 64, 72,
78, 87–89, 93, 106, 113, 119, 122,
127, 129–133, 136–137, 141, 145–
146, 173, 177–178, 212, 219, 220,

227, 231, 241, 243, 245, 247, 253,
267–268, 271
defined, 46–48
Disunity, defined, 11
Divided responsibility, or differential reactive attitudes, 110, 121,
269
Double effect, doctrine of, 141

Elster, J., 6, 115, 161
Empathy, 15
"Enslavement" of later selves by earlier
selves, 164–165
Episodic and programmatic, or life-
plan, autonomy (Meyers), 222–224,
236
Examples, real and imagined, 77–78,
272

First- and second-order desires, 16, 68,
92, 105–107, 222–223, 230, 236.
See also Real selves
Flanagan, O., 19, 26, 114, 218, 256,
262
Forensic responsibility (Locke), 34, 45,
92–93, 125, 269
Foreseeability and preventability, 89–
99, 104–105, 122
Forgetful person, case of (Rovane),
282 (n. 7)
Fragmentation, 23, 37–38, 205, 264,
267
defined, 38
Frankfurt, H., 16, 68, 105, 222–223,
230, 264, 265
Freud and Freudianism, 15, 42, 72,
216, 218–219
Functional disorders, 86, 89
Functional identity (James), 186, 190
Fusion of multiples. *See* Integration of
multiples

Gage, Phineas, case of, 60, 63, 176
Graham, G., 264–265
Grice, H. P., 9, 32, 41, 183, 187–188,
192–193, 270
Guilt and guilt feelings distinguished,
282 (n. 4)
Gutheil, T., 155, 157, 164–165

Hallucinations, 289 (chap. 16, n. 3)
out-of-body, 59, 248, 252–253, 255
Harm principle, 145, 162, 173–175
defined, 162
Heterogenous personality (James), 18
"Hidden observer." *See* Hypnoid
states, "hidden observer" in
Holmes, J., 220–221, 262
Homunculi and homuncular models
of the self, 42, 55, 82
Hume, D., 183–187, 192, 237, 255,
259–260, 270
Hypnoid states, 59, 67, 241
"hidden observer" in, 245–246, 253,
268

Identity of curtains, 26–27
Imagination, role of, 185–186, 217,
259–260, 262
Impulse control, disorders of, 68, 70,
106, 112, 176
Incompetence/consent proviso, 147,
177
Individualism, 6, 9, 11, 111, 119, 177,
194–196, 198–199, 204, 206, 209,
210–212, 224–228, 233, 270
methodological, 6
Individuation, interpersonal (or interself) and intrapersonal (or intraself),
40, 52, 63, 67–68, 70, 71–72
Insanity defense, 125, 128
cognitive elements in, 128–129,
130–133, 136–137, 139
Integration of multiples
analytic and synthetic stages of, 113–
114
confederacy model of, 213–214
criteria for successful, 287 (n. 6)
dissention over, 287 (n. 4)
Intentional explanatory framework.
See Rational or intentional
explanatory framework
Interself epistemology, 37, 47, 52, 94,
101, 250
Intimacy, special obligations of, 116,
121
Introspective alienation (Graham and
Stephens), 264

James, W., 17, 20, 32, 183, 185–187,
190, 195, 251, 256, 259, 260–262,
270
Johnson, Tom, case of, 94, 100, 134–
135, 137–139

Kant and Kantianism, 7, 185, 195,
227–228, 256, 259, 262, 270
Key/ring, case of, 246
Kierkegaard, S., 229–230, 235
Kluft, R., 113, 115, 215, 219
Korsgaard, C., 12, 195, 199–202,
237–238

Leibniz's law, 190
stated, 286 (n. 8)
Lindley, R., 220–221, 262
Locke, J., 34–35, 45, 78, 81, 86, 91–
94, 98, 101, 105–106, 109, 183–
184, 191, 269
Locke's principle, 93, 95, 99–104,
107
guarded formulation of, 104
as a hypothetical, 100

M., case of, 62–66, 101–103, 151
Macklin, R., 150, 158
"Made experiences." *See* Thought
insertion
Madell, G., 199–200
Marks, C., 88–89, 246–247
McNaughten's rule (*Regina v.
McNaghten*), 132
stated, 283 (chap. 8, n. 5)
Memory
contemporary wars over, 220
of ownership and agency, 98, 102–
103
snapshot model of, 95
Metaphysics
characteristics of, 183
meaning of term, 285 (n. 1)
Meyers, D., 222
Mill, J. S., 145, 156, 173
Milligan, Billy, case of, 131–132
Mind-body dualism, 86
Modernism, 6–7, 195–196, 199,
233

Moments when criminal law engages the mentally disturbed (pretrial, trial, sentencing) and criminal responsibility, 126–127, 131, 133, 140, 141

Mood or affective disorder, 59, 61, 62, 64–65, 86–87, 103, 105–106, 127–128, 162–163

Moore, M., 117–120, 129–130, 135

Multiple-personality disorder. *See* Dissociative-identity disorder

Multiplicity, 8–9, 21, 23, 29, 39, 42, 45, 52, 56, 59–60, 62, 64, 68, 77–78, 80, 82, 227, 267

criteria or conditions of, 37, 43–44, 46, 56, 91, 112, 118, 120, 179, 209

Nobel laureate, Parfit's case of, 279 (chap. 5, n. 2)

Numerical identity, refinements of, 275 (n. 3)

"One to a customer" rule (Dennett), 25, 30, 33–34, 143, 154, 192, 196, 228

Organicity, presumption of, 86–87, 122, 128, 132, 133, 137, 268, 271

Out-of-body hallucinations. *See* Hallucinations

Paranormal phenomena, descriptions of, 257–258

Parfit, D., 6, 9–10, 28, 32–34, 78–79, 81, 175, 183, 188–194, 200, 237, 256, 270

Particulars (Strawson), 27

Paternalism, 143

interpretations of, 144, 152, 162

Perspective, issues concerning, 12, 14, 65, 67, 102, 139, 153, 170–171, 189, 209, 224, 255, 268

Physics exam, Parfit's case of, 288 (chap. 15, n. 1)

Planning for care of future selves, 105

Possession, 8, 50, 70, 241–242, 248, 254–255, 257, 263, 268, 271

Postmodernism, 6, 7, 195–196, 233

Preference reversals, 21–22

Presenile and senile dementias. *See* Brain damage and disease

Prince, M., 48, 50–51, 212, 214

Promises and resolves, 168, 170–171

defined, 168

Psychiatric wills. *See* Ulysses contracts, or psychiatric wills

Psychological continuity and connection, theories of, 187–194

Putnam, F., 44–45, 105, 112–114, 116, 136, 179, 213–215, 217

Quine, W. V. O., 79, 81–82

Radden, J., 70, 166, 200, 232

Rational or intentional explanatory framework, 29, 67, 102

Reactive attitudes (Strawson), 87, 92, 96, 110, 112, 114–116, 121, 200–201, 206

cognitive and affective components of, 95–98

Real selves (Wolf), 89, 92, 105–106, 150, 223

Reflective equilibrium, 9, 83–84, 179, 272

Reid, T., 187, 198–199, 201

Reigning self, defined, 46

Relational individualism (Chodorow), 224, 226

Relational self, 195, 225. *See also* Relational individualism

Responsibility

in contrast to accountability, 126

for others' actions, explained, 281 (n. 1)

for others' care, 111, 116, 121, 146, 177, 178, 269

Retributivist framework, 125–126

and moments when criminal law engages the mentally disturbed (pretrial, trial, sentencing), 126–127, 131, 133, 140, 141

Sameness, 26–29

different interpretations of, 274 (chap. 2, n. 1)

Schelling, T., 69–70, 171

Schizophrenia, 38, 50, 59, 61–62, 64–65, 80, 86–87, 103, 105, 127–128, 150, 162–163, 249, 264
Schreber, Daniel, case of, 72
Self, selves
alternative definitions of, 274 (n. 4)
analyzed dispositionally, 45–46, 242
defined, 11
sequential or simultaneous, 45
thin and fat, 70
Self-assessment, emotions of (Taylor), 196
Self-deception, 14, 20–23, 54–56, 59, 66–67, 70–72, 99, 271
"one shot" and "full blown" (White), 278 (n. 18)
Self-determination, 220–225, 236
Self-understanding, epistemological models of, 217–220
Sentencing and diminished responsibility, 126
Separate-agency condition, 39, 41, 43, 44, 57, 63, 66–67
defined, 39
Separate-personality condition, 39, 41, 43, 57, 63, 66–68
defined, 39
Shoemaker, S., 12, 32, 97, 183, 190, 256, 262
Somnambulism, 133–135, 253
Specious present, 274 (n. 2)
Spence, D., 218–219
State v. Grimsley, 119, 120, 134, 135
Stephens, L., 264–265
Stevenson, R. L., 5, 42, 44, 82, 89, 99
Strawson, P., 96, 200
Stream of consciousness (James), 20
Substituted or proxy judgment, 143–144, 154–155, 157–158, 223
Successive selves
defined, 7
language of, 8, 25, 29–30, 33–34, 37, 63, 68, 151, 179, 183–184, 192, 227–228, 232–233, 270
metaphysics of, 9, 33, 154, 162, 164, 166, 171, 174–176, 179, 184, 191–192, 197, 200, 227–228, 232
Survival thresholds, 10, 189–193. *See*

also Psychological continuity and connection, theories of
Suspended personhood (Moore), 116, 120, 129, 133, 135–136
Sybil Dorsett, case of (Schreiber), 243, 245, 247

Taylor, C., 7, 203, 216, 234
Taylor, G., 196
Telescope case and patchy awareness, 138–139
"Thank you" theory, 158–159
Therapeutic monogamy (Yalom), 214
Thief, case of the (Tom Johnson), 94, 100, 134–135, 137–139
Thought insertion, 8, 39, 241, 248–249, 255, 257
Total temporary state (TTS, Grice), 187–188, 193
Trait paucity of multiples, 277 (n. 14)
Trust, judicious, 202, 206

Ulysses, 161, 163, 167, 169
Ulysses contracts, or psychiatric wills, 163, 171, 177–178
Unbidden thoughts, 265
Unconsciousness, legal defense of, 120, 129–130, 133, 135–137, 139
Unity and continuity, 11
why conflated, 273 (n. 3)
Usage, literal and figurative, of the notion of self, 28–33, 270
Utilitarianism and consequentialism, 127, 140

VanDeVeer, D., 148, 175
Virtues and vices
MacIntyre on, 286 (n. 4)
moral systems based on, 204, 235

Wanton acts (Frankfurt), 223
Waverings, 241, 244
Weakness of will. *See* Akrasia, or weakness of will
Wholeheartedness, 229–230
Wilkes, K., 12, 79–82
Wolf, S., 105–106, 150, 222–223

Yalom, I., 214